IN THE LINE

OF FIRE

TRAUMA IN THE
EMERGENCY SERVICES

CHERYL REGEHR

TED BOBER

OXFORD
UNIVERSITY PRESS

2005

D0209823

OXFORD
UNIVERSITY PRESS

Oxford   New York
Auckland   Bangkok   Buenos Aires   Cape Town   Chennai
Dar es Salaam   Delhi   Hong Kong   Istanbul   Karachi   Kolkata
Kuala Lumpur   Madrid   Melbourne   Mexico City   Mumbai   Nairobi
São Paulo   Shanghai   Taipei   Tokyo   Toronto

Published by Oxford University Press, Inc.
198 Madison Avenue, New York, New York 10016

www.oup.com

Oxford is a registered trademark of Oxford University Press

Library of Congress Cataloging-in-Publication Data
Regehr, Cheryl.
In the line of fire : trauma in the emergency services / Cheryl Regehr, Ted Bober.
    p. cm.
Includes bibliographical references.
ISBN 0-19-516502-0
1. Emergency medical personnel—Job stress.   2. Fire fighters—Job stress.   3. Police—Job stress.
4. Emergency medical personnel—Mental health.   5. Fire fighters—Mental health.   6. Police—Mental
health.   7. Psychic trauma.   8. Post-traumatic stress disorder.   I. Bober, Ted.   II. Title.
RC451.4.E44R44 2005
616.02'5'019—dc22   2004006827

9 8 7 6 5 4 3 2 1

Printed in the United States of America
on acid-free paper

THROUGHOUT THE PROCESS of preparing this book, we have experienced the fullness of life, including stresses and challenges of clinical and research work, the SARS epidemic, concerns of West Nile virus, technological problems such as a blackout that left one-quarter of North America in the dark, and, most importantly, the serious illness and death of family members. At the same time, babies were welcomed into lives of our extended family and friends, one child left for university, and others entered new and exciting stages of life. All the while, colleagues and friends were supportive, brought tea and humor.

THIS BOOK IS ABOUT RESILIENCE and strength in the face of adversity. It is dedicated to those important individuals in our lives who have taught us about resilience, grace, and gratitude. These are experiences that will continue to enrich our lives forever. To our families who have always provided the love and support and been our secure base—thank you—always.

Foreword

This book provides an objective, original, enlightening, and thought-provoking analysis of the full range of emergency and trauma recovery services practiced by social workers and emergency services personnel throughout North America. Cheryl Regehr and Ted Bober have made a major and significant contribution to the mental health and human services literature. This is the most thoughtful, compassionate, inspiring, readable, insightful, and original book I have ever read on emergency services, crisis management, and trauma recovery. This book is so engaging and well-written that I could not put it down until I read every page at one sitting.

Dr. Cheryl Regehr and Ted Bober have been on the front lines of community disaster intervention as co-directors of the Critical Incident Stress Team at Toronto Pearson International Airport for over 15 years. In addition, the authors' two decades of clinical work, training workshops and seminars, and research on trauma and emergency services are evidenced throughout this timely book. I was also delighted to see an emphasis on evidence-based individual and group interventions.

This gem of a book is a rare combination of outstanding writing, stimulating case illustrations, and an integration of qualitative and quantitative research. In sharp contrast to other academic trade books, the valuable information in this original volume is both superbly researched and eminently readable. Catastrophic events, trauma and coping case exemplars, emergency services and the continuum of early interventions and long-term follow-up, and the everyday lifesaving and recovery work of police, paramedics, firefighters, and emergency mental health practitioners are highlighted throughout this book. The figures, models, and graphs add an important conceptual and practical dimension to the book.

In summary, this book is essential reading for almost every mental health practitioner because of the continued threat of community disasters, emergencies, terrorist attacks, and trauma-precipitating events. Every informed citizen, student, and practitioner interested in mental health and emergency services should purchase this book. It is a pathfinding and seminal contribution to the most challenging societal problems of the twenty-first century.

Albert R. Roberts, Ph.D.
Professor of Social Work and Criminal Justice, Director of Faculty and Curriculum Development, Faculty of Arts and Sciences, Livingston College Campus, Rutgers, the State University of New Jersey, Piscataway, and editor in chief, *Brief Treatment and Crisis Intervention* journal (www.crisis interventionnetwork.com).

Preface

In the wake of disaster, emergency service workers including police officers, firefighters, and paramedics are first on the scene and last to leave. They are repeatedly exposed to violence and its aftermath and are expected to cope with it. They put concern for the lives of others over concern for their own lives, working tirelessly to recover the bodies of the missing. Their heroic actions save lives, provide comfort to and care for the wounded, and inspire onlookers, but at what cost to themselves? We now know that rescue workers who are exposed to mutilated bodies, mass destruction, multiple casualties, and life-threatening situations may become the hidden victims of disaster. The sequelae in terms of traumatic stress symptoms and depressive symptoms have the potential to be highly disruptive and long-standing both for the individual worker and their families and for the organizations in which they work.

Additionally, emergency workers are exposed to events involving human pain and suffering on a daily basis. These events often do not make the news or capture public attention. They do not result in an outpouring of public support for emergency services. While for the most part emergency workers are equipped to deal with these events, on occasion one particular event will have a lasting impact. Indeed, this one event may have a more lasting effect than other more dramatic events involving the loss of many lives. How do we understand such a process? How do we intervene to ensure that we do not lose these valuable resources for society?

This book is based on the authors' combined experience of over 40 years of clinical work in emergency departments and with emergency service organizations. This experience has included managing crisis intervention teams in both health care and emergency service settings, interventions following critical events in the workplace and response to disasters. In addition, the book is based on research conducted with more than 350 police, fire, and ambulance workers in two continents, 300 emergency mental health practitioners, and qualitative research interviews with more than 50 emergency service workers.

This book provides an overview of the issue of trauma in the emergency services. It is intended to serve as reference for social workers, psychologists, and other mental health professionals who provide services to emergency service organizations. It is also intended as a guideline for administrators and peer support team members within emergency service organizations. Issues addressed include the event-related, individual, organizational, and societal factors that influence trauma response. Various theoretical models for understanding trauma response are reviewed. In addition, practical advice is provided regarding planning intervention programs, developing trauma response teams, training both emergency service professionals and mental health professionals regarding providing mental health trauma response in the emergency services, and evaluating the effectiveness of services provided. Finally, the stories of emergency responders and the strategies for both self-care and care of significant others will resound and make the book of interest to both emergency services workers themselves and their families.

Acknowledgments

Many people have been instrumental in the development of this work. Members of the Pearson International Airport Critical Incident Stress Team and the Ministry of Natural Resources (MNR) Team have been valuable colleagues over the years. In particular the energy and commitment of Deane Johanis of the Greater Toronto Airports Authority, and the vision of Doug Hyde of MNR, have been invaluable. John Hill of Mississauga Fire and Emergency Services, Gerry Goldberg of Toronto Emergency Medical Services, and Chuck Bartram of Peel Regional Police have been important coinvestigators in the research projects. Other team members have shared their wisdom over the years and have shaped our thinking significantly. Ron Seymour of Toronto Fire and Emergency Services has inspired us with his dedication to peer support. In addition, we wish to thank all the emergency responders who have given us the privilege to share in their experiences through our clinical work, training, and research. We have tremendous respect for their resilience and ingenuity. Finally, thanks to Albert Roberts for his encouragement, facilitation, and enthusiastic support of this project.

The research reported in this book was generously supported through the Social Sciences and Humanities Research Council of Canada.

—Cheryl and Ted

Thanks to Graham, Kaitlyn, and Dylan for tolerance, support, and fabulous senses of humor.—CR
I also wish to thank colleagues and mentors David Hoath, Keith Travis, Liz White, Donna Little, Madeline Brynes, and Janina Bober. Thanks to Vicky Lynham and Clare Pirie for their research support. And thanks to the love and support of my partner Sue and daughter Jacqueline.—TB

Contents

IN THE LINE
OF FIRE

1

SETTING THE STAGE

Following the crash of two subway trains during rush hour, ambulance, fire, and police crews worked tirelessly in cramped and difficult conditions to move ambulatory victims safely from the tunnel, to carry out the injured, and to extricate those trapped in the debris. The response was time-consuming and hot. Paramedics held the hands of trapped victims and reassured them. In the end, however, three passengers died during the rescue attempts. As indicated by the advertisement in figure 1.1, which ran in newspapers one week later, the public response was overwhelmingly supportive towards emergency responders. People brought food and drink and offered their thanks. Emergency responders were called heroes. At the public inquiry that followed, however, it was suggested that altered fire and ambulance procedures during the course of extrications could have saved at least one life. It seems that heroism isn't necessarily forever.

On a hot August night, the crew on Engine 11 arrived at a blazing home. A woman on the lawn screamed that her children were still in the building. Firefighters immediately set about dousing the flames. Two firefighters entered the building and managed to rescue the children. A newspaper photographer managed to get a picture of Joe Driscol (not his real name) emerging from the flaming building with a three-year-old child in his arms. The picture ran on the cover of every local newspaper declaring that Driscol was a hero. Television and radio stations sought interviews and described his brave actions. But Driscol did not want to be heralded as a hero.

On Friday August 11, 1995 at 6:05 pm, tragedy struck on the Spadina subway line.

The Toronto Transit Commission extends heartfelt sympathy to the families and friends of our customers who died or were injured in this tragic event.

🙐

And to Metro's professional emergency response teams and the dozens of individuals from across the community, businesses, and TTC employees who reacted so swiftly to this disaster:
In the face of extremely difficult and trying conditions, you performed with courage and caring, providing comfort and assistance to those in need. To all those throughout the community – both professionals and volunteers – who contributed so courageously and selflessly during this tragic event, we wish to express our overwhelming gratitude. Your heroism will not be forgotten.

Figure 1.1. Toronto Transit Commission

He repeatedly stated that there is no one hero in such a situation; rather, everyone works as a team to manage risk, preserve life, and protect property. Other firefighters in the hall who also worked on that fire shared Driscol's sentiments, but expressed them by putting HERO signs on Joe's locker and bunk and playing Tina Turner's "We Need a Hero" over the loud speaker.

After another long day of body recovery on a handful of hours of sleep, a firefighter heads home, passing the American flags, the mountains of food and water, and the posters that say THANKS and THANKS, HEROES. As he has done every night, he arrives home, eats, and sits on the couch with his wife for a moment. His wife briefly brings him up to speed on the neighborhood, a new baby was born. Meanwhile, another firefighter's family grieves. He's trying to listen, trying to win the battle, but he's tired and loses. He is asleep, she's in midsentence. A few hours later he is up, sheepishly, when some people drop by to say thanks and offer support to the neighborhood hero. His wife asks, "Does the hero have time to take out the garbage tonight?" He smiles, appreciating his wife's sense of humor. It has been their way, her way, to help him stay steady, as he juggles the work, the thoughts of Ground Zero, and his role as a firefighter, as a neighbor, a father, and husband.

This book is about everyday heroism. It is about the work emergency responders do and the traumatic situations they face when serving the public. It is about the impact of this work on them and their families. We look at factors at multiple levels that make these jobs and the impact they have on individuals more difficult or less difficult. Our purpose is to show that it is not one event alone that causes trauma in people who work in the emergency services. Rather, trauma is a result of the interplay between an event, the person encountering the event, the public and media response to the event, the organization in which responders work, and the supports and life that they have outside the workplace. In the end, we attempt to provide suggestions for intervention that take into account these multiple levels of influence. The goal is to assist mental health workers, managers of emergency service organizations, and peer support team members to realize that there is no single, one-size-fits-all model for assistance. Interventions must fall on two continuums: one that spans prevention, early intervention after a traumatic event, and long-term follow up, and one that spans the individual responders, their families, the organizations in which they work, and the community as a whole.

The information contained in this book is derived from a series of research projects conducted on two continents with more than 350 police officers, paramedics, and firefighters, and with 300 emergency mental health practitioners. These projects involved quantitative data gathering through the use of questionnaires addressing various issues regarding exposure to traumatic events, public response to the events, personal and organizational supports, and levels of distress experienced by emergency service workers. In addition, qualitative research interviews were conducted with over 50 emergency responders to more fully understand their experiences, what aspects of the job they find most troublesome, and what forms of assistance are most useful.

More important, however, is our combined experience of over 40 years of clinical work in emergency departments and with emergency service organizations. This experience has included managing crisis intervention teams in both health care and emergency service settings. For instance, for 15 years we have shared the clinical director duties of an interagency, multidisciplinary crisis response team at Toronto Pearson International Airport, and through this experience we have had the honor of working with dedicated professionals from many emergency service organizations. We have also conducted interventions following critical events in the workplace and have provided mental health services in disaster situations.

In chapter 2 we begin with an overview of the types of critical events to which emergency responders are exposed. This chapter addresses human tragedies encountered in the course of everyday duties. One type includes dramatic events such as the death of a child, multiple casualties in a large traffic accident, a line-of-duty death, or situations where the responder's own safety is at risk. These events are easy to identify as distressing and are most likely to result in intervention services provided by peer support teams and mental health professionals. A second category involves low profile, individual tragedies, such as the isolated death of an elderly person or the despair of a suicide victim. These events may connect with a responder at a highly personal level, causing hidden distress that is generally not acknowledged or even identified by intervention programs.

The experiences of emergency responders and their subsequent reactions to these experiences are placed in a theoretical context in chapter 3. Here we review current theories for understanding response to adversity. *Stress theory* attempts to explain the biological and psychological reactions experienced by a person faced with excessive demands, often on an ongoing basis. From this perspective, stress occurs when there is a significant imbalance between one's demands and the type and amount of internal and external resources available to cope with those demands. *Occupational stress theory* further refines this concept and applies it to stressors encountered in the workplace. It suggests that when the requirements of the job do not match the capabilities, resources, or needs of the worker, harmful physical and emotional consequences can result. Thus, the ongoing demands of the job and the consistent exposure to suffering and tragedy can gradually wear on the emergency responder and in the long run create physical, emotional, and social problems. *Crisis theory* and *trauma theory* refer to more specific traumatic events. *Crisis theory* describes the psychological disequilibrium experienced by individuals as a result of a hazardous event or situation that disrupts normal patterns of behavior and cannot be remedied by using customary coping strategies. A crisis causes emotional distress and behavioral disruption but generally is resolved within a few weeks, as the individual, with or without assistance from others, develops new strategies for managing the event. *Trauma theory*, on the other hand, refers to a set of physical, cognitive, and psychological responses to a particular horrifying event. As a result of this exposure, individuals experience symptoms of intrusive thoughts and dreams, autonomic arousal, and behavioral avoidance of stimuli that may trigger memories of the event. Increasingly, however, trauma theorists are aware that people are highly individual in their responses to horrifying events, and that several individuals encountering the same event will have great disparity in the severity and duration of symptoms. Finally, *secondary trauma* or *vicarious trauma* refers to overwhelming emotions and thoughts experienced by people who are exposed to traumatic imagery through their work with others. From this perspective, the process of empathically joining with others who are suffering allows for the transfer or assimilation of traumatic symptoms in the worker. Thus, merely witnessing the distress of another, such as a grieving parent, can lead to distress on the part of workers.

Clearly all the theories discussed above—stress theory, occupational stress theory, crisis theory, trauma theory, and secondary or vicarious trauma theory—are highly relevant to understanding responses to stress and traumatic events in emergency workers. It is the premise of this book, however, that each of these theories in isolation is inadequate in explaining the complexity of the work exposures and subsequent reactions of emergency responders. Rather, we contend that individual responses to adverse events are best understood within the broad context of an individual's life experience. One approach to comprehending the complex interactions between people and their environment is the ecological framework. This perspective allows for multiple levels of influence in any one situation. For instance, emotional distress is rarely predicted by any one event. Certainly, as we discuss in this book, emergency responders are exposed to events far beyond the average person's experience. It is not surprising that people will be affected by such exposures. Yet reactions to even the most gruesome and devastating of events are highly variable. Thus, we must consider the personal history and concurrent struggles of the individual encountering the event. We must consider the organizational environment in which they work. We must consider the societal response to the event in terms of public attitude and media attention. We must also consider the social supports an individual has in terms of friends and family. From an ecological perspective, the relationship between these levels of influence is the best way of understanding response to any adverse event.

In chapter 4, we review catastrophic incidents, which in and of themselves affect many of those responding. Disasters are events that occur rarely if ever in the work life of the average responder; yet when they do occur, they have lasting impacts. Disasters are unique in terms of the extent of loss and devastation, the length of time and hours of work involved in the rescue and recovery efforts, and the disruption to the daily and family life routine of emergency service workers.

We continue our discussion of multiple levels of influence, which began in the chapters on daily exposures to events and disasters, by considering the individual encountering the event. Chapter 5, "The Right Stuff," begins by describing the types of reactions encountered by emergency responders exposed to stressors. The symptoms experienced by responders range from mild distress to symptoms that significantly influence functioning. Preexisting or concurrent vulnerabilities often contribute to the development of more severe symptoms. Someone who is also dealing with other losses or stressors may have reduced capacity to cope with additional traumas. In addition, coping strategies vary between individuals. Coping strategies discussed by emergency responders include the deliberate use of cognitive strategies. For instance, during a traumatic event, emergency workers describe conscious attempts to shut out the emotional reactions of family members of the victim and visualize the next technical step to be accomplished. They also discuss the need to shut down their own emotions. Following the event, an additional strategy involves reviewing the event from a technical standpoint and identifying learning opportunities. Other types of strategies involve having a positive personal life, talking to family, exercising, and blowing off steam with colleagues.

All workplace traumas are experienced within the context of organizational culture and climate. Recent advances in workplace health research have found that psychosocial factors in the workplace have a significant effect on work-related health problems. Occupational health research indicates that a lack of control over work demands and a lack of resources to work effectively seriously damage the health of workers. This is particularly true in the instances of high psychological demand. Higher rates of heart disease are evident in jobs that impose unpredictable and uncontrollable demands, particularly when one's skills and decision-making abilities are underutilized. Clearly high demand and unpredictability are central factors in the jobs of emergency responders. In addition, the organizational structure is frequently based on a hierarchical command model that demands high levels of accountability and low levels of autonomy and input into policies and procedures. The degree to which distress is acknowledged, accepted, and supported varies considerably between organizations and between departments within any one organization.

In the aftermath of September 11, 2001, the North American public is aware as never before of the stresses, danger, and potential for fatalities inherent in the work of emergency responders. While the initial public response to tragic events may be an outpouring of support and admiration for emergency workers, this support inevitably wanes and society begins to consider what might have been done to facilitate a more positive outcome to the disaster. Following the occurrence of a significant event such as a mass casualty or death of an emergency responder in the line of duty, frequently a postmortem inquiry is performed in the form of a coroner's inquest, an internal investigation, or a specially formed public commission. The experience of going through a postmortem review can be extremely stressful for workers. Emergency service workers are often faced with life-threatening and uncontrollable situations where quick thinking and reasoned action are required. Failure to deal with these acute situations optimally may result in professional condemnation, community sanctions, and possible legal actions. Chapter 7, "Heroes or Villains?," discusses inquiries into deaths that occur during a traumatic event and the media and public response to emergency service workers during these review processes.

A final level of influence that must be considered when discussing the impact of traumatic events on emergency responders is their personal support network, in particular their families. There is considerable evidence that family support is a key protective factor in managing the stresses of the jobs of emergency responders. However, families of responders are also significantly affected by their loved one's choice of work. Daily stressors include coping with shift work and long and unpredictable hours that can interfere with family activities and undermine a sense of support. Added to this is the constant fear for the emergency responder's safety. When critical events occur, these fears are heightened. Over time, the coping strategies employed by emergency responders can cause additional stress on families. One result of exposure to trauma described by workers is that they at times felt disengaged and emotionally distant from family members. Another issue is generalized anger and irritability, often vented on family. Further, responders describe generalized fears for the safety of family members and a tendency to become overprotective. In the chapter "Are You Coming Home Tonight?" we discuss the strains that emergency work places on families and strategies for maintaining this central resource.

Using the ecological framework, in chapters 9 and 10 we suggest a continuum of interventions aimed at addressing the multiple levels of influence that lead to trauma and stress reactions. Interventions for complex issues, such as trauma in the emergency service, cannot be simple, one-size-fits-all models. Rather, interventions must be offered at different times along the spectrum of prevention, before the event, during an event of massive proportions, and after the event has occurred. Interventions must not focus only on the individual, suggesting that they alone are responsible for their reactions. Rather, we must also address societal and organizational issues that support or hinder healthy recovery from severe stress. In addition, intervention must span from policy development and consultation, to training and establishment of support programs, to clinical interventions with individuals and groups. We suggest that any intervention must incorporate a thorough understanding of the situation, the organizational culture, the organizational response to the individual experiences of stress and trauma, and the level of stress and support individuals within the organization experience on a regular basis. One of the most effective ways of achieving this is through developing programs and trauma response teams that draw upon the experience and wisdom of members of the organization.

Next, in the chapters "Laying the Foundation" and "Keeping It Going," we discuss the development of trauma response teams within emergency service organizations and within communities. Team structure and responsibilities and support for the team must be carefully considered. In developing a credible program, team members must be chosen on the basis of their personal skills and abilities, the constituency they represent, and their reputation with others. Training must follow the principles of adult learning theory and focus on team building and ethics, as well as skills such as listening, assessing, and group leadership. Once teams have been established, continued work must focus on maintaining a strong administrative structure, on continuously upgrading the skills of team members, on maintaining the motivation and commitment of team members, and on assessing the quality of services provided by each team member. Finally strategies for self-care for team members must be developed and monitored.

We end with a chapter titled "Does It Work?," in which we review the evidence related to workplace interventions following traumatic events. Considerable controversy exists over the use of certain types of interventions, in particular the critical incident stress-debriefing model. The research literature is somewhat contradictory, in large part because different types of studies review different aspects of interventions. There has been a tendency for groups and individuals to consider only one aspect of the literature and conclude either that there is tremendous support for all aspects of the intervention, or that the intervention is not only useless but also harmful and must be abandoned. We attempt to find a middle ground in these discussions and seek to determine which aspects of early interventions are useful and have empirical support and which are potentially harmful. We believe that responsible practitioners in this area, both those with mental health backgrounds and those with emergency service professional backgrounds, wish to provide effective and responsible interventions. Therefore, in addition to reviewing research evidence currently available, we make suggestions for evaluating the programs each of us provide.

2

ALL IN A DAY'S WORK

Traumatic Events in the Line of Duty

Emergency workers are exposed to events involving human pain and suffering on a daily basis. They work to rescue individuals trapped in crashed vehicles, they extricate people from fires, they collect the remains of suicide victims, they care for victims of assault. While for the most part emergency workers are equipped to deal with these events, on occasion one particular event will have a lasting impact. In recent years, researchers focusing on the potential impact of emergency work have recognized that exposure to death and destruction can result in post-traumatic stress symptoms and depressive symptoms in emergency workers (Bryant and Harvey, 1996; Marmar et al., 1999; McFarlane, 1988; Regehr, Hill, and Glancy, 2000). Symptoms described include recurrent dreams, feelings of detachment, dissociation, guilt about surviving, anger and irritability, depression, memory or concentration impairment, somatic disturbances, alcohol and substance use, and reexperiencing of symptoms when exposed to trauma stimuli (Gersons, 1989; Solomon and Horn, 1986). These symptoms undoubtedly have an impact on the health and well-being of emergency workers and their families.

While most of us can imagine that emergency workers will be affected by an event involving mass casualty, it is frequently a smaller and less sensational event that triggers an emotional response. Such events as the lonely death of an elderly person or the suicide of a desperate individual do not make the news or capture public attention. They do not result in an outpouring of public support for emergency services. Yet these quieter events may have more lasting effects than other, more dramatic events involving the loss of many lives. In this chapter, we discuss the types of traumatic events emergency workers encounter and begin to consider the impact of this exposure on them.

Dramatic Events

The research literature and the popular press have focused a great deal in recent years on critical events that occur in the line of duty for emergency workers and the impact that this may have on them as individuals. This focus generally involves mass casualties, including natural disasters (McFarlane, 1998); bus crashes killing children (Dyregrov, Kristoffersen, and Gjestad, 1996); explosions on a naval ship (Ursano, Fullerton, Vance, and Kao, 1999); airplane crashes (Brooks and McKinlay, 1992); train wrecks (Tehrani, Walpole, Berriman, and Reilly, 2001); and terrorist attacks (Galea et al., 2002; Pfefferbaum, Doughty, et al., 2002). It is easy to see why such large-scale events would draw the attention of researchers, the media, and the public. While disasters of great magnitude are unlikely to happen often in the career of an emergency responder, most emergency responders are nevertheless exposed to many gruesome and dramatic events.

In the studies we have conducted with emergency responders, we provided a list of events that clinical experience and the literature have suggested may cause distress in those exposed while on duty. These events included the death of a patient in the responder's care, the death of a child, exposure to mass casualties, witnessing violence perpetrated against a member of the public, being personally assaulted by a member of the public, a responder feeling his or her life was threatened while on duty, and having a coworker die in the line of duty. Figure 2.1, "Exposure to Critical Events," demonstrates the rates of this exposure in three groups: 103 Canadian firefighters, 164 Australian firefighters (Regehr, Hill, and Glancy, 2000), and 86 Canadian paramedics (Regehr, Goldberg, and Hughes, 2002). As can be seen in this figure, paramedics, as a result of the nature of their work, report significantly higher rates of exposure to death of patients, multiple casualties, deaths of children, and violence against others, with over 80% reporting exposure to each of these events. In addition, paramedics were more likely to have been assaulted (almost 70%) and feel that they had been in situations where their lives were at risk (56%). Nevertheless, over 40% of the firefighters in Canada report being exposed to violence against others and witnessing multiple casualties; over 40% of firefighters in both countries had been exposed to the death of a child, and approximately 30% of firefighters report experiencing the death of a person in their care. These

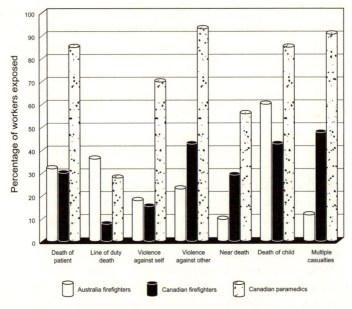

Figure 2.1. Exposure to Critical Events

findings are consistent with those of other studies. For instance, 56% of volunteer firefighters in New South Wales reported that their safety had been seriously threatened at some time, 26% in the last year (Marmar et al., 1999). Similarly, 82% of ambulance personnel in Scotland reported exposure to a particularly disturbing incident in the past 6 months (Alexander and Klein, 2001).

In addition to asking emergency responders whether they had been exposed to the events listed above, we were also interested in whether emergency responders would identify that these events were distressing for them. We therefore asked them to identify whether they had ever experienced "significant emotional distress" as a result of events on the same list. The results of this question appear in figure 2.2, "Workers Exposed Reporting Distress." It is clear from this graph that the event causing distress for the greatest number of people is the death of a child, followed by the death of a colleague in the line of duty and the death of a patient for whom the responder had responsibility. There is a fair bit of discrepancy between groups regarding the distress experienced as a result of multiple casualties, violence against themselves, and risk to their own safety. These findings come to light when we examine interviews held with emergency responders about their experiences and exposure.

The next sections report the results of 50 interviews conducted with paramedics, firefighters, and police officers. The interviews were 1–2 hours in length and were conducted in a place most convenient to the respon-

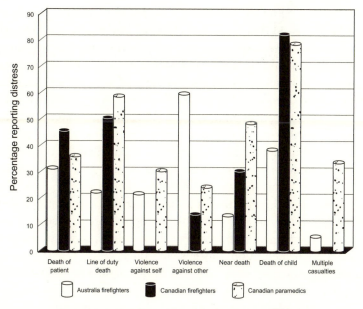

Figure 2.2. Workers Exposed Reporting Distress

der, often an office or their home. Interviews followed a semistructured interview guide that included questions about stressors encountered on the job, the effects of the stress on participants, organizational supports, and strategies for dealing with stress. The interviews were audiotaped and transcribed to ensure accuracy of data. Data were analyzed for themes using the Nvivo computer program. Throughout this research process, members of emergency service organizations have acted as community partners, working to develop the research questions and discussing data as portions of the analysis were completed. This process has provided an opportunity to confirm and expand upon the trends developed in the analysis, thereby enhancing the trustworthiness of the data (Erlandson, Harris, Skipper, and Allen, 1993).

The Death of a Child

In our clinical experience and in the research interviews that we conducted, the events emergency responders most commonly cite as causing traumatic reactions involve violence against children. In cases of child abuse and neglect in particular, responders are able to recall in specific detail aspects of the victim and of the environment in which he or she was found. One paramedic described a 10-year-old child whose throat had been slit by his father. Another described a dirty, neglected baby who was sleeping on a mattress on the floor with his parents in a basement squat and was smothered when the parents rolled over on the child as they slept. A third

described a baby who had been burned to death in an oven. A police officer described a child that had been viciously bitten and scalded to death
with boiling water. He explained that despite the fact that he had many
years of experience on the force and had seen many gruesome things by
that point, this particular event caused nightmares and distress. Another
officer described the sense of helplessness that he experienced when a baby
died. As he held the three-month-old in his arms, he states that was the
only time in his life that he felt overwhelmed by helplessness.

Emergency responders indicated that the impact of child deaths and severe abuse of children was due to the fact that they were unable to understand why something like this might have occurred. One recalled, "I
thought it was the child's father that had done this and I sat, just outside
the building for the longest time just trying to make sense of it and of
course that's the biggest trap in any of these things, trying to make sense
out of what are by definition nonsensical things."

Dealing with the grief of others adds to the trauma of child deaths. Responders described situations where parents were screaming and beating
on the backs of firefighters and paramedics as they were attempting to assist an injured child or a baby who died suddenly in the crib. One paramedic described his feelings toward the mother of a dead child. "It was just
heart-wrenching; I didn't want to talk to her, I didn't want anything to do
with her at all. I couldn't even look at her."

A firefighter described working on a child, although he knew it was dead.
"The parents are just looking at each other and looking at you to do something, but not saying anything. You put the baby in your hand and the kid's
head just fits in the palm of your hand. You look at it, and you look at the
parents, and you know that you're doing something just to pacify them, just
to show them that there's something you're doing. You're ventilating and
also doing compressions. The baby is dead but you're going through the
motions and you're just pumping away and everybody is looking at you and
the other crew members are just looking at you looking at them, because
they understand what you're going through. And they're going, 'Holy shit,
there's nothing you can do.' They know it's over."

Violence toward Others

While television shows such as Law and Order and Third Watch make it
appear that rape and murder are common-place occurrences in emergency
work, exposure to violence and inhumanities is described by responders as
highly distressing. One aspect of this is the shock associated with the first
exposure to the scene. In our studies, one firefighter described an incident
where his truck responded to a call in which they were told that someone
was having difficulty breathing. When they arrived on the scene, they dis-

covered a female real estate agent whose throat had been cut when show-ing a property to a client. "Surprise! . . . She wasn't having difficulty breath-ing, she was bleeding to death." He then described his reaction. "Suddenly you kick into a high gear, you go into an adrenaline rush, basically, and you're trying to keep a handle on everything, and it's around 2 hours, at the end of it you just try to breathe." A police officer and a firefighter both de-scribed their attendance at a murder-suicide. At first when they entered the property, they were confronted with a woman who had cut her throat and abdomen but was still alive. Upon further investigation, they discovered the dismembered body of her husband. "I saw in the bedroom this guy's leg leaning up in the corner. That's all I saw was a human leg."

Sewell (1994) adds that the impact of homicide investigations on police officers involves not only exposure to the sights and smells of the scene, but also the responsibility for dealing with surviving family members. This in-volvement can last for years as family members seek information on aspects of the investigation, arrest, and trial.

Multiple Casualties and Patients
Dying in Care

As can be seen in figure 2.1, which depicts exposure to critical events, ex-posure to multiple casualties within the work environment is an experi-ence shared by almost every paramedic and a substantial minority of fire-fighters. Those that have the greatest impact involve some aspect that is emotionally memorable. One paramedic described a multivehicle collision involving automobiles and a transport truck. As emergency workers re-moved the deceased man and woman from one vehicle, they discovered a dead baby in the back seat. Another described working to extricate a se-verely injured man who explained to the responders that it was the wed-ding anniversary of himself and his dead wife, who was trapped beside him. A firefighter described watching two severely injured teenagers die before his eyes. He discussed how this memory plagued him as he inter-acted with his own teenagers.

Multiple casualties occurring in the context of disasters have an even greater impact. This will be discussed in more detail in chapter 4. Briefly, however, responders in the Toronto area, where we conducted many of our studies, remember with vivid detail the crash of a DC-9 that occurred in 1972. One paramedic described the scene. "We were the third unit on the scene and we got to view the crater where the nose had gone down. It was about a 15-foot crater, and there were body parts all over the place. There was all kinds of debris flying around. It was a total scene of chaos. There were little children there, parts of them, and half bodies strapped into the seat. I still have dreams of that [30 years later]."

Line-of-Duty Death

A line-of-duty death has a profound impact on emergency service organizations and those who work in the organizations. We speculate that the levels of distress identified in the graph above displaying subjective reports of distress are in fact low, as many people responding to that question in our study may have had a death occur in their organization, but not of someone with whom they were closely associated. Other researchers have underscored the traumatic impact of a death on duty on other members of the organization (Violanti, 1999). A study of police officers suggested that the death of a partner, the line-of-duty death of another officer, or the suicide of a colleague were among the top 6 of 144 possibly stressful events on the job. Of other items in the top six, two related to the shooting or killing of another person by a police officer in the line of duty (Sewell, 1983). Violanti and Aron (1994) found that killing someone in the line of duty and having a fellow officer killed ranked first and second on a list of stressors for 103 police officers.

One responder recalled a situation occurring 23 years earlier in which three firefighters with whom he was acquainted died in a warehouse fire. A police officer discussed the loss of a colleague and friend when his vehicle was hit by a drunk driver who had a suspended license. Friends continue to carry a plaque commemorating him to annual police events. A paramedic described in detail the shooting death of a police officer.

> It happened so close to the police station that there was hundreds of police officers, or what seemed to be hundreds of police officers, there. All of them stressed to the maximum, because they could see themselves lying on the ground instead of him. We had everybody from the apartment complex standing out on their balconies yelling and screaming. We had a six-foot fence that we had to get around, which means our response was delayed. The officers were getting angry and yelling and screaming and trying to pull our stretcher over a six-foot fence. So we're trying to gain control of the officers, we're trying to gain control of the scene, we're trying to work on a patient with people screaming and throwing things above us.
>
> When we got to the hospital the media became a big issue. Everybody was there from every news station you could think of—that heightened the stress. The hospital trauma team is now part of the scenario, and they're interested in trying to figure out what's just gone on. So we're trying to update them, update the police chief, who was on the scene, the Internal Investigations Unit of the department. All of those things now add further stress on us. It sort of just kept piling and piling and piling throughout the entire call, it never let off once. It just kept getting worse in terms of stress.
>
> Then at the hospital was the time that the officers could finally just

break down completely. That impacts on you to see adult police officers, male and female, all over the hallways crying.

He was only 20 something years old, so that added further impact. Ultimately, by the time we left the hospital, his fiancée had arrived. I felt like I gave his spouse a chance to see him when he was still alive. If it hadn't been for our revival, he would have been dead at the scene and therefore she wouldn't have had a chance to see him, and nor would any of his family. Sometimes it's not the patient we impact, it's the family, and that kind of makes it all worthwhile at the end of the day.

Risk of Personal Injury

In general, emergency responders do not describe violence directed toward themselves as traumatic unless it threatens their lives. Responders indicate that they have been assaulted, particularly on domestic violence calls, surrounded by dangerous characters on the street, and threatened by people on drugs. However, these events do not stay with them as traumatic experiences. For the most part, emergency responders are physically fit individuals well trained in defending themselves. One paramedic described feeling fearful and carrying a flashlight for use as a club in the early part of his career. He indicates that he was "set straight" by a more senior paramedic and has now learned to talk his way out of situations. Another stated, "You have to be able to talk your way out of some fairly serious altercations, because drunks and junkies are not necessarily known for their demeanor."

Understandably, responders did experience distress when confronted with severe risk to life and limb. One paramedic described feeling "shaken up" when he and his partner were attacked by a man experiencing diabetic shock. He recalls the man's wife standing in the home holding her infant as the man punched out a window and destroyed furniture. In the end it took six men to subdue the patient. A police officer described how he and his partner were attacked. The officer was thrown over a balcony and believed his back was broken because he was unable to move. He watched helplessly as his partner was beaten until help arrived. While his back was not broken, the injuries caused him to be off duty for a period of time. Another officer was shot during an episode where a gunman was being contained in a building. The bullet did not penetrate his Kevlar vest, so he continued working to the end of his shift. Later, in retrospect, as he looked at the severe bruising, he realized the risk to his life. Firefighters described being in situations where their air supply was running low or a fire was burning too hot for them to safely remain in the building.

Another officer was involved in an incident where a civilian was shot and killed by an armed robber. He was off duty at the time and was an unarmed customer in the business where the shooting occurred. He described being in such close proximity that the bullet actually bounced off him after penetrating the victim.

> This thing started happening with the sound of a shot. When that happens, you hear one thing at a time, you don't hear everything. I don't know how else to describe it. In this particular case, one person was the major speaker, but there were other noises happening that I wasn't hearing, which were the employees screaming and the yelling that they were doing as they were told. I pretty much focused in because I wanted to know what he was saying. I had been lying on the floor at this point, and I had been watching everything step by step. When the shot went off, and I heard the shot ring, and I knew what it was, the best way I can describe it is my vision shut down to the carpet within about a foot around me, and I couldn't see anything else. I know a shot, and I've heard shots, and I've shot guns. I know what a gun sounds like, and the sound sounded very soft in comparison, even though it was in an enclosed area. It should be loud, like so loud it should ring your ears, but it wasn't. It was muffled, in a big way. And then the adrenaline or fear or whatever it is that runs through your body when that happens, shut everything down to the point where I could only see in the immediate area of me. And then again I began doing some conscious things because I'm a policeman. I started looking for what had hit me. And after that, the field of vision became open again.

One officer emphasized the feeling of helplessness in a shooting incident in which he and several police officers were "just basically trying to get cover, and not knowing where this guy was, and he fired over the twenty minutes about six rounds, and that one shook me up a little bit because it was kind of tense, not knowing where this guy was going to pop up . . . what are we going to do, how do we find this guy, how do we get out of here, and stop this guy from doing it."

Responses and Interventions in Traumatic Events

There is no question that emergency responders describing these events are profoundly affected. In our studies, 64% of police, firefighters, and paramedics indicated that they had experienced significant emotional distress as a result of an incident that occurred on the job. Firefighters were least likely to indicate that they had ever experienced significant distress as a result of an event encountered at work such as the death of a child, multiple casualties, or risk to themselves (45.6%); paramedics were most likely (83.7%). This is not surprising when one takes into account that only 67.1% of firefighters reported encountering events and 100% of both police and paramedics in our studies had encountered one of the events listed. Police and paramedics were also far more likely to have encountered multiple tragic events. The effects of these exposures are described in detail in chapter 5, "The Right Stuff."

As a result of the exposure that traumatic events get within emergency service organizations and in the popular press, it is not surprising that many of the intervention efforts have been directed at these types of events. The most well known of these approaches is the crisis debriefing group model, an early-intervention strategy designed to mitigate post-traumatic stress reactions (Bell, 1995; Dyregrov, 1989; Mitchell, 1982; Raphael, 1986). This model offers a brief group treatment approach, usually limited to a single session. It is based on the premise that emergency service professionals possess the internal resources to deal with most work-related events but can benefit from limited extra assistance in extreme circumstances. Other aspects generally included in intervention programs include preventative education, informal group opportunities to discuss the event (defusings), family outreach, and follow-up counseling.

Quiet Losses and Despair

Emergency responders experience many of the traumatic events discussed above throughout the course of their careers. In interviews we have conducted with police, fire, and ambulance workers, we began by asking them to describe events in which they have been involved that they believed others would classify as traumatic. Most responders discussed horrific events that contained much blood and gore, but many were quick to add that these were not the events that "have left me sleepless." Frequently, the events that do lead to distress are quiet events that connect in some way with the emergency responder on an emotional level. As mentioned above, often this relates to the pain experienced by parents who lose a child. One firefighter talked about his realization that this loss will change the lives of these parents—that a part of their life was over because their child had died. Another firefighter vividly recalls the looks of two children whose mother had died in a car crash. "The kids are looking at me. Like, 'Do something.' Who else can they look to for help? But that's the kicker, I can't do anything."

Others talked about worrying about family members who had lost a loved one close to Christmas. One paramedic in particular recalled an elderly Eastern European man dying in the emergency room and his son, a tough-looking construction worker, was crying and saying "Daddy, Daddy, Daddy" in his own language. The responder's parents were from the same country and he spoke the language. "That one still chokes me up a bit." A firefighter described attending to a dead alcoholic who was still clutching a bottle in his hand. The man had been found by his daughter. The firefighter recalled, "That was in the days when I was trying to get my father to stop drinking."

The death of a patient in care can also have a lasting effect. One paramedic described working with a cardiac patient. The man said to him, "I'm going to die." And the paramedic responded that everything was under control and that he was fine. "Then his last words to me were 'goodbye,' and that was it. That really struck me." Another recalled the routine transfer of a woman with a chronic lung condition who was on a ventilator. En route she went into distress and died. "She was looking at me, like she was pleading for me to save her. That was early in my career before we had our current equipment. It really bothered me."

Another type of event recounted by some respondents was that of people dying alone. "Loneliness, people being alone and very ill, that bothers me." One paramedic described taking an elderly man who lived alone away from his apartment for the last time and transporting him to a palliative care unit. Other workers described the despair they felt when discovering a suicide victim and wondering what had happened that might have lead to this solution. "You're wondering why would [he commit suicide]—look at this, he's got everything, why would he do this? . . . there was no indication . . . that was like, wow, life is really frail."

Summary

The descriptions above make it clear that emergency responders are exposed to tragic events far beyond the experiences of most people. In addition, they are not simply exposed to one tragic event in the course of their careers; rather, a career involves a string of horrifying exposures outside the average person's experience. These events involve various types of human tragedy, including the abuse and death of innocent children, severe violence perpetrated by one individual against another, accidents caused by negligence, suicide, and lonely deaths. One police officer summarized his experiences by stating that he had probably dealt with 100 sudden deaths; he has seen people decapitated, severed limbs, and shootings and that no one had ever asked him to talk about it before. While each of these events in and of themselves has the capacity to cause reactions, it is frequently the accumulation of events that continues to wear on an individual, until one event is the final straw. A firefighter described how his chief left the job after the death of a child—he had stated that he had seen just too many children die.

While those individuals who select a career in the emergency services are in many ways prepared for the types of events they will encounter and over the course of their careers develop strategies for managing the impact of these events, they are still human and are unlikely to be unaffected. In this book we attempt to shed some light on the following questions:

What is the impact of exposure to tragic events in the lives of others on emergency responders?

What individual, institutional, and community factors influence response to traumatic events?

How can mental health professionals assist emergency responders, their organizations, and their families to manage responses to tragic events?

3

BUILDING A FRAMEWORK

Health, Stress, Crisis, and Trauma

As anyone who has undertaken a major home renovation knows, there is more to the work than starting off with a couple of hammers, a carton of nails, a load of wood, and the goodwill of friends and family. With resourcefulness and ingenuity, a few people may "reconstruct" a house under these circumstances. Usually, however, it is helpful to have a drawing of the existing structure and the plans for changes and additions. A useful plan provides a framework to understand the overall structure and gives a sense of how things may come together. And as any "do-it-yourself" enthusiast knows, a framework is not the same as having the right tools and skills to be in the trenches pouring a foundation or, later, framing a roof. The best-made plans may not anticipate the changes and adjustments required in marrying old and new structures, nor do plans consider how a couple or family will adapt to the stresses of a major renovation. Theories, like good framework and plans, can help us to understand how things work the way they do. A useful framework can make sense of the complex process of how people and their environment interact, adjust, and adapt over time.

This chapter provides the foundation for our discussions of trauma in the emergency services during the remainder of this book. We begin by looking at the theories that have been advanced for understanding stress. These theories consider the cumulative impact of working and living in stressful environments. Next we review models for understanding the influence of acute events, including crisis theory, trauma theory, and secondary or vicarious trauma theory. Since emergency responders work in complex or-

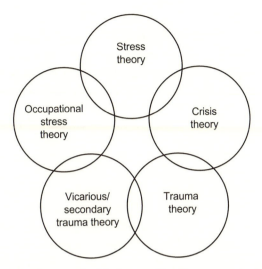

Figure 3.1. Theories for Understanding Responses to Adversity

ganizations that have rules, norms, and cultures that also influence response to adverse events, we then review occupational stress theory. While each of these theories adds to our appreciation of the experiences of emergency service workers, we suggest that they are too limited in providing a comprehensive understanding of the multiple forces that influence their response to events that occur on the job. As a result, we offer the ecological and population health frameworks to put trauma responses in the broad context of people's lived experiences and to use this broader understanding to direct our efforts at intervention.

Theories for Understanding Responses to Adversity

Stress Theory

To survive and prosper, our ancestors collected and hunted food, crafted tools, and gathered in small groups to take advantage of environmental resources and overcome environmental challenges. When acute threats were encountered, biological adaptations served as protective mechanisms. Respiration and blood pressure increased; oxygen and energy shifted to large muscles from the immune, digestive, and reproductive systems, less essential for immediate survival (see Bremner, 2002). Today, the biological mechanisms that have evolved to confront danger are remarkably similar to those of earlier times (Dubos, 1980) and are often summarized by the concept "flight or fight" (Cannon, 1932). Academic focus on these biological responses led to the development of the theory of General Adaption Syndrome (Selye, 1936), a three-stage model for stress adaptation involving (1) alarm and mobilization, when the body prepared for action, (2) resistance, in which the body's stress response diminished and returned to normal functioning, and (3) exhaustion, which occurred if stress was unrelenting or repetitive.

More recent work has substantiated the view of our biological ability to cope with adversity but has noted that earlier research focused on short-term biological responses that did not adequately account for ongoing stress and adversity, often caused by psychosocial factors, not only acute physical risk. The ongoing strain that leads to 'wear and tear' on a person has been called the allostatic load (McEwen, 2000; Sterling and Eyer, 1988). Earlier stress theories also failed to account for the buffering effects of social relationships in the experience of such stress (Repetti, Taylor, and Seeman, 2002; Ryff, Singer, and Seltzer, 2002). Further, earlier research ignored differences between male and female responses to stress, as most studies on stress were conducted on men. Although women and men may begin with a similar alarm reaction to stress, Taylor, Kemeny, Reed, Bower, and Gruenewald (2000) identified biobehavioral differences between men and women in how they continue to respond to stress. These researchers found that men often do react to stress with a "fight-or-flight" response, but women are more likely to manage their stress with a "tend-and-befriend" response. That is, females respond to threat by tending to or, in other words, protecting and nurturing children and by befriending or affiliating with others, particularly women, for social contact and support (Taylor, 2002). Fight and flight was necessary for our survival for thousands of years, and tending and befriending behaviors were equally protective of the well-being of children and families in danger. Taylor suggests that these differences are influenced by our biology and the behavior modeled in our society, and that these gender patterns are not permanent; they can be learned and developed in both men and women.

While early work on stress considered the biobehavioral aspects of stress, Lazarus and Folkman (1984) shifted attention to the cognitive aspects of stress response by defining stress as a relationship between the person and the environment that is appraised by the person to taxing or exceeding his or her resources and endangering his or her well-being. They observed that stress was an interaction and people assessed their circumstances by asking 'what's at risk and what can I do about it?'

Lazarus and Folkman identified two appraisal processes that lead to experiencing stress: a primary and a secondary appraisal process.

The *primary appraisal* considers whether an event is perceived as irrelevant, benign, positive, or stressful and considers whether the stress is a harm/loss, a threat, and/ or a challenge. *Harm/loss appraisals* include both physical and emotional features, such as diminished esteem or loss of a significant relationship. *Threat appraisals* involve the anticipation of continuing social, emotional, or economic losses, such as those related to a chronic illness or harmful exposure to a toxic substance. *Challenge appraisals* involve the potential of positive events to result in a risk of a negative outcome, such as accepting a job promotion in an unfamiliar city.

Through *secondary appraisals*, a person estimates his or her ability to deal with harm/loss by identifying the coping options available and the potential to successfully implement the preferred coping response (Lazarus and Folkman, 1984).

Stress occurs when there is a significant imbalance between one's demands and the type and amount of internal and external resources available to cope with those demands.

Lazarus and Folkman (1984) viewed stress as the balancing act between demands and resources. This addition of the cognitive process of appraisal to the theoretical formulation of stress recognizes that people are not merely on a physiological autopilot at times of stress but rather have the ability to alter their responses. Bandura's work (1997) recognized the power of a person's belief in his or her own ability to cope effectively as important to coping successfully. Belief in one's own competence, also referred to as self-efficacy, is associated with lower levels of distress following an exposure to a threat or extreme stress (Benight, Ironson, Klebe, Carver, Wynings, et al., 1999; Regehr, Cadell, and Jansen, 1999). Self-efficacy has recently been expanded to include the importance of communal efficacy in responding to large-scale stress events.

Hobfoll's (1989, 2002) Conservation of Resources (COR) theory enriched the appraisal model by introducing the importance of resources, community, and culture. In COR theory the loss and gain of personal, social, and material resources are key determinants in the experience of stress. COR's central premise is that people strive to obtain, retain, protect, and foster resources—that is, the things that they value. Resources are generally defined as objects such as property or other belongings, conditions such as a good job, personal attributes such as self-acceptance, or social skills and energies such as time or knowledge. Stress occurs when there is a threat of resource loss, actual resource loss, or the failure to regain resources after a significant loss (Hobfoll, 1989).

Research has demonstrated that after the initial exposure to extreme stress, resource losses predicted ongoing distress among disaster victims, combat veterans, rape victims, and the general population (Ironson, Wynings, Schneiderman, Baum, Rodrigues, et al., 1997; Holahan, 1999; King, King, Foy, Keane, and Fairbank, 1999; Norris and Kaniasty, 1996; Monnier, Resnick, Kilpatrick, and Seals, 2002). Individual losses, like dominoes, may quickly cascade down into a series of losses without the timely injection of resources. For instance, in a police shooting where an officer is injured, there will be multiple losses and disruptions (Travis, 1993). The injured officer's personal and work roles are disrupted, and there are risks to self-esteem and confidence as a number of investigations into the event proceed. Meanwhile the other officers have temporarily lost a colleague, perhaps a support person or mentor, and the organization has one less officer. Without supports including medical intervention, physiotherapy, or post shooting peer support, the recovery of the officer may be delayed or seriously disrupted.

One of the aspects distinguishing COR from an appraisal model is that a loss of something such as reputation, self-esteem, health, security, or home, is perceived as meaningful to both the individual and the workplace community. The community to which we belong influences what resources we value and aim to protect or "hang onto." In some workplace contexts being independent and self reliant are seen as a valued qualities, whereas in other workplaces, relationship skills and getting along with the team may be most valued (Hobfoll, Jackson, Hobfoll, Pierce, and Young, 2002). Adaptation by an individual, group, or organization is seen as the ability to use resources effectively and in a culturally appropriate manner. Workplace culture will influence people's perceptions of which resources are significant and, when these resources are lost, what the idioms of distress are. The loss of a firefighter in the line of duty will be expressed differently than a loss due to retirement. The unanticipated death of a police services dog will be experienced differently by the handler than an administrative office staff. Culture, in the broad sense of race, ethnicity, age, nationality, spiritual orientation, gender, or socioeconomic power, is an aspect of the workplace that influences which skills, abilities, characteristics, tools, or equipment are valued in a workplace community (Cohen, Deblinger, Mannarino, and de Avellano, 2001).

Crisis Theory

Crisis theory has had an interesting history in that it has been an integral part of the work of social work, psychiatry, psychology, and the community volunteer movement. One of the pioneers in the development of crisis theory was Erich Lindemann (1944), who worked with the survivors of a 1942 fire in the Coconut Grove nightclub in Boston, in which close to 500 people died. Lindemann observed and documented the reactions of the survivors, which included somatic responses, behavioral changes, and emotional responses such as grief and guilt. In describing the process of their recovery, he noted the importance of grieving, adapting to the loss, and developing new relationships. Lindemann's work contributed greatly to our understanding of crisis as the response to external, unpredicted challenges to the individual. Gerald Caplan (1964) built on the work of Lindemann and expanded crisis theory to include both developmental crises such as birth and adolescence and accidental crises. Caplan's work was based in preventative psychiatry and gave prominence to the community's role in supporting health and recovery.

Roberts (2000) defines a crisis as "a period of psychological disequilibrium, experienced as a result of a hazardous event or situation that constitutes a significant problem that cannot be remedied by using familiar coping strategies. A crisis occurs when a person faces an obstacle to important life goals that generally seems insurmountable through the use of customary habits and coping patterns" (p. 7). In the workplace, a crisis may result from an event that is sudden and unexpected such as an accident, or from the accumulation of multiple events such as an employee going through a company restructuring, and job redesign followed by a job loss. As a result of exposure to crisis-producing events, people may feel a sense of disorganization, confusion, anxiety, shock, disbelief or helplessness, which may increase as usual ways of coping appear ineffective. Pearlin and Schooler (1978) describe observable consequences of ineffective coping: (1) emotional distress, (2) impaired sense of personal self-worth, (3) inability to enjoy interpersonal contacts, and (4) impaired task performance.

Crisis = the event + the individual's crisis meeting resources + the individual's perception of the event + other concurrent stressors.

Crisis theories suggest that crises have the following characteristics:

- They are perceived as sudden. Even if one anticipates a particular developmental event, when it arrives, the changes that accompany it are perceived as sudden. For instance, although one may be forewarned about the risk of a child's death at an accident scene, as a paramedic the impact and the feelings upon encountering the child's death may be sudden and unexpected.
- The individual is not adequately prepared to handle the event and normal coping methods fail. An event does not become a crisis if the individual has coping strategies that match the situation. Early retirement can be a crisis for some and an opportunity for others who had been planning to start a small business for some time.
- Crises are limited in time, lasting from 1 day to 4–6 weeks. In general, it is thought that people cannot function at a heightened level of arousal for prolonged periods of time. Individuals, particularly emer-

gency responders, are resilient, work hard to cope and seek social support from others such as co-workers and family. Those who are unable to adapt may develop other more serious mental health or emotional problems.

- Crises have the potential to produce dangerous, self-destructive or socially unacceptable behavior. In times of disequilibrium, people may be so distressed that they feel suicidal. Some may express their distress by lashing out at others and undermining social support networks.

- Crises lead to a feeling of psychological vulnerability which can be an opportunity for growth. Crises are said to offer both danger and opportunity. Frequently people emerge from a crisis situation with a greater confidence in their own strengths and abilities and new strategies for life.

At times there is confusion over crisis as a concept, since it may appear as an umbrella term encompassing hazardous events such as traumatic events, workplace critical incidents, or traumatic crisis (Hendricks and Byers, 2002; Flannery and Everly, 2000). Nevertheless, crisis theory and crisis intervention models have been useful in understanding and supporting people in the process of learning new adaptive skills. However, the short-term nature of response implied by this theory does not fully account for the responses people have to life-threatening and horrifying events.

Trauma Theory

The experience of psychological trauma in response to exposure to horrific events is a theme that can be found in the earliest of literature. Achilles in Homer's *Iliad* and Hotspur in Shakespeare's *Henry IV, Part 1* are frequently cited as excellent portrayals of what we now understand to be traumatic stress reactions secondary to involvement in combat. Psychiatrist Pierre Janet wrote in 1919, "All famous moralists of olden days drew attention to the ways in which certain happenings would leave indelible and distressing memories — memories to which the sufferer was continually returning, and by which he was tormented by day and by night" (quoted in van der Kolk and van der Hart, 1989, p. 1530). In the late eighteenth and early nineteenth centuries, many physicians began describing reactions to traumatic events including both physical responses such as "irritable heart" (Da-Costa, 1871; Oppenheimer and Rothschild, 1918), post-traumatic spinal cord injuries due to nervous shock and without apparent lesions (Page, 1885), and "neuraesthenia," a physical disorder associated with fear (Mott, 1918), and psychological reactions such as "war neurosis" (MacKenzie, 1916) and "shell shock" (Southward, 1919).

Two main theories emerged out of this literature. The first was proposed by Freud who suggested the concept of "anxiety neurosis" or "hysteria" in which a horrific psychological event leads to physical consequences (Turnbull, 1998). The second suggested that the impact of physical forces on the central nervous system experienced during a traumatic event such as a rail disaster or combat resulted in a temporary neurological dysfunction which in turn lead to symptoms (Turnbull, 1998). However, this interest in the effects of psychological trauma on individuals subsided after the end of the First World War and did not resurface again until the Second World War and again in the mid-1970s. At that time both interest in the effects of war on Vietnam veterans emerged resulting in the concept of "post-traumatic stress" and interest in the effects of rape on victims emerged resulting in the concept of "rape trauma syndrome" (Burgess and Holstrum, 1974). Together, the pressures arising from the needs of these two highly divergent groups of sufferers resulted in official recognition of post-traumatic stress disorder in the third edition of the *Diagnostic and Statistical Manual* (DSM-III) of the American Psychiatric Association in 1980.

When an individual is exposed to an event that involves actual or threatened death or serious harm to themselves or others during which they experience fear, helplessness or horror, they may subsequently experience traumatic stress.

One aspect of trauma response is viewed as neurophysiological. As a result of exposure to an experience of fear or danger, individuals undergo neurophysiological changes that enhance the capability for fight, flight or freezing. These biological responses generally return to normal levels within a period of hours. In individuals suffering from post-traumatic stress, however, several biological alterations remain including an enhanced startle response that does not habituate, increased activation of the amygdala, alterations in the hypothalamus, and decreased cortisol levels (van der Kolk, 1997; Yehuda, 1998; Yehuda, 2002). Thus, autonomic hyperarousal mechanisms related to the event continually recur and are exacerbated by traumatic memories and images. Sufferers thus find themselves alternating between states of relative calm and states of intense anxiety, agitation, anger and hypervigilance (Roberts, 2002). In part the neurophysiological influence is evidenced by the disorganization in trauma memory and the difficulty in producing a coherent narrative (Brewin, 2001). As individuals attempt to reconstruct events they discover gaps and experience spontaneous flashbacks. These flashbacks can be controlled, primarily through attempts to manipulate the probability of their being triggered by stimuli (Brewin, 2001). Thus, in order to cope with the symptoms, an individual frequently attempts to avoid exposure to stimuli that are reminiscent of the event or tries to shut out memories of the event. From this perspective, reactions to traumatic events are expected and viewed as normal.

What is problematic about this formulation, however, is that there is considerable evidence that not all people will have traumatic stress reactions to a catastrophic event. Several studies have shown that 50–80% of men and women experience potential traumatic events, but that the majority does not develop post-traumatic stress disorder (PTSD), which requires that the symptoms continue for more than 1 month (Kessler, Sonnega, Bromet, Hughes, and Nelson, 1995; Resick, 2000). For instance, a nationally representative study of 512 Israelis who had been directly exposed to a terrorist attack and 191 who had family members exposed demonstrated that while 76.7% had at least one symptom of traumatic stress, only 9.4% met the criteria for PTSD (Bleich, Gelkopf, and Solomon, 2003). In this study, the majority of people expressed optimism and self-efficacy regarding their ability to function in a terrorist attack. Similarly, a study of Latino primary care patients in the United States revealed that of those who had experienced political violence in their homeland, 18% met the criteria for PTSD (Eisenman, Gelberg, Liu and Shapiro, 2003). The reported lifetime prevalence of PTSD in the general population of the United States is reported to be 5% for men and 10% for women (Kessler et al., 1995). This is not to say that individuals are unaffected by the events, but rather that they have symptoms of distress that for the most part subside within a relatively short period of time. These findings led researchers (Litz, Gray, Bryant and Adler, 2002; Shalev, 2002) to suggest that "traumatic events" may be more appropriately called "potentially traumatizing events." Thus, the evidence is that most people are resilient and adaptive following a traumatizing event. Those who continue to have difficulty with symptoms frequently also experience other problems. It is reported that approximately 80% of men and women with post-traumatic stress disorder have co-occurring problems including depression, anxiety, significant health problems, and/or substance abuse (Schnurr and Jankowski, 1999).

It has been suggested that the ability to contain disruption caused by trauma within reasonable boundaries is associated with a cluster of personal attributes including mastery, control and flexibility, and optimism. This understanding of trauma response is primarily cognitive in nature. That is, a traumatic event violates assumptions that individuals hold about the world, such as "If I drive safely, I will not get into a horrific accident." As a result of this disjuncture between an individual's view of the world and the event that has occurred, his or her normal adaptive mechanisms fail to be activated. Sensory images of the event are stored in active memory, where they are repeatedly experienced. These intrusive thoughts and images give rise to feelings of anxiety, guilt, and fear (Horowitz, 1976). From this perspective an individual attempts to cope with the traumatic imagery in one of three ways:

1. Failing to be sensitive to the discrepant information ("It did not really happen," or "It wasn't so bad")
2. Interpreting the meaning of the information in a way consistent with current beliefs ("I brought this on myself" and "I will be more careful next time")
3. Altering existing beliefs to match the experience ("The world is really a bad place" or "Bad things happen to good people") (McCann, Sakheim, and Abrahamson, 1988)

Those individuals who are able to maintain a sense of control and optimism regarding the outcome of the event are thus expected to fare better. However, this formulation ignores other factors that influence the individual and his or her response to trauma. For instance, there is an important difference in the development of trauma symptoms when the event is attributable to human rather than natural causes. Most people believe it is profoundly different to be hit by a rock thrown by a volcano than one thrown by another human being (Briere, 2000). Secondary losses or stressors, in particular the loss of resources and the failure to replenish lost resources, are another crucial factor in trauma response (Brewin, Andrews, and Valentine, 2000; Hobfoll, 2001). For instance, people surviving a tornado may have lost loved ones, their possessions, and their community, losses that continue to influence their ability to recover. In addition, the degree of support in the environment regarding the event is important. This support includes the individual's personal network, the workplace, if it is a job-related traumatic event, and the community response to the event.

Secondary Traumatic Stress, Vicarious Traumatization, and Critical Incident Stress

Trauma theory was advanced to understand the experience of people who encountered tragic and horrifying events in their lives. In the past 20 years, the focus has broadened from considering only the victims of an event to include those who were on the scene attempting to help. A variety of concepts have arisen in the literature in recent years aimed at identifying occupational mental health issues related to trauma exposure in health care and emergency services workers. These concepts include critical incident stress, secondary traumatic stress, compassion fatigue, and vicarious traumatization. At the front lines, these terms often have been used interchangeably. At the research level, there is lack of consensus about these terms and the factors that contribute to these work-related problems.

Secondary or vicarious trauma *refers to the overwhelming emotions, thoughts, and reactions of individuals who, through their work, relate empathetically to traumatic events and survivors.*

Saakvitne (2001) suggested that it is useful to distinguish direct, secondary, and vicarious traumatization in the following manner:

- *Direct traumatization* refers to the effects of direct exposure to traumatic events or its consequences.
- *Secondary traumatization* refers to the effects of loving or feeling responsible for someone who is directly traumatized and consequently experiencing their symptoms (Saakvitne, 2001; Figley, 1999). This term is sometimes applied only to those who have a personal relationship with the victim and sometimes also includes emergency responders.
- *Vicarious traumatization* refers to the transformation of a worker's inner self as a result of empathic engagement with a traumatized client or patient (McCann and Pearlman, 1990b; Pearlman and Saakvitne, 1995; and Saakvitne, 2001).
- *Compassion fatigue* is a term used to describe the results of caring for traumatized individuals over a period of time (Figley, 1995).

Vicarious traumatization is based on theories related to trauma and constructivist self-development theory (McCann and Pearlman, 1990b; Pearlman and Saakvitne, 1995). This concept was originally used to describe the experience of mental health workers who develop symptoms of traumatic stress as a consequence of working with traumatized individuals. That is, through the process of hearing the graphic details of other people's horrifying experiences, the worker can begin to experience symptoms that include intrusive imagery, generalized fears, sleep disturbances, a changed worldview, and affective arousal (Chrestman, 1995; Regehr and Cadell, 1999). Over time vicarious traumatization leads to a diminished sense of hope. Similar to burnout, vicarious trauma may also lead to pervasive cynicism and pessimism. More recently, the term has been applied to emergency service workers who not only hear of traumatic material described by others but also witness gruesome events and experience personal risk on the job.

Critical incident stress theory applies directly to responses experienced by emergency service and health care workers encountering critical events on the job. A *critical incident* is defined as a "stressor event (crisis event) which appears to cause, or be most associated with, a crisis response; an event which overwhelms a person's usual coping mechanisms. The most severe forms of critical incidents may be considered traumatic incidents" (Mitchell and Everly, 2001, p. 3). *Critical incident stress* is the stress reaction a person or group has to a critical incident. The range of reactions includes cognitive, physical, emotional, and behavioral signs and symptoms. Sources of stress can include physical and psychosocial stresses. The model draws on Lazarus's work and states that only events appraised as challenging, threatening, or aversive will become stressors.

A *critical incident stress debriefing program* is described as crisis intervention "specifically designed to mitigate and, if possible, to prevent the development of dysfunctional and potentially disabling post traumatic syndromes and stress disorders" (Mitchell and Everly, 2001, p. 2). "CISM and the group process CISD is seen as applicable to emergency professionals, business, industry, school systems and communities to prevent post traumatic stress reaction and accelerate the recovery process for those who have experienced significant psychological trauma" (p. 85). At this time, however, there is a lack of consistent evidence for the use of critical incident debriefings as an effective means to reduce or prevent post traumatic stress. We discuss this issue in greater detail in chapter 13, which evaluates the research on interventions.

Conceptual clarity is muddled at times as the terms *crisis, traumatic stress,* and *critical incident stress* are interchanged. One important contribution of the three concepts of secondary traumatic stress, vicarious traumatization, and critical incident stress is that they raised awareness of occupational health issues relevant to traumatic events and emergency professionals. In addition to traumatic events that occur with more limited frequency, however, emergency workers are also faced with ongoing stressors in the workplace. It is the premise of this book that emergency professionals possess a resiliency, as they encounter numerous "traumatic" events in the course of their work. Nevertheless, their resources for coping can be diminished by many factors, not the least of which is ongoing workplace stress.

Occupational Health and Stress

Historically, occupational health literature was primarily concerned with the "micro" view of employee health, such as accident prevention and stress management for individual employees. Increasingly, however, occupational health researchers find workplace stress to be a multidimensional process between people and their workplace environment. This recent view is illustrated in a workplace study of the automobile industry. In five assembly plants in Ontario, employees generally had similar jobs and created similar goods. Nevertheless, results showed a five-time difference between the best and worst companies in their workers' compensation time loss claim rates (Shannon, 2000). Studies like this one are considering the role of the psychosocial determinants of employee health.

Occupational stress *is the harmful physical and emotional responses that occur when the requirements of the job do not match the capabilities, resources, or needs of the worker.*

Shannon (2000) described macro level influences as "firm-level organizational practices" linked to workplace health and safety. Firm-level factors include organizational structure and philosophy on occupational health and safety, labor markets and unions, legislation, risk and physical conditions, and financial performance and profitability. Workplace health is affected by the changing environment, which includes workplace reorganization, increasing work role complexity and redesign, the role of information and technology, labor and economic markets, and political climate. There are changes in work-related health risks, from a concern with accident prevention to biochemical hazards, infectious diseases, workplace violence and harassment, and threats of chemical, biological, radiological/nuclear, and explosive (CBRNE) terrorism. Sullivan and Frank (2000) state that insurance approaches to workplace health and injury are important, although beyond the scope of this discussion. Among the models of workplace health and well-being that have been well investigated are the demand/control/support model, the effort-reward imbalance model, and a social role theory approach.

Karask and Theorell's (1990) *demand/control/support model*, also referred to as the *job strain model*, considers the physical and psychological demands on individual workers, including the workload pace and intensity. Control is examined in terms of how much control a person has over his or her work, the extent to which the person's skills are utilized, and the variety of tasks within the job. Work that consists of high demand and low control produces high job strain and the increased risk of physical and psychological morbidity. Research with thousands of men and women in a variety of occupations has indicated that low control, high demand, and low support occupations predict high rates of sick absence and cardiovascular disease (Karasek and Theorell, 1990; Bosma, Peter, Siegrist, and Marmot, 1998). In times of workplace reorganization and redesign, when people have less control of their work and frequently perceive less possibility of advancing their position or competencies, there will be a greater risk of health-related problems (Thereoll, 2002). Social support from coworkers and supervisors may buffer the workers under high demand–low control work conditions.

Siegrist (1996) proposed the *effort-reward imbalance model*, which suggested that the perceived imbalance between the efforts and rewards associated with work leads to job strain. Effort may include both situational factors and the personal exertion required to fulfill the work role. The work role creates opportunities for rewards such as money, opportunities, increased self-esteem, and efficacy. Persistent high cost, low reward conditions result in impairment in one's work role or self-efficacy, decreased self-esteem, and less positive social connections (Siegrist, 1996). Siegrist and Peter (2000) suggest three reasons people may be remain in high cost/low gain conditions: (1) there are few career alternatives; (2) a person may intentionally choose this position to improve the likelihood of a future promotion or other rewards; or (3) a person overcommits to work in an effort to gain approval. Underestimating the demands of the job while overestimating personal ability to cope will lead to job strain.

Researchers are finding an overlap between the demand-control and effort-reward models of job strain. Studies incorporating elements of both demand-control and an effort-reward imbalance predicted a significant increase in cardiovascular disease in men and women in diverse populations, such as nurses, sawmill workers, physicians, and civil servants (Bosma, Peter, Siegriest, and Marmot, 1998; Quick and Tetrick, 2003; Sullivan and Frank, 2000). It is postulated that under these adverse work conditions the immune system is compromised.

From a social-role theory perspective, Dobreva-Martinova (2002) investigated work stress and work roles in the Canadian military. Like most professionals, those in the military have multiple roles in the workplace. Stress was related to role ambiguity or unclear work expectations, conflicting work role priorities and expectations, and role overload—that is, the amount and quantity of demands. This may be relevant as one considers how work strain has changed as the role of emergency professionals has changed. For example, the role of firefighters has increasingly changed from fire suppression to emergency medical response (Gist and Lubin, 1999). As work roles change there is likely an accompanying shift in the balance of job demands to employee control and effort to rewards, which may promote or disrupt health.

The prevailing climate of fairness and safety in the organization is also an important aspect of workplace health. Zohar (2000) suggests the safety of employees is reflected in organizational climate, which refers to shared perceptions of coworkers with regard to the policies, procedures, and practices of a workplace. Zohar (2002a, 2002b, 2003) suggests employees will view "safety climate" as the congruency between policy and day-to-day practices and priorities of the immediate supervisor and the organization. In a workplace intervention, when managers were trained to be attentive to safety there was a reduction of injuries and improved safety climate and practices (Zohar, 2000). Although the research has focused on injury rates in manufacturing, this concept may be relevant to the climate of safety in emergency services. Professionals will quickly learn whether both their physical and psychosocial well-being are priorities and protected. Research on organizational justice or equity has found that employees are aware as to whether procedural and relational fairness is a priority. Employees are able to recognize consistency and fairness in decision making (procedural equity) and respectful, attentive, and honest relationships with their supervisors. A low quality of organizational fairness has been related to increased sick absences and mental health problems (Kivimaki, Elovainio, Vahtera, Virtanen, and Stansfeld, 2003).

This section has advanced the view that psychosocial factors in the workplace such as high effort/low reward, high demand/low control, low organizational/coworker support, a poor climate of safety, and a sense of unfairness lead to an accumulation of stress and in turn are detrimental to one's health. Consequences can include emotional exhaustion, cynicism, and decreased productivity, or as once described as the career phases of 'recruitment, rookie, resentment and retirement' (Lee and Ashforth, 1996; Maslach and Leiter, 1997; Maslach and Jackson, 1981). As will be discussed in the coming chapters, emergency service organization and professionals typically experience daily hassles, at times chronic organizational stress, along with the routine exposure to traumatic events. There is a need for integration of the promising models advanced by occupational stress and trauma stress research and interventions, to better address the range of health risks to emergency professionals.

Comprehensive Theories for Understanding Human Experiences

Ecological Framework

To this point we have discussed specific theories regarding stress, crisis, and trauma that help us understand particular adverse events that individuals encounter. Each of these theories focuses on a particular type of stressor— for instance, general stress or workplace stress, a personal crisis such as a sudden and significant life change, or an event that is life-threatening to oneself or someone else. The various theories have differing understandings of the nature of the experience of the adverse event and how difficulties stemming from the stressor are resolved. These are summarized in table 3.1. We contend, however, that individual responses to adverse events are best understood within the broad context of an individual's life experience. One approach to comprehending the complex interactions between people and their environment is the *ecological framework*. This framework is derived from ecological and systems theory, which evolved from the biological and social sciences. Drawing on these theories, people as individuals, families, and groups in a workplace or community are viewed as systems, much like systems in nature. Systems theory and ecology each contributed several key concepts to the ecological framework: context, interrelatedness, adaption, and goodness of fit.

One key premise in ecological theory is that throughout our lifespan, change is constant, and it occurs in a context—people grow, learn, stay well, or become ill within the context of their environment. The context includes the entire physical, social, and cultural environment (Germain and Gitterman, 1980). Human development is not just a genetic blossom independent of the weather and water; rather, it is highly reliant on the environment. Focusing only on the individual does little to advance our understanding of what keeps individuals, families, communities, and workplaces healthy. Ecological approaches recognize that "all aspects of human life are interrelated" (Dubos, 1980, p. xii). Bronfenbrenner, in his influential book *The Ecology of Human Development* (1979), proposed that people live and develop in multiple contexts or settings that are layered within each other. In the immediate setting, a person has a direct contact through relationships with people and places, such as family and work settings. Settings such as home life and work life are interconnected and continually influence each other. The settings of everyday life are layered within and are influenced by larger systems, such as organization policy, or regulations or public legislation regarding safety standards, or a coroner's inquests. These structures interact within the "macrosystem" that is the social political, economic and cultural context (see also Salazar and Beaton, 2000). There are a multitude of everyday conditions and interactions such as the experience of the person, their gender, the physical environment of the workplace, shift work, the overall job demands, the effort and reward systems, organizational policies, leadership styles, and the culture and political climate that interact to influence people's well-being. Within all these multiple interacting systems are individuals, possessing their own unique sets of influences, such as their physical and emotional health, the coping strategies they have acquired through life experiences, and their disposition and approach to challenges and hardships.

This model argues against a simple cause-and-effect model of people and their behavior. While a linear cause-and-effect model offers comforting simplicity, it is limited by eliminating a great deal of contextual information on the interactions and interrelatedness between people. Although simplicity and predictability is often desirable, in nature there are multiple

Table 3.1. Theories for Understanding Responses to Adversity

Stress	Crisis	Trauma	Occupational	Related Concepts
• Stress arises from sudden, intermittent, or continuous events that range from low to extreme levels of physiological, social, emotional, cognitive demands	• Temporary or ongoing events overwhelm personal resources including customary coping strategies	• Events that provoke fear, helplessness and horror and the threat of injury or death	• Workplace events and processes that create physical and psychological hazards	• Secondary Trauma refers to the trauma like effects of supporters or helpers for people experiencing traumatic stress. Concept applied to both family members and helpers such as disaster and emergency personnel
• Survival mode response includes fight, flight or freeze responses followed by nurturing, affiliating, and cooperating behavior (tend and befriend)	• Personal and environmental resources are not replenished in a timely manner	• Reexperiencing, arousal and avoidance symptoms are common	• Work related physical and psychosocial factors influence employee health and injury rates	• Vicarious traumatization refers to the therapist's or helper's experience of distress and most importantly, to the changes in their belief systems or world views occurring as a result of their empathic engagement with traumatized clients
• Stress increases as personal or community resources are threatened, harmed, or lost	• Response may include confusion, disorganization, anxiety or helplessness	• Distress followed by resilience and adaption to trauma is the usual response	• Occupational stress affected by workplace factors such as leadership, role clarity, decision making latitude, social support, sense of fairness or injustice, balance of efforts and rewards, and the organizational safety climate	
	• Increased risk of harmful behavior or re-victimization during acute phase	• Trauma related to intentional human actions such as violence or neglect increases the risk of PTSD and co-occurring health problems		
	• Vulnerability increases as crisis events persist without adequate resources			

Table 3.1 (*continued*)

Stress	Crisis	Trauma	Occupational	Related Concepts
• Persistent or extreme stress can weaken the immune system, increase health problems and disrupt important relationships	• Crisis intervention focuses on the here and now aspects of crisis	• Secondary health, social and economic problems disrupt recovery and undermine relationships, a sense of safety, competency, identity, and self-worth	• Prevention and interventions require multiple level efforts at the organizational, team and individual level.	• Critical Incident Stress refers to cognitive, physical, emotional and behavioral responses to a critical incidents, that is, a work-related crisis or an event that may be potentially traumatizing for emergency professionals
• A supportive, validating and resourceful environment enhances prevention, mitigation and resiliency	• Development of new adaptive skills and relationships may occur in the resolution of the crisis	• A supportive, non blaming and resourceful environment enhances prevention, recovery and resiliency	• Aspects of stress, crisis and trauma theory relevant	• Burnout refers to accumulation of work related stresses leading to exhaustion, cynicism and ineffectiveness. Does specifically address traumatic stress
• Recent developments include the integration of mind-body, gender, cultural factors, community and population stress and resiliency	• Some elements of stress theory relevant	• Specific trauma treatments available		
		• Some elements of crisis and stress theory relevant		

Figure 3.2. Shiftwork Causes Social Disruption and Stress

paths to an outcome depending on the conditions, time line, or settings. For example, one may make the statement that shift work causes social disruption and stress. However, this ignores the reality that many factors influence the experience of shift work, including the family structure in which one lives, the ability of the spouse to manage a shift work routine, social activities in which the individual engages, the sense of satisfaction that the individual attains from the job, the extrinsic rewards of the job (social status, pay), and the ability of the individual to adapt to changing sleeping/working patterns. Thus, a more contextual or ecological systems approach might look like figure 3.3.

Using an ecological systems approach not only directs our way of understanding a situation, but also influences the approaches that we might take for intervening when problems arise. A practical application of this principle is to develop numerous actions or interventions to deal with any one situation. For instance, construction bylaws, smoke alarms, fire drills, extinguishers, and teaching children not to play with matches all work to create one outcome—a safer home. From the perspective of managing shift work, a reality of round-the-clock emergency services, we would want to assist people to determine whether their family, social-recreational activities, and per-

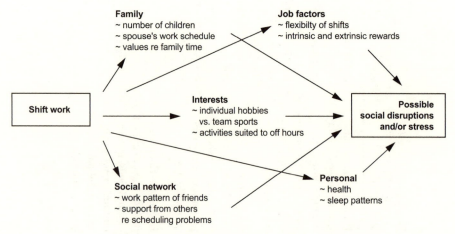

Figure 3.3. Ecological Systems Approach

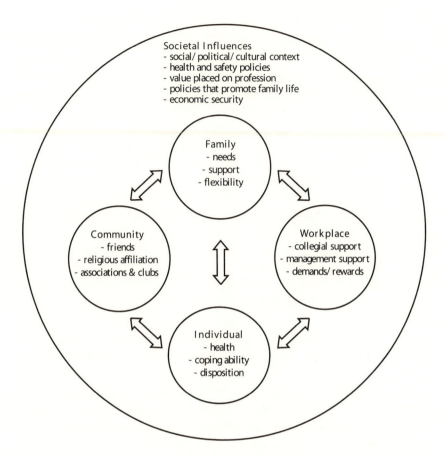

Figure **3.4.** Ecological Systems Theory

sonal biological clock can adapt to the rigors of shift work. We would help families develop strategies for dealing with disruption. We would work with organizations to develop flexible, people- and family-friendly shift work schedules and policies. We might intervene with other systems that are making life more difficult for shift workers, such as advocating for advance polls for voting and extended hours for health care services. Ecological perspective guides scientists, health practitioners, and emergency professionals to be attentive to interrelatedness and context—what are the surrounding conditions and relationships that promote or deplete health? A central process is the "goodness of fit"—that is, how well people and their environment can adapt and balance needs, capacities, and resources to promote or restore health (Germain and Gitterman, 1980; Hobfoll, 2001).

The ecological framework is well supported by research in population

---

1. Social position and economic circumstances are related to health.
2. Stress harms health.
3. The effects of early development last a lifetime.
4. Social exclusion creates misery and costs lives.
5. Stress in the workplace increases risk of disease.
6. Job security increases health, well-being, and job satisfaction.
7. Strong supportive networks improve health at home, at work, and in the community.
8. Individuals turn to alcohol, drugs, and tobacco and suffer from their use, but use is influenced by the wider social setting.
9. Healthy food is a political issue.
10. Healthy transportation reduces driving and encourages more walking and cycling, backed up by better public transport.

Figure 3.5. Social Determinants of Health—World Health Organization

health, an approach concerned with the social determinants of health and well-being (Evans, Barer, and Marmor, 1994). Numerous other community-oriented researchers and practitioners recognize that community values, culture, and structures can promote health and well-being or create adversity (Caplan, 1964; Hobfoll, 2001; Norris and Thompson, 1995; Stokols, 1992). For instance, McKeown (1979) studied the significant decrease in mortality rates in the 200 years since the industrial revolution and concluded that improved social conditions, rather than advances in health care, were the paramount reason for longer life span. The World Health Organization concurs that the health and longevity of people are strongly influenced by the circumstances of life and work (Wilkinson and Marmott, 2003). These ten key social determinants of health are summarized in figure 3.5. These conditions can be influenced and improved to promote health.

Public health and health promotion approaches are concerned with how individuals, organizations, and communities can shape policy and practices to promote well-being. Public health approaches work along a continuum of primary, secondary, and tertiary prevention across multiple settings and times (Norris and Thompson, 1995). *Primary prevention* attempts to reduce the incidence of new health problems in a population. The aim is to lower the risk of the population as a whole by reducing vulnerability factors while building resiliency and resources. *Secondary prevention* is aimed at the early stages following an event and targets groups that are at most risk. *Tertiary prevention* looks at improving and sustaining health after the event has occurred and distress or damage has taken place. The goal would be to reduce the duration of the problems or distress and improve the quality of life.

Health promotion focuses on healthy people to develop community practices to maintain and enhance well-being. In the past, health promotion emphasized encouraging individual responsibility for lifestyle changes such as eating a low fat/high fiber diet or committing to regular exercise. Health promotion may also develop strategies to change community norms, such as seat belt use or attitudes toward cigarette smoking. Most workplace health promotion campaigns have focused on individual lifestyle changes or stress management programs. From the perspective of ecology, population health, public health, and health promotion, occupational health suggests that individually focused interventions are too narrow in scope to promote health, as will be discussed further in chapter 6, "Help or Hindrance?"

Summary

In this chapter we have reviewed some of the most popular theories for understanding responses to adverse events, beginning with theories addressing stress and crisis, moving to theories addressing trauma and workplace-related trauma, and finally looking at occupational stress. We then turned to ecological theory, a more comprehensive approach for understanding human experiences, well-being, and health. That is, individual health cannot be viewed as separate from the context in which people find themselves. We learned that stress comes in many forms, physical, social, cognitive, and psychological aspects and from many sources or interactions between our home, work, and community surroundings and us. Each of us, as humans, has limits in our capacity to cope with physical demands, and in our ability to process new information and powerful feelings. Our limits and strengths are both a reflection of our personal and community or workplace supports and resources.

In the remaining chapters of this book, we discuss the experiences of trauma and stress in the working lives of emergency responders. The sources of stress and trauma are discussed, the consequences of these experiences are reviewed, and strategies for intervention are proposed. However, it is important that in all discussions we understand that critical events on the job are encountered in a context that includes ongoing work stressors, family needs and supports, individual strengths and vulnerabilities, and a changing sociopolitical environment. No two individuals will experience an event the same way, because no two individuals possess the same context. Ecological theory guides our understanding of work-related trauma and the interventions that we propose. Within this broad framework, however, we draw upon the valuable contributions of theories regarding stress and occupational stress, trauma, crisis and secondary trauma, or critical incident stress. Each of these theories assists with our understanding; nevertheless, no one theory is adequate to explain the complexity of trauma encountered in the line of fire.

4

DISASTROUS EVENTS

Mass Emergencies and the Emergency Responder

It has been said that disasters shape human behavior and human behavior shapes the disasters we face (Oliver-Smith, 1996). Yet how relevant are disasters to most lives? Growing up in Toronto, we rarely heard stories about disasters in the community. Disasters, when they occurred, seemed sudden, unexpected, or likely to happen in places where nature could be troublesome, like Tornado Alley, a coastal area, or along a fault line in California. In Ontario, hurricanes usually lose their destructive strength before arriving as just a rainy day. When Hurricane Hazel arrived in Ontario, early in the fall of 1954, it did not follow expectations. There was extensive flooding and damage to Toronto and southern Ontario as 81 people died and more than 4,000 people became homeless. One street in Toronto was completely washed away by the rains, and an overflowing river killed 32 people. Years later some of the neighbors still recall that day, sometimes when the rains are heavy. Today, people running on a park path beside a Toronto river may not realize they are passing by the area where flood damage and deaths occurred 50 years ago. The park is now a conservation area that also serves as a flood-control plain created after the hurricane, in an attempt to avoid a repeat of that disaster.

On the morning of December 12, 1985, Arrow Airlines flight 1285 crashed on the east coast of Canada, soon after takeoff from Gander, Newfoundland. The passengers were American soldiers returning home for Christmas following peacekeeping duties in the Sinai. All 248 soldiers and the 8 crew members were killed in the crash and ensuing fire, which took

47

4 hours to bring under control and 30 hours to extinguish. The crash was ranked as one of the worst military air disasters in U.S. history ("Tragedy at Gander," 2003). A small and isolated community, led by the Royal Canadian Mounted Police, began the task of recovering human remains. With the assistance of U.S. military personnel, all remains were returned to American soil within the month. The lingering effects of the disaster were felt not only by the families and friends of the lost American soldiers, however. The impact on recovery personnel had profound implications for disaster support in the United States and Canada.

In the fall of 1989, the Toronto airport, Canada's busiest, established a critical incident stress response team to support the local airport community, particularly in the event of an air disaster. This became the first team of mental health, airport, and emergency professionals in Canada responsible for providing support to the airport on a range of incidents. A few team members responded to their first major air disaster, which occurred off the east coast of Canada, Nova Scotia, in 1998. On September 2, Swiss-Air 111 crashed into the ocean, and its 229 passengers and crew members were killed on impact. The local Nova Scotia health services and peer support programs worked with the community and emergency response, recovery, and investigative personnel. The postdisaster needs exceeded the best local efforts and led to directed invitations for support. Whatever a Toronto-raised mental health worker had learned about crisis and trauma did not fully prepare any of us for the magnitude of the deaths and thousands of local volunteers, military personnel, air industry, emergency, and law enforcement professionals involved in the ocean and land recovery work. During the year of follow-up services, we consistently observed the emergency professionals' dedication and resilience in the face of loss and disaster. We also learned about the usefulness and limitations of posttrauma interventions, as we will discuss in later chapters.

September came to represent another tragedy on September 11, 2001. In one single, coordinated terrorist attack, thousands of Americans lost their lives in the Pentagon and in New York as the World Trade Towers crashed to the ground. During the rescue efforts in New York, more than 343 firefighters and 75 police officers were killed. Emergency responders worked tirelessly to recover bodies of the missing, and numerous communities offered their support. Greater Toronto Airports Authority (GTAA) team members, several of whom responded to Swiss Air, provided on-scene support in New York during the weeks after the terrorist attacks. Yet our acquired knowledge and experience still did not fully prepare us for an event of such mass violence.

Up the coast at the Gander airport, a smaller, though significant story unfolded. A community of 10,000 people, now no strangers to disaster, effectively accommodated 38 additional trans-Atlantic flight landings. Overnight Gander and surrounding communities supported an additional 6,600 people who were grounded over 5 days following the attacks (Scanlon, 2002). The stranded people represented diverse nations, ethnicities, and races. For months afterward, the passengers offered their admiration and appreciation to the people and efforts that emerged to support them. Disasters may also bring out the best in people: efforts, caring, and cooperation.

Disasters come in many forms and sizes. They have common elements, and yet each community and disaster will have a unique combination of characteristics and effects. The effects may range from minor, localized disruptions to severe, widespread destruction of communities. People and resources in the community converge onto the disaster area to deal with their circumstances. As their own resourcefulness is depleted, the replenishment of resources will determine the quality and speed of recovery (Hobfoll, 1998; Kaniasty and Norris, 1999). Yet while community members tend to be heavily involved in early disaster response, emergency service professionals remain central to the entire on-scene rescue and recovery process. The magnitude of disasters and mass emergencies, the circumstances in which they occur, and the prolonged recovery period create unique chal-

6 billion people and growing with over 15,000 births every hour

Growing upward toward 500 cities with over 1 million residents

An average of more than 1 disaster each day

Over 200 million people affected by disasters yearly

In the past ten years 1/3 of Earth's population was affected by disasters

Disasters are complex interactions between nature, the manmade environment, and social processes that lead to significant harm to people and their sustainable environment. Disasters reflect the quality of adaptability and resiliency between people and the environment.

Figure 4.1. A Dynamic Earth

lenges for emergency responders. This chapter provides an overview of disasters, mass emergencies, and their effects on communities and emergency services.

The Daily Planet

From 1992 to 2000, the United Nations reported 4,989 disasters throughout the world, approximately 500 disasters each year, many of which are not widely reported in North America. During the past 10 years 2 billion people, a third of the planet's population, were affected by a disaster in their community (International Strategy of Disaster Reduction [ISDR], 2002). There is some good news in the figures: the number of people killed in disasters, excluding wars, has decreased worldwide. Nevertheless, reports indicate that an average of 60,000 people were killed each year by "natural disasters" in the past 10 years. In the 1990s, over 200 million people each year were affected by disasters, three times as many as in the 1970s (ISDR, 2002). From 1980 to 2002, the United States alone experienced more than 54 weather-related disasters, each of which cost over a billion dollars, and which cost over $300 billion total.

In addition to disasters caused by natural events and human error, collective or mass violence such as armed conflict, terrorism, and genocide are at times included within the definition of disasters. Collective or mass violence would add 500,000 deaths related to war, terrorism, and genocide (Reza,1991). In his review, Reza estimates that 191 million people lost their lives in the 25 largest violent events of the twentieth century. Since the Second World War, there have been 190 armed conflicts throughout the world. Throughout this century civilian deaths have steadily increased as military casualties have declined. Additionally, greater numbers of people are physically, socially, and psychologically at risk following mass violence, due to injuries, lack of health care, economic instability, family and community disruption, and other war-related difficulties. All of these disaster-related injuries and deaths do not include the millions of incidents of homicides, fires, industrial, and motor-vehicle accidents emergency professionals respond to each year.

From these statistics, it would be reasonable to say that every community is in the process of ignoring, identifying, or preventing potential disasters or recovering from previous disasters, as noted in figure 4.1. Most of the world's population of women, men, and children have had or will have their lives affected by disasters, for some subtly and for millions severely. What are disasters and how do they affect people?

Disasters: Nature and Human Nature

Over time there has been a change in the models of understanding disasters. The roots of disasters were historically seen as one of nature's "one-off" events that occurred unexpectedly to overwhelm a community. These events, much like the early views of stress, were seen as the result of an outside force that exceeded the coping ability of the community, and recovery was a means for a community to rebalance itself. One possibility is to take a fatalistic view that disasters are not preventable. However, beginning with the work of Carr (1932), many people now recognize that human actions contribute to the occurrence and effects of disasters. Carr posited that "so long as the city resists the earth shocks, so long as the levies hold, there is no disaster" (1932, p. 211). Damage from natural disasters such as hurricanes or earthquakes can be tempered or avoided by technological advances. Technology can be seen as a resource to provide earlier warnings and better tools to prevent and repair the destruction. An earthquake may not be preventable, but better building regulations and improved construction could have greatly reduced the extent of damage and losses in quakes like that which struck the Bam region in Iran in 2003, or the 2001 disaster in northwestern India. Other events, such as the structural collapse of a dam or walkway or "nuclear accident," are the primary result of human action. Human factors such as urbanization, population growth density, and resource development can create new opportunities, such as faster travel or higher-yield crops, as well as new hazardous risks, such as toxic chemicals or, when accidents occur, higher fatalities. Manmade events may also include disasters that result from intentional harm or violence, such as terrorism, genocide, or environmental damage stemming from dumping toxic chemicals (Bankoff, 2001; Hewitt, 1997). The harm and reactions in communities and emergency services will vary according to the perceived causes of the disaster. Human factors postincident also affect the severity and outcome of disaster. Large-scale disasters including mass violence will have municipal, regional, and national levels of emergency response and law enforcement. Factors such as interagency communication and coordination influence the effectiveness of the immediate and long-term rescue and recovery responses.

Figure 4.2 illustrates the interactions between nature (e.g., weather conditions), the human-built environment (e.g., a house), and social processes (e.g., enforced building codes) that contribute to the development of a disaster. Disasters begin with a potential hazard—that is, any natural or manmade action that "threatens people and the resources for health and well being" (Cutter, 2000, p. 2). Vulnerability—that is, the risk of harm from

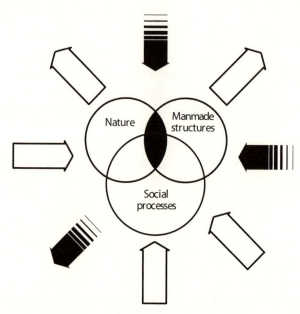

Figure 4.2. Natural and Human Factors Interact to Create Disasters

disasters and the resources to prevent or mitigate the risk—will vary in a community. However, as we will discuss later, vulnerability, like community resources, is not distributed equally or randomly among children, the elderly, those with chronic health conditions, or socioeconomically disadvantaged groups (Kaniasty and Norris, 1999).

Disasters and Their Characteristics

"What are disasters?" is a question raised by Quarantelli (1950, 1998), who has researched disasters for almost 50 years. The answers have been discussed from diverse perspectives of emergency services, architecture, geography, engineering, social work, psychology, anthropology, sociology, the media, politics, economics, medicine, and nursing. Though there is not a consensus definition, there are common features among the definitions. Considering several important reviews, for our purposes, disasters are complex interactions between nature, the human-built environment, and social processes that lead to significant harm to people and their sustainable environment (Norris, Friedman, and Watson, 2002; Oliver-Smith, 1996; Quarantelli, 1998; IDRC, 2002). There are several key elements of a disaster: natural and human factors, intentionality, predictability, timeframe,

Contributing factors
Natural, human-built, and social factors

Intentionality
Neglect
Malice
Human error

Predictability

Time frame
Development
Onset
Duration
Frequency

Degree of threat
Predisaster
Future fears / health risks

Location
Urban/rural
Accessibility
Localized/national/global

Extent of disruption and destruction (harm/loss)
Property loss
Witnessing injury/death
Injuries
Social networks
Economy
Psychological
Disruption to sense of safety/trust/esteem

Timeliness and Sustainability of Resources / Support

Figure 4.3. Characteristics of the Disasters

degree of threat, location, extent of disruption and destruction (harm/loss), and the timeliness and sustainability of the outside resources. The interplay of these factors affects the community and the emergency service responses during the rescue, and the recovery and long after the event has ended. This chapter will refer briefly to the unique challenges of CBRNE related terrorist attacks, however for a fuller examination see Moghaddam and Marsella (2003) or Ursano, Fullerton, and Norwood (2003).

Contributing Factors and Intentionality

As we have discussed, nature and human nature or actions may be more or less implicated, and both are always involved in the course of a disaster. As humans, we go through many steps to safeguard our well-being. For example, we expect to be protected through design, safety procedures, training, administration, management, organizational practice, health and safety policy and practices, safe locations for producing goods, a system of health care, rapid emergency response, public and scientific regulations, policies, and public inquires. The perception that we are safe and secure is vital to our sense of well-being. The tragic losses related to disasters seen as acts of God will be experienced differently than acts of intentional harm, typically related to higher levels of anger, blame, and distress (Weisaeth and Tonnessen, 2003). How these issues of responsibility and blame emerge during public inquires will be further explored in chapter 7.

Intentional acts to horrify, threaten, or harm people, such as terrorist attacks, are particularly distressing. Green and colleagues (2001), in a study of traumatic death, found that intentional violence related strongly to the lasting distress of the family members. The study found that it was the violence directed at the victim, not the unexpectedness of their death, that was a more important a factor in predicting PTSD. Stroebe, Schut, and Finkenauer (2001) concur that traumatic grief develops when a death occurs as a consequence of violence, mutilation, or destruction. The different responses among emergency service workers and other members of the public regarding two of the disasters mentioned at the outset of this chapter are telling examples of this. At the SwissAir disaster in Peggy's Cove, Nova Scotia, the overwhelming feeling was grief and mourning regarding the tremendous human loss; yet for many this crash was viewed as a tragedy caused by material and equipment failure. This was later confirmed by the Canadian Transportation Safety Board through the painstaking process of reconstructing the aircraft. By the time the second aircraft hit the second tower of the World Trade Center in New York, it was clear that this could be no accident. The grief and mourning of workers was mixed with anger and outrage. Workers were on a mission to find fallen comrades, joined by the fact that they were Americans. Those at Ground Zero and others throughout the country sought justice.

In 1995, Aum Shinrikyo, a Japanese doomsday religious cult, released deadly sarin nerve gas into the Tokyo subway system, killing 12 people and sending more than 5,000 others to hospitals. The group had recruited both wealthy followers and young scientists whose combined resources led to the development and stockpiling of biological weapons and a helicopter to distribute the gas over Japanese cities. The subway attack came at the peak of the Monday morning rush hour and left commuters lying on the ground with blood gushing from their noses or mouths, gasping for air. The fact that a small cult or group of terrorists with limited means could and would engage in chemical warfare and harm so many sent waves of fear throughout Japan and the rest of the world (Lifton, 1999; Council on Foreign Relations, 2003).

Predictability

Disasters have at times been described in terms of timelines and phases, which is helpful in understanding and organizing the process of disasters. The phases, including preparation, detection, rescue , and recovery, often make sense in the context of natural disasters, particularly those that occur in areas vulnerable to certain types of conditions. In these cases, there is often a preparation phase, which involves becoming aware of hazards, the risk of exposure, and the vulnerability of the community, followed by improved steps to prevent or reduce harm. Detection of threat focuses on the recognition of the impending disaster or an awareness of how a hazard may potentially become a disaster. Protective action can be taken given an effective early warning and communication system and responsive, trusting relationships between the public and government or corporations.

From an outsider's view, disasters may or may not appear predictable. Consider an earthquake that occurs suddenly in Turkey or California. The dozen or so tectonic plates that make up the earth's crust are in motion every day, moving at the pace of few centimeters per year, about the speed of a fingernail growing. On the surface the earthquake can be a sudden, unexpected event, though below the surface the event may have been centuries in the making. The risks we identify and manage are related to a number of technological, economic, political, and social factors. Predictability can lead to better preparation. However, when disasters become predictable because they are chronic events, communities and responding organization will become over taxed and perhaps defeated without outside support.

While there is no question that the destruction caused by events that come with advanced warning continue to have a devastating impact on many of those affected, other events come without warning and without preplanned community resources for recovery. The bombing of an office building in Oklahoma was not only unexpected, but it also fell outside the imagination of possible disasters in North America. When people are unprepared, not only do they suffer from the losses associated with the event, but in addition their worldview is shattered and forever altered (North and Pfefferbaum, 2002).

Time Frame

The time frame of a disaster may be experienced on several different levels. There is clock and calendar time of minutes, hours, days; the half-life of radioactivity; or the half-life of how long a life sustaining drug will stay in your body; or, psychological time when "time passed slowly" or " time stood still." The following is a counselor's journal entry that reflects the changing sense of time frames:

New York—September

At an office building there are four clocks on the wall, each one another city, another time zone. It feels like I am living in multiple time zones. Listening to counselors who were near Ground Zero. They say the day passed before they realized it. It was an uneventful day. I came to learn that it means no fires, no injuries, no obvious human remains found. It is too soon to speak of loss, the dead, or biohazards. I ran into a spouse of a recovery worker, a firefighter. She was on school time, waiting for kids and later taking a night class. She stated that she and her spouse exchange lots of care, though not conversation about Ground Zero. In the evening at Washington Square a family member lights another candle. He sits among thousands of candles, pictures, and poems. He hopes, he grieves, he waits, thinking over and over about the last day. He too is in many time zones—his body, mind, and heart in past, and trying to imagine a future. After 10 days, I am also tired like a jet-lagged traveler working across multiple psychological time zones.

In addition to differences in predictability that affect preparation and detection time, the response and recovery time can vary substantially between disasters. Rescue and recovery operations continue 24 hours a day, 7 days a week. During the rescue phase, many emergency responders may refuse to go off shift and continue working long beyond what might be considered safe and healthy. When they do agree to rest, frequently emergency responders cannot or do not return home, rather sleeping and resting in temporary housing located near the scene of the disaster. While the urgency may reduce as the weeks progress, this commitment can go on for prolonged periods of time. Family members can initially be supportive and understanding; as time continues, however, the reality of their own unmet needs grows. Three months after the SwissAir crash, the final identifications of victims were completed, and another year later the recovery operation was called to a close. Several of the investigative staff stayed there the entire time, with only short trips home to see family. The prolonged, seemingly unending days associated with disaster response have tremendous effects on emergency service workers and families. At times, individuals who are unable to see the impact that the event is having on their well-being must be relieved of duties.

Lieutenant General Roméo Dallaire, who led the Canadian peacekeeping mission in Rwanda, suggested that when individuals are faced with inhumane and atrocious situations, one strategy both individuals and commanders use is to keep people working until they drop. He indicates that in order to survive the emotional impact of this type of work, it can be important to ensure that one does not have time to think about the reality of what one is doing. Nevertheless, he states, when certain individuals reach a point where they can no longer function effectively and are in psychological trouble, they must be relieved of duties and sent home. In large part this is for the well-being of the individual. However, it is also important so that these individuals' distress does not permeate the rest of the troops and impede the ability of others to continue the grueling and gruesome work. While these strategies may very well serve the public at times of great need, it is not difficult to see how they will have a lasting impact on those who perform the service. General Dallaire is candid in his discussion of what this has cost him and of his present struggle with traumatic stress symptoms.

Timing affects not only the emergency workers, but also the community in which they reside. The frequency and duration of an event will influence the opportunity for a community to prepare and recover. Repeated disasters or ongoing and unrelenting risk may not allow for a community to restore its resources and resiliency. Recovery is not successful if repeated disruptions diminish the community's coping capacity. Similar to the concept of wear and tear, there may be damage to a community's adaptive flexibility as a result of the cumulative impact of periodic disaster events (Dyer, 2002)

Degree of Threat

While the risk associated with some events is eliminated or at least minimal once the flames have been doused and the dust has cleared, for other events the risk continues indefinitely. These include events such as the toxic chemical spill at Bhopal or the widespread dispersal of radioactive material from Chernobyl. Such toxic disasters are invisible and threatening, with no clear end point (Havenaar, 2002). To the thousands of emergency response personnel and public, the duration may seem indefinite, with no single peak impact. The effects on health may be dispersed over years. The disaster may not have begun on the day of the accident, but may have started much earlier through a combination of human and technological processes which have resulted in increased health risks. The lack of knowledge regarding certain types of chemical warfare, the lack of training among emergency service professionals regarding this type of disaster, and the lack of equipment and resources to manage the disaster have potentially high risks for emergency responders. While the first response of emergency professionals is to rush in and save as many people as possible, such action may increase the risk to responders and to the public as a whole as toxic elements are spread further afield (Henry and King, 2004). Information about biohazards, for example, can bring relief or dread about the future. These unknowns challenge the trust between the public, emergency responders, business, and government (Cwikel, Havenaar, and Bromet, 2002).

At times risk occurs due to the unknown hazards associated with another type of disaster. At other times it is the health risk alone that creates the disaster situation. Neila Laroza, a 51-year-old nurse working on the orthopedic ward of a Toronto hospital, died of Severe Acute Respiratory Syndrome (SARS) on June 30, 2003 (Galloway and Alphonso, 2003). Her death had a profound impact on health care workers throughout Toronto, who had been battling the illness since it first emerged on March 7, 2003. A study of health care workers at Mount Sinai Hospital (MSH) in Toronto during the SARS outbreak reported that within the hospital environment, the perception of personal danger was exacerbated by the uncertainty about the disease. "Modification of infection control procedures and public health recommendations day-by-day and at times hour-by-hour, increased uncertainty. The perception of personal danger was heightened by the known lethality of the syndrome and intense media coverage of the outbreak and its effects" (Maunder et al., 2003, p. 1248). In this study, health care workers expressed feelings of fear, anxiety, anger, frustration, and a conflict between their role as health care workers altruistically caring for those in need and their need to protect their own family. In addition to those caring for SARS patients in hospitals, health care workers in the community also faced risks—in some ways, greater risks—due to the uncontrolled environments in which they work. One example was Toronto Emergency Medical Services (EMS), which employs approximately 750 paramedics. Paramedic Greg Bruce contacted SARS on March 16 and subsequently spent 10 days at MSH in the intensive-care unit battling fever and struggling for breath (Fowlie, 2003). The SARS outbreaks completely reorganized the way EMS operates. Many hundreds of staff members were quarantined, approximately 200–250 in the first outbreak and 400 in the second outbreak. All staff members still need to follow procedures that add a great deal of extra stress to their job. The large number of quarantined staff meant that enormous amounts of overtime were needed and no lieu time was permitted for more than 100 days.

The Centers for Disease Control and Prevention in the United States reported the profound risk to rescue workers in the aftermath of 9/11. The most immediate risk was the building collapse that took the lives of 343 Fire Department of New York (FDNY) rescue workers. During the next 24 hours, 240 rescue workers sought emergency medical treatment, and 28 required hospitalization. Ninety percent of the 10,116 rescue workers assessed in the first 48 hours after the attack reported respiratory problems. As of August 2002, 90 FDNY rescue workers continued to be on medical leave or light-duty assignments as a result of injuries occurring during the 3 months of work at Ground Zero (Centers for Disease Control and Prevention, 2002).

Location of Disasters

The location will influence the accessibility, availability, and sustainability of resources critical to the prevention of harm. Not all communities or groups have acceptable levels of resources prior to the onset of a disaster, which lengthens the recovery timelines and need for sustainable support (De Jong, 2002). In North America the number of emergency resources available and ongoing physical, economic, and health resources are significantly higher than in developing countries. Urban areas with a higher population density may be at greater risk for losses, though this will be moderated by the preparation and protective actions that the community has taken.

When disasters occur in small communities, such as the SwissAir crash in Peggy's Cove, certain types of resources will naturally be limited and the community must rely on national efforts to provide assistance. However, while accessibility of large-scale resources in terms of specialized equipment and manpower may be limited, the access to informal supports is often greater in smaller communities. People know who has sustained losses and can offer assistance. Community members are aware of which families have one or more members who are emergency workers and can provide relief and assistance. When support sessions are offered, people notice who is missing and seek them out individually to ensure that they are all right. Large-scale disasters bring together hundreds of public and private agencies and thousands of professionals and volunteers. Accessibility to the site, resources, coordination, and communication will be affected by the setting of the disaster.

Extent of Disruption, Destruction, and Loss

Disasters reduce support both to the individual and within the community because of injury or death, relocation, disruption of the social network, and, over time, the potential of increasing secondary losses. As personal loss and community destruction rise, and as the ratio of victims to nonvictims in a community increases, distress will become widespread and severe among individuals as well as within the community at large. This suggestion is consistent with a study by Briere and Elliot (2000) examining the long-term effects of natural disasters. After a mean of 13 years postdisaster, three conditions—fear for one's life, personal injury, and major property loss—were significantly associated with psychological symptoms. Similarly, Norris (2002) suggests that the severity and duration of the distress were the greatest when two of the following four disaster-related factors were present: extreme and widespread damage to property; serious ongoing financial problems for the country; intentional harm; and significant prevalence of injuries, threat to life, and loss of life. As previous discussed, secondary resource losses such as of security, safety or property often deepen the effect of the initial disaster. One aspect of loss repeatedly shown to affect disaster experiences for rescue workers is the loss of a colleague (Sewell, 1983; Violanti and Aron, 1994). The impact of a profound loss of colleagues in an event such as 9/11 cannot be underestimated.

Timeliness and Sustainability of Resources

One of the key resources in a disaster situation is the public. There is considerable evidence that during disasters, ordinary people are the first rescue workers. Following earthquakes in Mexico and Turkey, the public quickly and spontaneously began to extricate trapped people. At the Loma Prieta earthquake in California, most of the people trapped in their cars were rescued by strangers: people who worked nearby and bystanders. In New York after 9/11, we often heard stories of an injured or disabled person who was assisted by others. Later, the same stories helped victims to counter the depth of the loss and harm felt. In the example at the beginning of this chapter, Newfoundland communities effectively supported more than 6,000 passengers for 5 days. In New York, thousands of people were evacuated from lower Manhattan by people with boats who spontaneously coordinated their rescue efforts. One of the key lessons learned is the importance of seeing the public as initially eager and resourceful. Coordinating the resourcefulness of the public is an important aspect to disaster response.

At disasters, it is usual for a convergence of volunteers and supplies to arrive. In 1956 Fritz defined convergence as the informal, spontaneous movement of people, messages, and supplies toward the disaster area (Auf der Heide, 2003). From a disaster preparation viewpoint these volunteers and supplies may appear uninvited or unexpected (Cone, Weir, and Bogucki, 2003). This is an important social process that requires coordination. When emergency services arrive, the challenge is not to just put up yellow tape but to channel the energies and efforts of the public. There are safety issues. Efforts must be directed into managing the disaster site and risk. Freelancing at a disaster scene without knowledge or coordination brings a high risk to oneself and others. The point is to channel convergence, rather than eliminate or reduce it. Communities require information and opportunities to help; with good coordination and communication, the public and professionals may take constructive action while reducing the risk of harmful communication and actions. While civilian assistance is vital in the initial stages, Norris and Thompson (1995) explain that emergency responders must sustain the operation beyond the initial outpouring of assistance, and governmental support and resources are key once the generously donated free food and supplies dwindle away.

At the community level, initial supports are also being depleted, as people face the delicate balancing of mobilization versus the deterioration of resources for ongoing community recovery. How well the ebb and flow of resources are balanced will have a strong influence on the long-term health of the community. Communities will also have a history regarding which groups face neglect and vulnerability and which groups are well resourced (Norris and Kaniasty 1996; Kaniasty and Norris, 1999). History also influences the emergency operations. Another important factor is the coordination of the emergency service resources. Henry and King (2004) document the coordination problems between emergency service organizations at Ground Zero, which occurred in part as a result of historic conflicts. These coordination difficulties are acutely felt by emergency service workers, who must attempt to function in the absence of a clear chain of command.

Effects of Disaster

According to Dynes, "the best predictor of behavior in emergencies . . . is behavior prior to the emergency. Emergencies do not make sinners out of saints, nor Jekylls out of Hydes" (1994, p. 150). There are several well-researched findings about how the public responds at the time of a disaster. The public initially is prosocial, helpful to each other, as people collect and form emergent groups that undertake helpful tasks and converge support at the disaster sites. We are not sure how certain urban myths began— for example, that at the time of a disaster people will behave recklessly and irrationally as when someone screams *Fire!* in a crowded theater. Fifty years of group behavior after disasters have shown that the public rarely panics; instead, people act responsibly (Quartelli, 1950; Fisher, 1998; Perry and

Lindell, 2003). A smoke-filled crowded stairwell seems like the most likely place for people to feel helpless or perhaps show an "every person for themselves" attitude, disregarding others. Yet in two attacks on the World Trade Center, the 1993 bombing and the September 11 terrorist attacks, the vast majority of people moved in an orderly fashion down the smoke-filled stairs. Despite the fact that during several education and support sessions people were overheard to describe their reactions as "I panicked" or "I had a panic attack" and appeared to describe the usual physiological alarm reactions related to threatening and frightening circumstances, the vast majority of people were not immobilized or incapacitated by their feelings or the circumstances. Significantly, people described their actions as adaptive, looking for exits, joining coworkers and strangers in finding a way out of a damaged office floor, moving in a deliberate and cooperative manner. Public panic may nevertheless occur under conditions in which there is perceived immediate severe danger, few apparent escape options, and escape routes are closing.

Norris and her colleagues (2002a, 2002b) reviewed 20 years of studies of disasters. The review encompassed 102 different events with more than 60,000 individuals. Overall, the findings indicated that people experienced a wide range of difficulties and disruption to their physical, psychological, social, and economic health. These effects were experienced on multiple levels: the individual, family, and community. The disasters were ranked on a 4-point scale regarding their severity of impairment. Disaster effects ranged from minimal transient impairment to a significant level of clinical distress and impairment. Mass violence was a particularly distressing event for people, with moderate to severe levels of distress being reported. Not all populations were equally at risk. Youth generally were the most vulnerable to distress, whereas rescue and recovery workers were least vulnerable. Following the World Trade Center attack, 20% of people living closest to Ground Zero had symptoms consistent with a diagnosis of post-traumatic stress disorder 5–9 weeks after the attack. This reduced to 9.7% and 7.5% as the researchers moved away from the epicenter (Galea et al., 2002). Throughout the rest of the United States, the rate for PTSD was 4.0% (Schlenger et al., 2002). Rescue workers at the Oklahoma City bombing who were directly exposed to the disaster, unlike most of those in the studies of civilians post-9/11, had PTSD rates of 13% (North et al., 2002a). As noted in an earlier section, exposure to a hazard or disaster and the vulnerability of the person and community exposed interact in the development of distress. One might speculate that emergency professionals have a higher exposure to traumatic events but are less vulnerable because of their training and experience.

Disasters and Recovery Workers

As the EMS workers and I [Dr. Prezant] began to set up the mini-triage area in the middle of West Street, there was a soft rumbling that sounded like a freight train. Everyone started to run across the street away from the tower. I had nearly reached the cover of a pedestrian bridge when I was blown off my feet and completely buried in debris. I knew that I was going to die but it seemed to be taking forever. I pushed myself up to my knees and tried to maintain a position that could trap enough air to breathe. Several sheets of construction materials covered me up and I was able to wedge myself out. I was surprised that I could stand up. It was dark as a tunnel and the air was thick as soup. Despite repeatedly scooping chunks of debris from my mouth and nostrils, I inhaled and swallowed large quantities. I heard screams to my left and I began to walk towards them and met several firefighters. Together, we helped several civilians out of the debris. After walking one or two blocks, the sky lightened to a grayish color, and it became obvious that I had been trapped in a massive dust cloud. We were coughing continuously, and it was hard to see. I do not remember hearing the second tower collapse. (Prezant and Kelly, 2002, p. 1582)

Research findings indicate that rescue and recovery workers are a resilient population in the aftermath of a disaster. Nevertheless, they are affected by the prolonged exposure to tragedy and difficult conditions. Consistent with the findings reported in chapter 2, certain disaster-related conditions increase the risk of distress. These include event-specific factors such as the death of children, disasters related to intentional harm, the death of a colleague, risk of personal injury, and sense of control and competence in dealing with the situation. Working with human remains under grotesque conditions is a significant stressor, especially for inexperienced rescue workers (McCarroll, Fullerton, Ursano, and Hermsen, 1996). Performance guilt is also related to subsequent distress (Davidson and Veno, 1980). Work related "what if"s and "if only"s are among the common remarks heard after disasters. At times, the efforts of responders are lauded by the public and the media and they are crowned heroes. However, this hero status is often accepted with ambivalence at best. Members of the Israeli National Police discussed the pressures associated with being considered a hero and the self-doubt it engenders. The chief superintendent is reported as saying, "The line between success and failure is so close . . . when an individual becomes a hero, he or she is under pressure to be the best, and maybe someone can't be the best" (Lewis, Tenzer, and Harrison, 1999, p. 622). Family stresses are also reported to increase. For instance, following the Oklahoma City bombing, it is reported that the divorce rate of Oklahoma City police officers increased 25–30% (Lewis, Tenzer, and Harrison, 1999).

For some professionals, a disaster is both a tragic event and a moment that they have prepared for over the years. It becomes a moment to use all of one's personal and professional skills and energies in helping, investigating, and recovery work. The team and the work come together at a pivotal challenging time. At the SwissAir crash site, an investigator said he was on a "mission," a step-by-step process that may prevent future air disasters and "provide information that could bring relief and support to the family." This person saw himself or herself as having multiple yet congruent roles. In chapter 3, we discussed theories of occupational stress and suggested that when professionals feel trained, supported, and have roles that are congruent, it is likely they will resist the stresses. Professionals who find themselves in roles they do not feel prepared for, or do not view as congruent with their professional expectations, will find increased challenge at a disaster. As one recovery worker said, "I was OK; not even the human remains bothered me, but then I found the kids' clothes, pieces of kids' clothing. Later that day some family members approached me away from the site and asked for information. I was not ready for that. Months later it was when I thought about that day I cried." Loss is a current that runs through most of chapter 3.

Loss may not be experienced only in terms of a death. Loss has many meanings: a loss of beliefs or values, loss of loved ones, loss of self-esteem or efficacy, community or social fabric. There are numerous secondary personal, social, and economic losses that develop as the disaster occurs. When losses occur as a result of a disaster recognized as a public tragedy, there will be public grief and rituals. As discussed in chapter 2, for emergency responders not all losses are recognized. One professional felt unsupported as he struggled with the transition to another department a year after the death of a retired colleague. The office represented the last link to his friend, "a link I am finding hard to give up." This can perhaps be best understood as disenfranchised grief. Doka (1989) defined *disenfranchised grief* as the process when grief is not socially acknowledged or supported and the loss is not validated and grieved by others. In a similar way, Stein (1999) asks, in a disaster "who counts? Who is treated as though they do not matter? Who is remembered? Who is forgotten? Who is, or becomes, a social symbol?" He adds that losses and suffering may be "speakable, unspoken and unspeakable" (p. 167). We would add that some losses are supported, others unsupported, and some do not exist. Recently, we worked with a professional who was unable to drive to a particular part of the city because of the tragic death of a family member. He was able to avoid the neighborhood for many years until recently. His losses were not just for the deceased but also carried self-doubt and other detrimental self-beliefs. Although he discussed this at the time of the death, he believed everyone had quickly grown weary of his thoughts. His sense of loss accumulated to a tipping point toward distress. At times the distress may be evident in the increased use of alcohol among some emergency professionals after incidents of traumatic events as we report in the next chapter (see also North et al., 2002).

Summary

In chapter 2, "All in a Day's Work," we described some of the experiences emergency service workers encounter in the line of duty and the impact that these experiences may have on them as individuals. When a disaster occurs, these same experiences are not isolated incidents. Death, destruction, and human suffering occur at catastrophic levels. Personal resources are taxed to the limit as the rescue and/or recovery continues for days, weeks, and months. Generous support is often felt at the beginning as large numbers of citizens in the community offer their services and instrumental support. In the end, however, these people go home and the emergency workers are left to finish the job that they started when conditions were too dangerous for civilians. Families of responders involved in the long rescue attempts can begin to feel neglected and shut out as the operation grinds slowly along. While emergency workers are highly trained and highly resilient, it is not surprising that these events take their toll and remain imbedded in the memories of those who served.

5

THE RIGHT STUFF

Trauma and Coping

Traditional approaches for dealing with trauma in emergency workers tended to ignore the problem or attribute the traumatic reactions to inherent character flaws. These tendencies are most evident when one considers the history of awareness of traumatic reactions related to exposure to horrifying events in the line of duty in the military. Military historians in Canada have documented the shocking treatment of distressed personnel. During World War I, 25 soldiers in the Canadian Army are reported to have been executed for cowardice. Current analysts now assume that the label of cowardice was applied to dysfunction caused by psychological distress, including PTSD symptoms of hyperarousal, avoidance, and dissociation (Copp and McAndrew, 1990). By World War II, army medical corps had begun to deal with stress reactions. However, commanding officers still asked whether "demoralizing malingering cases cropping up whilst in action should be shot on the spot as an example" (Birenbaum, 1994, p. 1484). While no Canadians were executed for cowardice in World War II, controversy continued about whether to treat soldiers with battle fatigue. In the end, many received a dishonorable discharge on the grounds of LMF— lack of moral fiber (Copp and McAndrew, 1990). Col. F. H. van Nostrand, an army neuropsychiatrist, said in 1947, "Although we are interested in rehabilitation . . . our primary function is early diagnosis, early treatment, and above all, early disposal of the mentally unfit" (Birenbaum, 1994, p. 1489).

The Vietnam War and concern for military personnel in its aftermath sparked a new interest in the issue of traumatic stress reactions and the impact of combat exposure (Figley, 1978, 1980; McFarlane, 1990; Keane, 1993). In 1970, two New York psychiatrists initiated "rap groups" with recently returned Vietnam veterans in which they talked about their war experiences. These groups spread throughout the country and formed the nucleus of a network of professionals concerned about the lack of recognition of the effects of war on these men's psychological health (van der Kolk, Weisaeth, and van der Hart, 1996). Information gathered formed the basis for development of the diagnostic category post-traumatic stress disorder in the third edition of the *Diagnostic and Statistical Manual of Mental Disorders* (American Psychiatric Association, 1980). Concern about the well-being of these veterans resulted in a wide array of services, including, in 1995, 25 specialized inpatient PTSD units for veterans (Fontana and Rosenheck, 1997). The literature on the impact of war-related trauma on military personnel is now rich and extensive and emanates from countries throughout the world.

While the approach of emergency services to trauma was in no way as dramatic as that of the military, there has been a traditional notion that a person suited to the job of police officer, paramedic, or firefighter should be immune to the effects of trauma. In many organizations, the culture has not allowed for the expression of distress. This resulted in an atmosphere in which someone had to be tough enough for the job, emotional reactions were suppressed, and those who did not suppress reactions were ridiculed and penalized.

The effects of disaster and horrifying life events on victims is well established in the professional literature and has led to a myriad of self-help books and treatment manuals for professionals. This attention to the experiences of victims has been important for the development of effective treatment modalities and the funding of programs aimed at reducing distress. In addition, awareness of traumatic responses has led to the modification of legislation and case law dealing with victims (Regehr, Bryant, and Glancy, 1997; Regehr and Glancy, 1995).

To a lesser degree, researchers have documented the effects of traumatic events on rescue workers. In 1967, Lifton described the emotional distress of rescue workers following the Hiroshima devastation. It was not until the 1980s, however, that attention to this issue became widespread. Subjects in studies included police officers following a shooting incident (Gersons, 1989; Solomon and Horn, 1986); firefighters following large blazes (Fullerton, McCarroll, Ursano, and Wright, 1992; McFarlane, 1988); nurses following the death of a child or colleague (Burns and Harm, 1993) and ambulance workers recovering bodies following mass disasters (Thompson, 1993). This research has led to the recognition that rescue workers who are exposed to mutilated bodies, mass destruction, and life-threatening situations may become hidden victims of disaster. Traumatic stress reactions stemming from this exposure have important implications for individual workers and their families who are attempting to deal with the aftermath of traumatic events. In addition, these physical, emotional, cognitive, and behavioral reactions in emergency responders have a profound effect on the ability of emergency service organizations to continue to respond to the needs of the public.

Distress Reactions

In chapter 3 we discussed various theories advanced for understanding response to adversity. Some of these theories refer to ongoing exposure to stressful events in life in general or in the workplace; others referred more specifically to response to tragic and sudden events. In this chapter, we will discuss response to traumatic events, relying primarily on trauma theory and vicarious trauma theory. Trauma theory was originally formulated to explain the experiences of victims of life-threatening and horrifying events. This concept has been expanded and now includes not only reactions of those who are victims, but also those individuals who witness horrifying incidents that leave them feeling helpless to change the course of events. From this perspective, exposure to life-threatening events overwhelms the coping capabilities of an individual, resulting in psychological and physiological symptoms. A second process that may occur when an individual is exposed to the tragedy of others is secondary trauma (Figley, 1995a) or vicarious traumatization (McCann and Pearlman, 1990b; Saakvitne and Pearlman, 1996), discussed later in the chapter.

When individuals are exposed to events that threaten the life or cause serious injury to themselves or others, and they consequently experience great fear, helplessness or horror, it is not uncommon for this to result in post-traumatic stress reactions. Post-traumatic stress disorder is a cluster of symptoms defined in the *Diagnostic and Statistical Manual of the American Psychiatric Association* (*DSM IV-TR*). The *DSM* defines three clusters of symptoms related to PTSD.

Reexperiencing symptoms are those in which memories of the event intrude upon the individual through recurring thoughts; distressing dreams; flashbacks of the event that may be visual, olfactory, sensory, or auditory; and reactivity to cues that symbolize the event.

Avoidance symptoms include efforts to avoid thoughts, feelings, or conversations about the event or avoidance of places that serve as reminders, inability to recall certain aspects of the event, diminished interest in activities, feelings of detachment from others, and sense of a foreshortened future.

Crisis or Adjustment Disorder	Acute Stress Disorder	Post-traumatic Stress Disorder	Chronic PTSD
- identifiable stressor - marked distress - impaired functioning - lasting less than 6 months	- exposure to a traumatic event - intrusion, avoidance & arousal symptoms - lasting 2 days to 4 weeks	- exposure to a traumatic event - intrusion, avoidance & arousal symptoms - lasting 1-3 months	- exposure to a traumatic event - intrusion, avoidance & arousal symptoms - lasting more than 3 months

Figure 5.1. Continuum of Traumatic Responses

Arousal symptoms can include difficulty getting to sleep, irritability and anger, difficulty concentrating, hypervigilance, and exaggerated startle response.

While post-traumatic stress disorder has now become part of common language, not all trauma reactions can be considered PTSD. Rather, traumatic responses are seen to fall on a continuum from crisis response (also called adjustment disorder in *DSM IV-TR*) to acute stress disorder, to PTSD and chronic PTSD. An excellent review of distinctions among these responses can be found in Yeager and Roberts (2003). They are briefly summarized in figure 5.1.

Various scales are used to attempt to determine the levels of symptoms experienced by individuals who have faced a traumatic event. One such scale is the impact of event scale (IES), developed by Horowitz, Wilner, and Alvarez (1979). This scale measures both intrusion and avoidance symptoms of PTSD by asking if people have experienced certain symptoms in the past 2 weeks. Each symptom is rated on a four-point continuum. The score places the symptoms of PTSD in one of four categories: low, moderate, high, or severe. In our studies with firefighters, police, and paramedics, we found that at any given point not immediately following an event, 57.1% had no to low levels of symptoms, 18.3% had moderate levels of symptoms, 4.2% had high levels of symptoms, and 20.4% had symptoms that fell in the severe range. These findings are summarized in figure 5.2.

There were no significant differences in the scores of police, firefighters, and paramedics. This means that at any given time, 24.6% of emergency responders in our studies had high or severe levels of symptoms. Other studies of police, fire, and ambulance workers confirm that at any time, somewhere between 25% and 30% of members of the organization report high

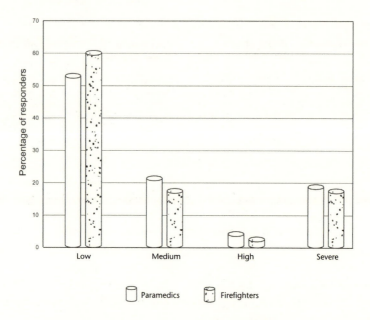

Figure 5.2. Levels of Traumatic Stress

or severe levels of trauma symptoms (Alexander and Klein, 2001; Bryant and Harvey, 1996; Stephens, 1997). Following a critical event such as a police shooting, trauma symptoms in the high or severe range can affect as many as 46% of those officers involved (Gersons, 1989). This leads to the question of how these symptoms are experienced by emergency services workers.

Intrusion Symptoms

Sleeplessness as a result of intrusive images is one of the most commonly reported symptoms experienced by responders after a traumatic event. At times this results in difficulties getting to sleep, and at other times responders are awakened by graphic nightmares. One paramedic stated, "I'd go to bed, I'd close my eyes and there would be the lady doing a swan dive off the balcony again, as clear as you sitting in front of me." A firefighter added, "I can remember the first murder that I did, I couldn't sleep for three nights, I remember seeing the body over and over and trying to shut it off, but I couldn't." One police officer reported crying when a dead baby was removed from a home by paramedics. He stated that for the first month he had repeated nightmares about the baby and had visual images of the baby. At the time we spoke, 8 months later, he continued to have the occasional nightmare.

Flashbacks are another common intrusion symptom. Some responders described visual flashbacks to the actual event; others described seeing people on the street who, for a fleeting moment, they thought was the victim of the traumatic incident. Lieutenant General Roméo Dallaire, who led the Canadian peacekeeping mission in Rwanda, speaks passionately about the atrocities he and his soldiers witnessed. Describing visual flashbacks of sights including dismembered children, he says "the scenes come back with digital clarity." When he closes his eyes to sleep, he says, "Thousands of eyes come back to haunt me." Very commonly emergency responders describe olfactory flashbacks. They are able to recall vividly the first time they smelled a human brain or burned flesh. After a traumatic call, they frequently report an inability to rid themselves of a disturbing smell. "I couldn't get the smell out of my nose for months, it's like a burnt bacon smell." Older firefighters and police officers who attended the DC-9 crash in 1970 report that they are still able to smell that event at times.

Avoidance Symptoms

One avoidance symptom is trying to limit exposure to certain events. This may involve volunteering for duties least likely to result in a particular type of exposure, for instance, remaining busy with transfers in order to be less available for trauma calls. In addition, taking sick days may be a means of limiting exposure for a period of time. One paramedic recalled, "It was the first time that I ever approached the department and said, I'm not coming in tomorrow because I just don't want to deal with anybody who's sick or got injuries. I just don't want to be here. I need 24 hours off."

Another form of avoidance is trying to block out memories of the event by refusing to speak about the job or event, by attempting to distract oneself, or by self-medicating with alcohol or drugs. Responders reported, "I was drinking more than I should." "I finally had enough to drink so that it put me to sleep." "I was off for the weekend, so I just tried to keep myself busy so I wouldn't think about it. Mind you, it didn't work."

Arousal Symptoms

Arousal symptoms described include physical symptoms of anxiety, generally high levels of stress and tension, tearfulness, and extreme anger toward the perpetrators of the tragedy. Two responders described psychological arousal that resulted in difficulty concentrating, sleeplessness, and fearfulness: "I couldn't make any sense of the map; it was just a bunch of lines, and cold sweats." "I used to wake up in the middle of the night, at home, in a cold sweat, breathing as if I'd been running, not knowing what was happening. Then, on the job, being quite frightened to the point that I couldn't really discuss it with my partner." These symptoms often continued for a prolonged period of time: "It was literally months before I could drive by that building without crying."

Finally, anger is a commonly reported arousal symptom. Emergency responders can describe in vivid detail, with a great deal of emotion, what they would like to see happen to perpetrators of violent crime. They express considerable rage at parents whose children are mortally wounded through neglect due to indifference or intoxication. They express anger toward systemic problems that interfere with effective responses. This anger is frequently misdirected toward coworkers, managers, or family members.

Longer-Term Reactions

Longer-term effects are also described by some emergency responders. These included a reduced capacity to handle stressful events, depression, and substance use. While many of the responders described the use of alcohol as a short-term coping strategy, there was a recognition that this at times became problematic. "I just basically burned out and fell into a pot of booze. Then I quit because it was killing me, killing my family, killing my work."

In order to ascertain the possible effects of event exposure on mental health and substance use, emergency workers in our studies were asked to rate their experiences before and after exposure to traumatic events. Responses are outlined in figure 5.3. While only 1.9% of workers indicated alcohol-related problems before exposure to a particular traumatic event or series of events, 8.4% identified these problems after exposure. Similarly, mental health stress leave rose from 1% to 16.3%, and the rate at which workers took psychiatric medication went from 1% to 6.8% after exposure to traumatic events.

Other research has pointed to high divorce rates among police officers. One study reported divorce among 60% of officers in Seattle during their first three years on the force (DePue, 1979). However, research in other cities reports rates of divorce among police officers as being 1 in 3 or 1 in 4, closer to the national average (Sewell, 1983). Suicide rates among police officers are also frequently pointed to as indicators of long-term distress. Nevertheless, while rates of suicide among police officers are found to have risen over the last 50 years, several studies in various parts of the United States have found that reported police suicides remain lower than the national average (Marzuk, Nock, Leon, Portera, and Tardiff, 2002; Josephson and Reiser, 1990; Loo, 1999). It has been suggested, however, that officially reported rates may not actually reflect the rates of suicide within the profession (Violanti, 1995).

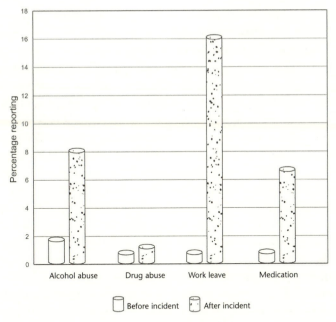

Figure 5.3. Outcomes of Events

Families of responders are also significantly affected by these incidents. One impact is the fact that the exposed worker at times feels disengaged and emotionally distant from family members: "You almost treat your spouse like another call . . . there is a [emotional] deficit there." Another issue is generalized anger and irritability, often vented on family. While this is mostly limited to "grumpiness" and argumentativeness, one responder in our study disclosed that this contributed to family violence perpetrated by him. Further, responders describe generalized fears for the safety of family members and a tendency to become overprotective: "You realize that . . .wow . . . my son is at the age that this could happen." Other responders describe the way that exposure to traumatic events causes them to reevaluate and value family relationships in a more positive manner. The experiences of families are discussed in detail in chapter 8, "Are You Coming Home Tonight?"

Factors Influencing Reactions to Trauma

The emergence of the diagnostic category PTSD heralded an important shift in psychiatry by acknowledging the contribution of environmental stressors to mental health problems. Implicit in the criteria for diagnosis was the assumption that PTSD could occur in any individual who encountered a catastrophic event, regardless of any pretraumatic considerations (Yehuda, 1999). This assumption has been supported by a body of research literature that concluded that the development of post-traumatic distress is correlated with the "dosage" of traumatic exposure (Mollica, McInnes, Poole, and Tor, 1998; Resnick, Kilpatrick, Best, and Kramer, 1992; Marmar et al., 1999). For instance Orcutt, Erickson, and Wolfe (2002) found that higher levels of combat exposure in Gulf War veterans was related to high rates of PTSD. Similarly, Mollica and colleagues (1998) found that there was a relationship between the degree of post-traumatic stress and the degree of violent exposure experienced by both Vietnamese and Cambodian survivors of mass violence and torture. Blanchard and colleagues (1995) demonstrated that survivors of motor vehicle accidents had higher levels of trauma symptoms if they had greater injuries or were at greater risk of death. Among emergency responders, Bryant and Harvey (1996) found that volunteer firefighters who were exposed to multiple traumatic events were more likely to report symptoms of traumatic stress.

However, other authors argue that the dose-effect model is inadequate in explaining post-traumatic distress. These critics point to methodological limitations of dose-effect studies, small amounts of variance explained by the severity of the traumatic event, and low incidence rates of PTSD following shared events (Bowman, 1999; Paris, 1999; Yehuda and McFarlane, 1995). Our studies also demonstrate that while many responders state that they experienced distress as a result of certain events, such as mass casualties or the death of a child, not all do. In addition, anyone with experience working in emergency organizations has observed that people respond differently to tragic events on the job; some people are more affected by any one event than others are.

Although many studies have supported the view that the intensity of the trauma has a bearing on the severity and chronicity of trauma symptoms in rescue workers (Fullerton et al., 1992; McCarroll et al., 1996; Weiss, Marmar, Metzler, and Ronfeldt, 1995), it is becoming increasingly clear that trauma and distress do not have a simple cause-and-effect relationship. Rather, traumatic events may act as precipitants, while the severity of response is determined by individual differences and the environment in which the affected person finds himself or herself. Figure 5.4 models the relationship between event factors, individual factors, and environmental factors.

The social environment in which responders find themselves is a key factor in understanding response to trauma. For instance, McCarroll and colleagues (1996) found that spousal and coworker support were important predictors of trauma response in workers handling the remains of bodies following mass suicides in Waco, Texas. Marmar et al. (1999) similarly

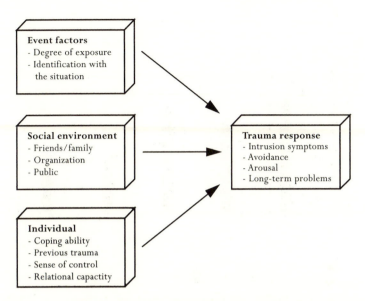

Figure 5.4. Model for Understanding Reactions to Traumatic Events

found that social support was negatively associated with traumatic reactions in rescue workers following a freeway collapse—that is, as social support went up, trauma symptoms went down. In our study of firefighters in Australia, social support from spouses, family, and friends was also significantly associated with trauma scores (Regehr and et al., 2000). Figure 5.5 demonstrates the relationship between support and trauma symptoms reported on the impact of event scale for 139 police officers, firefighters, and paramedics. On this scale, 1 represents the lowest level of perceived support from spouse, family, and employer, and 5 represents the highest level. It is clearly evident that as perceived support from others increases, trauma scores decrease. Support experienced from within the organization is also important and will be discussed in chapter 6. Furthermore, public and media responses to the event also have a profound effect, covered in detail in chapter 7, "Heroes or Villains?"

In addition to external factors such as social supports, the environment, and the strength of the stressor, who it is that encounters the event is also critical. Each individual has strengths and vulnerabilities that serve as risk factors or protective factors when traumatic events are encountered. Recent reports have highlighted the importance of individual differences in determining the intensity and duration of trauma-related symptoms (Paris, 1999; Bowman, 1999; Yehuda, 1999; Regehr, Hemsworth, and Hill, 2001). Mediating variables identified by researchers include a history of trauma before the event (McFarlane, 1988; Luce, Firth-Cozens, Midgley, and Bruges,

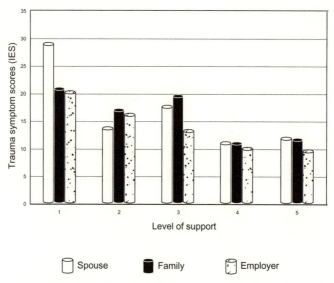

Figure 5.5. Level of Support and Trauma

2002), previous mental health problems and/or a family history of mental health problems (McFarlane, 1988; Luce et al., 2002), and the personality of the affected worker.

One aspect of individual response to events encountered in the workplace is the way in which the event connects with the personal history and life experience of the worker. This experience can perhaps best be understood in the context of secondary or vicarious trauma theory (Figley, 1995a,b; McCann and Pearlman, 1990b; Saakvitne and Pearlman, 1996). These concepts were originally used to describe what Figley (1995b) called the *costs of caring* among mental health professionals. That is, through the process of hearing people's stories of violence, torture, terror, and abuse, therapists begin to experience feelings of fear and suffering similar to those of their clients. As a result, they can develop symptoms including intrusive imagery, generalized fears, affective arousal, changes in their relationships, and a changed worldview (Chrestman, 1995; Regehr and Cadell, 1999; Sexton, 1999). More recently, Figley (1999) has applied this concept to emergency service work in general, and to the work of police officers in particular. Vicarious trauma, as we have stated earlier, is understood to occur in part as a result of prolonged exposure to traumatic material. In addition, however, it is understood to occur as a result of the empathic engagement between the worker and the victim (Figley, 1995a; Saakvitne and Pearlman, 1996). Figley (1995b) noted that those who have the greatest capacity for caring and empathy are at greatest risk of experiencing stress and trauma as a result of their compassion.

Empathy is an elusive concept long been examined by philosophers and psychotherapists alike. In general, however, empathy is conceptualized as involving two different components, *cognition* and *affect* (Davis, 1983). The first aspect is a cognitive process, in which an empathic individual has the ability to accurately perceive the plight of others. From this perspective, empathy can be an objective, detached, analytical process (Kant 1949; Rogers, 1957). As a result of this understanding, one can behave in a manner that conveys concern and caring. The second component of empathy is a vicarious emotional process, in which the person develops an affective connection with another and subsequently has an emotional response to the other's suffering (Hume 1966; Keefe, 1976). In emergency workers' work with victims of violence, the two components of empathy may be expressed as a cognitive awareness of the distress of victims while maintaining an emotional distance, or, alternately, may involve an emotional connection with the victim.

The concept of vicarious trauma and the vulnerability caused by empathy are useful in understanding our research into events that cause the greatest distress in emergency responders. Frequently the events that are most troubling for emergency workers involve not multiple deaths in a dramatic incident but rather the death or injury of someone the worker contextualized in relationship to others. That is, an individual who died alone, without the support of others; a child who did not live in a loving, caring environment; a family devastated by loss, or an individual so alienated that he took his own life. These reactions can be triggered by the responses of other people or by objects that connect the victim to others, such as vacation photos spread across the road in a motor vehicle accident. In this process of contextualizing, the emergency responder develops an emotional connection to the individual or bereaved family members. This emotional connection results in experiences of distress that remain with the worker. Other research conducted with body handlers has confirmed that developing an emotional link between the remains or identifying the remains as someone who could possibly be a friend or loved one increases trauma reactions (Ursano et al., 1999; McCarroll et al., 1995). One of the problems with reactions to this type of event, however, is that they are less obvious to outside observers. As a result, the support mechanisms that might be in place for a dramatic occurrence are not made available, and the worker suffers alone.

Another factor specific to the individual worker is style of coping. Rutter (1993; Rutter, Champion, Quinton, Maughan, and Pickles, 1995) proposes the concept of resilience as a way of understanding how individual personality characteristics influence the ability to manage stressful life events effectively. He suggests that resilience results from having previously encountered serious life challenges and having coped successfully. That is, when individuals have successfully coped with events in the past, they develop a sense of self-efficacy or a belief that they will be able to overcome new challenges (Lazarus, 1966). As we indicated in chapter 3, "Building a Framework," a cognitive appraisal of an event as manageable and within one's coping ability reduces affective arousal, influences a person's expectations of success, and consequently changes their behavior. Thus, a sense of optimism shapes a person's reaction to a crisis and subsequently influences the outcome. In the instance of body handlers at Waco, Texas, those individuals who had more previous experience in handling human remains had lower levels of trauma (McCarroll et al., 1996). Presumably, individuals who have faced and managed trauma in the past are familiar with feelings of distress and discomfort and understand that these will pass with time. In addition, they have undoubtedly learned mechanisms that assist them in reducing distress, such as distraction, talking to others, or relaxation. These strategies increase the sense of control that an individual has over the healing or recovery process.

The sense of control individuals experience over an event or over their reaction to an event is important in understanding trauma reactions. The concept of *locus of control* is frequently discussed in the literature and has been subject to research in many domains. Locus of control is conceptualized as the patterned ways in which an individual perceives the sources of control over unforeseen stressors (Rotter, 1975). Locus of control ranges on a continuum between internal ("All my successes and failures are the result of my own abilities and efforts") and external ("Everything that happens to me is a result of fate"). This concept is especially relevant for understanding responses to critical events due to the challenge of the person's belief in a controllable and predictable world. Individuals who retain a belief that they can control outcomes in the face of disaster have been found to manage the experience far more effectively than individuals who believed they were controlled by external forces (Gibbs, 1989; Regehr, Regehr, and Bradford, 1998; Regehr, Cadell, and Jansen, 1999). Firefighters experience difficulty coping when they perceive a loss of control (Bryant and Harvey, 1996). Clearly, however, when we apply the concept of locus of control to emergency responders, we must take into account that many things are clearly outside of their control, and this can add to stress and distress experienced. In this regard it is helpful to differentiate between stable and global perceptions of control or lack of control (such as "I am a born loser") versus situational control (such as "There are aspects of this situation that are outside of my control"). While a global sense of control is adaptive, accepting that there are situations outside of one's control can help reduce self-blame when things end less than ideally.

A final individual characteristic is the individual's ability to develop and sustain interpersonal relationships or relational capacity. This capacity is useful in understanding individual differences in obtaining social support. From the perspective of relational capacity, attachment experiences, especially in childhood, become incorporated into perceptions of self and other. When early relationships with caregivers are marked with hostility, victimization, and blaming, later relationships are bound to be seen through the filter of these past experiences (van der Kolk et al., 1994). That is, individuals who have experienced negative relationships with others are more likely to be suspicious of the motives of others and are less likely to trust that others are truly interested in their welfare. For instance, individuals who have had abusive or neglectful parents are likely to have developed self-protective mechanisms to reduce the possibility that they will be hurt. These same individuals will find it more difficult to open themselves up to warm and loving relationships with others, for fear they will again be emotionally harmed. Consequently, social support is increasingly viewed as a process of cognitive appraisal or a property of the person, rather than an actual reflection of the transactions between individuals in a particular situation (Coyne and DeLongis, 1986). That is, individuals with limited relational capacity may emphasize negative factors in relationships with others and consequently underestimate the amount of support they receive. Further, the nature of individual expectations and relationship skills plays a large part in determining both the types of people with whom one will associate and how they will be accepted (Bowlby, 1979). Thus, the ability to garner and use social support is in itself a strength and an effective coping resource.

Coping Strategies in Emergency Responders

Earlier in this chapter we discussed the increased risk of trauma reactions when emergency responders developed an emotional or empathic connection with the victims of violence or tragedy. In our work with emergency responders, we have discovered that many of the coping strategies employed by respondents involved the deliberate use of cognitive techniques that reduce the risk of developing an emotional connection. In the midst of a crisis situation, emergency responders must maintain their focus and enhance their ability to function. To this end, one emergency responder described to us the manner in which he used "visualization" to help determine the next course of action when confronted with a scene where people are in a state of high anxiety and hysteria. That is, he would picture the next task to be done rather than take in the scene around him. Other responders describe the conscious process of emotionally distancing themselves and ensuring that they did not become emotionally attached to the victim or the victim's family. One paramedic recalled, "[the mother of the victim] wanted to climb in the ambulance and I just said no, the police will transport you. . . . I just didn't want to see her at all." Another responder stated, "You have to really suppress your emotions at that time . . . you got to really concentrate on blocking her out because her emotions may affect yours at that time."

One subject posited, "We tend to be heartless in what we do and people say, 'Well didn't that affect you?' It probably affects us all, it's just that we've developed sort of a nice thick skin to a lot of the calls, as a protective mechanism. If you want to use the word *thick skin*, that's really what it is . . . you don't let it bother you cause you're not supposed to let it bother you." In the long run however, this strategy has consequences.

> This tends to make [my] family feel like they don't mean something. . . . That's not the reality of how I feel, but that's the way I make them feel, and that's tough, to bring about that division. When you walk through the front door of your house, you're a different person, 'cause you can't turn it on and off, so the coping mechanisms that I've developed for work unfortunately can have a slight negative impact at home because I'm utilizing a coping mechanism that probably shouldn't be utilized in that setting. But I can't go back and forth, and that's a problem, so that's certainly the downside.

Humor is another strategy for maintaining a sense of distance. Each type of emergency service organization has its own brand of humor, shared among members. Jokes tend to focus on the most gruesome aspects of the job as a protective strategy for reducing the impact of the work. Emergency responders are well aware that others outside the organization would be appalled at the material, and they are cautious to keep the jokes in house. Following an event, they are conscious that the public and media are scrutinizing their reactions, and thus they are careful not to be caught laughing.

Following a traumatic event, one emergency responder identified the need to obtain information about the situation in order to get a "sense of closure" by understanding why the person committed suicide. Others discussed a process by which they reviewed their work during the event to ensure that they had done everything right and to learn what could be done better next time. In this way they positively reframed the event as a learning experience and an opportunity to improve services. Further, they used tragic events as an opportunity to reframe their own lives, focusing on the positive and downplaying the aggravations. In a similar vein, one responder described that in order to cope with the lack of control over the job, he ensured that other aspects of his life were in control and that his family was prepared for possible disaster.

Summary

In summary, when exposed to tragic events, emergency responders will frequently develop some symptoms of distress. These include intrusion symptoms such as repetitive thoughts or nightmares about the event, avoiding situations that remind them of the event or trying to block out memories using deliberate cognitive strategies or substance use, and arousal symptoms such as anxiety and fears. Occasionally these symptoms may reach a level of intensity and continue for a sufficient period of time to be considered post-traumatic stress disorder. Many factors influence the intensity and duration of symptoms. One set of factors relates to the type of exposure—how bad, how often, and how long it lasted. A second set of factors relates to the recovery environment, including personal social supports and organizational supports. We will be discussing these factors in greater detail in the coming chapters. A final set of factors relates to the personal life experiences of the individual responder. What does this event remind them of? How competent do they feel in coping with the event? How adept are they at establishing and using social supports? In the end, most emergency responders are extremely well suited to the work that they have selected; consequently, they are adept at developing and using coping strategies in order to manage most events they face. These coping strategies in general are highly effective. At times, however, event, environmental, and personal factors converge to overwhelm coping strategies. The coping strategies themselves can become problematic over time. This is why intervention programs are necessary in these high-voltage work environments.

6

HELP OR HINDRANCE?

Stress and the Emergency Service Organization

Critical events encountered in the line of duty and the possible subsequent traumatic stress symptoms have been an area of focus for emergency service workers, unions, management, and mental health professionals over the past decade. While there is considerable evidence that these events have an impact on workers, many research studies suggest that it may be the everyday hassles encountered by emergency service workers within their organizational structure that occasion considerable stress and strain and form the foundation on which critical events are heaped (Liberman et al., 2002). Critical events encountered by those who are already experiencing stress and who perceive that they do not have support from their colleagues, managers, and/or union in good times, and especially in bad times, are more likely to result in traumatic stress reactions than are critical events encountered by individuals at their optimal level of functioning who know they can count on others when they are facing challenges.

In 2000, we conducted research on stress and trauma experienced by child protection workers in a large, urban child-welfare organization. Child protection workers in this organization were responsible for investigating allegations of child abuse reported to the agency by professionals or the general public. Investigations involved going to homes, often in dangerous areas of the city, and insisting upon interviewing the parent and seeing the child. If it was determined that the child was at risk, the child would be removed from the home. Alternately, protection workers provided ongoing

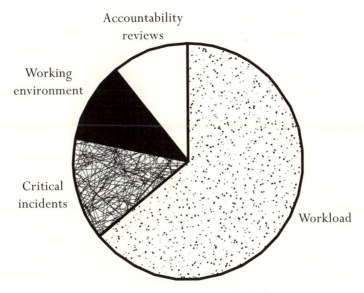

Figure 6.1. Relative Stressors in Child Protection

monitoring of high-risk cases in which parents had previously been abusive or were at risk due to their substance abuse or mental health issues. This involved regular home visits and at times the necessity to obtain a court order to remove a child. Child protection workers in this city work alone. They infrequently requested police back-up. Not surprisingly, these jobs were perceived as dangerous and stressful.

The 175 workers who participated in this study reported frequent exposure to critical events. Among intake workers, half of whom had been with the agency less than 1 year, 20% indicated that they had been assaulted by a client, 50% indicated that they had been threatened with violence , and most had also been involved in situations where children had been severely abused or killed. On average, the most recent event occurred within the past 8 months for the intake workers and within the past 18 months for the family support workers. Rates of traumatic stress among these workers were extremely high and far exceeded those of studies we conducted with firefighters, police, and paramedics. Yet when asked what factors were most distressing in their jobs, these workers referred to high caseloads, overwhelming paperwork, public accountability reviews, and inadequate community resources to support families in distress. When asked to rank stressors, 68% of child protection workers identified workload as the most stressful component, 11.5% identified the working environment as most stressful, 11.5% identified accountability reviews as the most stressful, and only 15% identified that the critical events were the most stressful (Regehr, Leslie, Howe, and Chau, 2000).

As a result of the findings above, we attempted to identify what factors contributed to the extreme levels of traumatic stress symptoms encountered by these workers. Using a statistical method called linear structural equation modeling (SEM), we included a variety of factors we thought might contribute to traumatic stress, including characteristics of the individual, organizational stressors, and incident factors. While all these factors contributed to traumatic stress symptoms, the strongest predictors were organizational factors including workload, union support, and management support (Regehr, Hemsworth, Leslie, Howe, and Chau, 2004). We concluded from this that critical events in this child welfare organization were encountered by individuals already coping with high levels of challenge and stress. In this context, individuals who consistently face adversity on the job may no longer have the resources to manage and overcome post-traumatic stress reactions when faced with a traumatic event such as the death of a child or a threat of personal injury. As a consequence, they report higher levels of symptoms. This is vital to consider when we are planning comprehensive programs for dealing with trauma in the workplace. If we do not address the foundation, making sure workplaces are healthy, we will not be nearly as effective in dealing with crisis situations as they arise.

Workplace Stress

Workplace stress has been identified as a clear health and safety issue and has been a major area of focus for health and safety organizations such as the National Institute for Occupational Safety and Health (NIOSH), mandated by the U.S. Congress to study workplace stress. NIOSH (1999) reports studies that indicate that between 29% and 40% of workers in the United States rate their workplaces as very or extremely stressful. Factors identified that lead to workplace stress include task design factors such as long hours and overload, a management style that communicates poorly and dissuades employee participation in decision making, lack of support within the organization, conflicting roles, job insecurity and lack of opportunity for growth and promotion, and environmental concerns (NIOSH, 1999). The consequences of work stress include high turnover, absenteeism, and impaired quality of service for those who remain on the job (Rees, 1995). Physical conditions can include cardiovascular disease, musculoskeletal disorders, gastrointestinal problems, impaired immune functioning, and possibly increased vulnerability to illnesses such as cancer and diabetes

(NIOSH, 1999). For instance, cardiac responses such as elevated heart rate have been identified in emergency service workers following a stressful event on the job. These responses do not diminish by the end of a shift but rather are carried home (Anderson, Litzenberger, and Placas, 2002; Roberts and Levenson, 2001). Researchers caution about the use of alcohol, illegal drugs, prescription drugs, and over-the-counter medications as a coping strategy due to the risk that they may contribute to high rates of substance abuse in emergency responders (Davidson and Veno, 1980).

Workplace stress, including both cumulative daily stress and post-traumatic stress, is compensated by both public and private insurance schemes and has serious cost implications for employers and society. It is estimated that work-related stress costs American companies nearly 10% of their annual earnings. Annually $26 billion is paid out in disability claims related to stress in the workplace in the United States. In 1998, the Workplace Safety and Insurance Board (WSIB) of Canada amended its regulations to include, for the first time, mental health stress leave secondary to a traumatic event on the job that was not associated with physical injury (Workplace Safety and Insurance Board, 1998), leading to a large increase in claims and in insurance costs to employers. Other, more indirect costs come from loss of work time due to both stress and physical illness resulting from stress. For instance, heart disease alone accounts for 135 million lost workdays each year (Knott, 2003).

Recent U.S. case law has expanded the definition of workplace stress and workplace injury to include psychological trauma. In a landmark case, a paramedic challenged definitions of occupational injury and illness (Fairfax County Fire and Rescue Department v. Mottram, 2002). During the first 10 years of his career, the plaintiff, Mr. Mottram, had responded to approximately 12 calls per day, many of which due to his level of training and experience, involved serious injury. Beginning in the 1990s he was assigned to administrative positions but continued to work one paramedic shift every 2 months in order to maintain his certification. During one of these shifts, he responded to a fatal fire that triggered memories of an earlier fire where six members of a family were killed. The Worker's Compensation Commission denied his claim for injury due to PTSD and ruled that the PTSD he suffered could not be causally linked to either fatal fire—the more recent one that was less serious, or the earlier one for which he did not previously experience symptoms. Mr. Mottram then attempted to claim that PTSD was an occupational disease arising out of his employment. Again the claim was denied. On appeal to the Virginia Court of Appeals in 2001, the court reversed the commission's decision, noting that in some cases PTSD may be compensable as an injury and in some as a disease arising from occupational risk. This was upheld by the Virginia Supreme Court and sets a precedent for employer liability for PTSD not only as a form of workplace injury, but also as an ongoing occupational hazard (Dreisbach, 2003).

The costs of losing highly trained staff members are not limited to worker's compensation and insurance claims. The Canadian military has recently estimated that the cost of training and preparation for overseas deployment of one soldier is approximately $315,000. This means that if within one garrison 80 soldiers presently identified as suffering from PTSD as a result of peacekeeping missions are discharged from the armed forces, the cost in terms of personnel losses alone would be $25 million ("Stressed Soldiers Shunned," 2003). Added to that, of course, are the health care and social costs associated with caring for individuals suffering from combat-related PTSD.

Everyday Hassles as a Source of Stress

Several research studies point to the fact that emergency service workers identify everyday hassles as the primary source of stress in their jobs. For instance, in a study of 733 police officers in 3 U.S. cities, researchers concluded that exposure to routine administrative, bureaucratic, and organizational aspects of police work is at least as stressful as the inherent dangers of the work (Liberman et al., 2002). The most common stressors noted by 100 Cincinnati officers were courts, administrative policies, lack of management support, inadequate equipment, community relations, and changing shift work. They reported being troubled by offensive policies, lack of participation in decision making, and adverse work schedules (Kroes, 1985). Similarly, 2,000 officers in Maryland and Virginia rated administration the most stressful part of their job. Stressful organizational events were found to be more highly correlated with psychological distress than were stressful field events for a group of 233 officers in the northeastern United States (Patterson, 1999). This same group of officers was asked to identify the most stressful event that they had encountered in the past 6 months, and the majority reported an organizational event—not a field event. In a study of 954 English police officers, researchers noted, "It is of interest that the police men and women interviewed about potential stressors identified organizational and management features as stressful more often than operational police duties—in a ratio of 4 to 1" (Brown and Campbell, 1990, p. 316). Similarly, in a study of New York police officers job satisfaction predicted stress 6.3 times more than acute stressors (Violanti and Aron, 1993). Another study noted "for police officers, the most serious stressors seemed to be problems in relationships with colleagues and superiors rather than other events, such as dealing with victims of serious accidents, being attacked by aggressive offenders or dealing with protesters" (Buunk, and Peeters, 1994). Obviously major traumatic events, such as the terrorist attack on the World Trade Center, will have a greater influence on well-being than will organizational policies and politics; nevertheless, these ongoing concerns presumably undermine resources for dealing with such events.

While studies of organizational stressors in the emergency services have focused largely on policing organizations, the studies that do address these issues with other emergency services confirm the findings of policing studies. Ambulance workers involved in body recovery duties following mass disasters in England, for instance, identified that poor relationships with management, not being valued for their skills, and shift work were the major stressors they encountered (Thompson, 1993). In the course of our interviews with emergency responders regarding stress on the job, one paramedic stated, "But more than anything is the frustration of I'm doing too much and other people are not doing their fair share, management is not providing us with the appropriate number of people, there's not enough cars, and the dispatchers are stupid." A firefighter reported, "I think for me the job itself doesn't stress me out at all. I can say that with 100% confidence, it's more some of the people that I work with that stress me out—more than the job." What is it about the organizational structures and the jobs of emergency service professionals on the front lines that make their jobs so much more difficult?

Organizational Structure and Stress

The hierarchical nature of emergency service organizations is one factor that leads to increased stress. The chain of command and the levels of authority result in a feeling that the individual worker has little influence over decisions that affect their work and lives. Workers view organizational stressors as unchangeable and less within their control than events that happen in the field (Patterson, 1999). "It is just the perception that they don't listen to you, don't hear you, they come down with silly commandments." "There is a lack of logic, a lack of fairness, of rationale . . . you just feel alienated."

This stress is not felt equally throughout the organization. Typically studies conclude that supervisors, sergeants, and chiefs report the highest levels of stress and trauma (Kirkcaldy, Brown, and Cooper, 1998). In part this is because they are involved in both frontline duties and frontline supervision of workers. This means that the consequences of their decisions are immediately apparent. It also means that they are sandwiched between upper management and workers and frequently must enforce decisions and

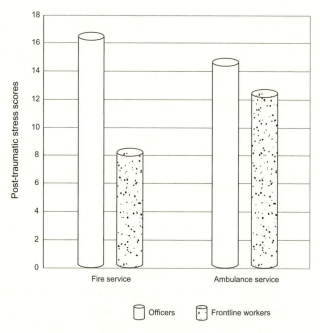

Figure 6.2. Post-Traumatic Distress by Rank

policies that they did not make. In our studies, officers in the fire service had significantly higher traumatic stress scores than frontline workers, but while officers in the ambulance service reported higher levels of symptoms, this was not statistically significant.

Another interpretation of the finding that supervisors and managers report more distress is that officers are also older and have more years of service. Our studies and others of emergency service organizations indicate that years of service is directly related to more negative attitudes about the job, more stress, a greater sense of alienation, and more sick time (Alexander, 1999). Over time, emergency workers experience a progressive loss of belief in being able to make a difference in the organization (Kroes, 1985). In our recent study comparing new fire recruits with experienced firefighters, we encountered what we considered to be a perplexing finding. That is, as years of service increased, self-efficacy, or confidence in oneself and one's abilities, decreased (Regehr, Hill, Knott, and Sault, 2003). While this surprised us as researchers, it does not appear to surprise those in the emergency services. One ambulance dispatcher explained, "I tend to deal with crews who are much older with lots of seniority and who are largely disenchanted, *burnout* is, I suppose, the best description of them. They do everything that they can to minimize the amount of work that they do." Part of this is simply the physical burden of the job on the body. "Old age, bad knees, my own health told me it was time to slow down." "The average life span of a paramedic is 10 years, then you get injured."

One factor that leads to disillusionment over time is the lack of career advancement opportunities in emergency service organizations. As we indicated in chapter 3, the effort-reward imbalance model (Siegrist, 1996) suggests that when it is consistently perceived that efforts do not lead to opportunities for rewards, such as money and promotion, the results can be reduced self-efficacy and self-esteem. Emergency responder organizations require many highly skilled frontline workers, but very few supervisors and managers. "There's no incentives except promotion, even if you work hard," explained one police officer. "The last 3 years running this unit, I haven't been home. I might as well have sold my place and bought a Winnebago to park in the lot because I'm here all the time. But it doesn't matter when it comes to promotion. . . . Just learn to accept it." This results in a high sense of competition between colleagues (Brown, Fielding, and Grover, 1999). As one firefighter stated, "I find that it is a job where people are very critical of one another, and there [are] a lot of people who measure themselves against one another." A police officer added, "There's lots of inside politics in policing; subsequently there's lots of backstabbing that goes on, so I always say I've never lost a day's sleep over anything any dirtbag did to me on the street, but I've lost sleep from time to time over what guys have done on the job. We're going through the promotional process right now and all the backstabbing and sniveling and carrying on." Yet skills acquired in emergency service work are not easily transferable (Alexander, 1999), so opportunities in other public-service or profit-making organizations are limited and people begin to feel trapped within their organizations and professions. One firefighter with many credentials within the department explained, "If I left this job today, I couldn't get a job, not with my credentials, neither could anyone else, you're just a glorified nobody."

A perception then arises that people who move through the ranks are promoted for political reasons and not for reasons of competence or experience. A group of recruits are hired together, pass the training period and examinations, and learn to support one another and work as a team. Then within a few years, these same colleagues are forced to compete for the very few middle management positions. People report that announcements of opportunities for advancement are removed from bulletin boards and communications books in order to try to limit the number of people who might compete for a job. In the end, former colleagues, now superiors, are viewed as corporate watchdogs who impose confining structures and consequences for those who step outside of those structures.

Job Content Factors as a Source of Stress

Shift work has been found to be a major source of stress in the professional and personal lives of many occupational groups (Alexander, 1999). Shift work leads to problems of fatigue, sleep disturbances, and workplace accidents, as well as health problems such as weight gain, cardiovascular problems, and gastrointestinal disturbances (Penn and Bootzin, 1990). One paramedic explained the impact of shift work on a person's ability to do competent work. "Sometimes when you are working a night shift and you're really late into the shift, you're tired, and you may document something and when you go home, you go over the documentation in your mind and you think jeez, did I leave that out or did I put that down? And so you worry about it." Further, as people attempt to deal with shift work and manage both sleep and alertness, they may begin to abuse substances such as nicotine, caffeine, and a range of drugs, including over the counter, prescription, and illegal. The nature of shifts in fire services differs from the other services due to the 24-hour shift pattern. These long work shifts also contribute to boredom and tedium secondary to the various routine housekeeping tasks that are undertaken by highly trained personnel (Murphy, Bond, Beaton, Murphy, and Johnson, 2002).

Extended shifts and compressed working weeks that occur in many emergency service organizations have the benefit of freeing up time for leisure, home, and family activities. However, the capacity of workers to enjoy that time off is frequently limited by the fact that shift work is not synchronized with the regular rhythm of society. "It's difficult to have a normal life. Most of my friends work Monday to Friday days, so they're off every weekend and every night. That's when they do things, so it's difficult for me to participate in their lives in the same way." The inability to participate in social and family life is one of the greatest sources of family/work conflict (Pisarski, Bohle, and Callan, 2002). "Shift work plays on your family life, when the rest of the family is having dinner, you're at work, when the children are up, you're not home, when you get home, they've gone to bed. So you have some separation from your children and long-term separation from your spouse and then their stress becomes your life when you get back home. So you have stress at work and then you've got the personal stress when you get back home, and that's consistent." Shift work affects not only those with families, but also single workers. "The shift work is a huge stress on a lot of guys' relationships. Good looking girl sitting at home, [and you have to say] I gotta work Friday, Saturday, Sunday again, or I'm tired." Karasek and Theorell's (1990) demand/control/support model, discussed in chapter 3, suggests that when workers perceive that they have less control over their work and its impact on their lives, increased stress and strain result. This can in turn lead to increased absences and impaired physical health. Control over shift choices and supervisor support can go a long way in alleviating many home/work time conflicts.

Role clarity is an aspect of work that has been investigated repeatedly by researchers in a variety of work contexts. From this perspective, it is argued that generally speaking, people can cope with higher demands and experience less stress when the expectations of their jobs are clearly defined. The greater the ambiguity regarding performance expectations, the greater the stress people feel. This was recently demonstrated in a study of over 1,700 U.S. Army soldiers. These individuals reported feeling less strain despite high demands when the tasks to be completed were well defined (Bliese and Castro, 2000). In the emergency services, competing demands frequently lead to lack of clarity. Should a paramedic do this transfer as directed or redeploy to a critical call? When a police officer encounters a homeless person sleeping in a bank entrance with an ATM on a subzero-degree night, should he be more concerned with the perceived security risk to the bank patrons or the physical health of the homeless individual?

It is important to note, however, that role clarity is not the same as being closely monitored or repeatedly instructed by a supervisor. Rather, another important factor that moderates job stress is autonomy within the work environment. Related to autonomy is the degree of control over the workplace environment that individuals experience. Those in areas with the lowest levels of control experience the highest levels of stress. Thus, paramedics cannot control where the dispatchers send them, and dispatchers cannot control whether the ambulance will get to the call in a timely manner. Both feel frustrated, angry, and stressed. While role clarity is a factor that reduces stress, instrumental leadership—leadership that creates excessive structure around the job—actually serves to reduce satisfaction and increase distress (Landeweerd and Boumans, 1994). "At the beginning of training you're basically told how to think and how they don't like people questioning them because you're just a grunt on the road, and so when you bring up a logical argument, they get defensive, which is very frustrating, and it affects your job satisfaction and feeling good about the work." One influence that reduces autonomy among individual workers and frequently results in stress and disillusionment among workers is the increased need for accountability, careful note taking, and endless report writing that follows each event. "The Monday morning quarterback is going to come and say that you should have done this . . . that kind of big brother mentality auditing your performance." A paramedic noted, "I always find that fault or blame or remedial action is taken with the frontline worker rather than having any kind of support or backup. Morale is low as a result." This is discussed in detail in chapter 7, "Heroes or Villains?"

Uncertainty is a function of emergency service work. Unpredictable, high-stress emergency tasks frequently occur between long periods of readiness (Lusa, Häkkänen, Luukkonen, and Viikari-Juntura, 2002). One police officer described his work as 2 hours of boredom followed by 2 minutes of sheer terror and 3 hours of report writing. In some services or some areas of a particular service, stress is experienced as a result of a high call volume. "We do 1,300 calls a day [in this ambulance service] and there are not enough trucks to do the calls. It is a constant juggle." In other areas, low call volume is the problem. As reported by one paramedic, "It may sound strange, but boredom is sometimes quite a large stressor . . . inefficiency." A firefighter concurred. "The station that I manage is a slower station and you may not have a working fire for 2 months because it is a newer neighborhood. That can be very stressful; you still keep active, but you want to be more than active, you want to do the job we're trained to do." The uncertainty is not all negative, however; the excitement, fast changing environment, and need to think on one's feet draw many people to the emergency services.

Stress is experienced differently by people in various parts of the organization. While we might expect that working on the tactical squad or the criminal investigations unit in a police service may carry the highest levels of stress, more stress is actually reported in areas that also report less job satisfaction, such as traffic or headquarters support departments (Kirkcaldy et al., 1998). The higher the status associated with the job area, the less likely people are to report stress. For example, a British study looked at stressors experienced by community police officers whose role was crime prevention. They reported that they were not viewed as "real" police officers because they did not make arrests and "pick up the bodies" (Fielding, 1994). Added to the stress of low-status jobs is the fact that frequently people are transferred to these details as a form of discipline or redeployment due to injury or illness. Certain areas of the organization then become employment ghettos.

Organizational change and shifting demands and expectations are an additional source of stress. Expanding cities that progressively engulf smaller communities on their outskirts combined with shrinking public funds are resulting in an amalgamation of services between jurisdictions and within jurisdictions, such as the joining of fire and ambulance services. These changes affect seniority, union contracts, opportunities for advancement, and the composition of the work team.

> The municipality has to prove that they are the most cost-effective method of providing the service. So now we have to go through a similar process that we have been through before. [Last time] everyone went through a lot of job stress when they amalgamated services.

Everyone had to reapply for their own jobs; now we have to do it again. No sooner have you proven yourself but they say now you have to prove it again. . . . In the end we've become kind of numb to it, we know our abilities, we are the best, and we'll be able to prove it, but it causes stress.

A Swedish study examined the physiological reactions of police inspectors during a time of organizational change. Survey questionnaires and blood samples began to be collected shortly after the change and continued at specified time intervals until 3 years after the change. Over the 3 years, worry about employment and workload decreased as the organization settled into the new routine. Significantly, cholesterol levels, cortisol, and testosterone were highly correlated with worry and workload. That is, as worry and workload decreased, cholesterol also decreased and testosterone increased (Grossi, Theorell, Jusisoo, and Setterlind, 1999). Cortisol levels also decreased, which is significant as elevated cortisol is associated with anxiety, depression, and PTSD.

Limited resources within the health and emergency sectors lead to frustrations regarding the ability to do the job in the best way. "We don't have enough paramedics on the road," mentioned one ambulance service worker. Hospital emergency departments become overloaded due to staffing and resource shortages and therefore go on critical care bypass—meaning that they are closed to ambulance crews. As a result ambulances are forced to travel considerable distances with critically ill and injured individuals. Yet the stressors felt by the other services are not always immediately apparent to emergency workers. "You don't have the staff? Well, that's not my problem. My problem is that I have to find a bed for my patient. And the crew goes in, and you could shoot a cannon down the [hospital] hallway, and it wouldn't hit anybody, but they say they are out of service and can't take anybody. It's really frustrating." There is a sense that management is unaware of the stresses caused by the resource crunch. "They write a policy for everything, but there are no resources there. They say, 'Oh, you could take a truck out of service, but you have three critical calls pending.'" This creates conflict within and between departments. As one worker stated, "They try to be sympathetic, but people are just trying to keep their eyes on their own fries." As we indicated in chapter 3, Zohar (2000) suggests that an important factor in employee satisfaction is the congruency between policy and day-to-day operations and the perceived priorities of the immediate supervisor and organization. This in turn leads to an increased sense of safety in the organization and an actual decrease in workplace accidents.

In the past decade, fire services have moved toward providing advanced life support, changing not only the qualifications of firefighters but also the pace and type of work. Police are increasingly hiring individuals with university degrees, and computer literacy is a must. In ambulance services expectations and qualifications have risen dramatically. In Toronto, Canada, the first group of paramedics graduated in 1984. Since that time, all ambulance workers have been expected to return to school to upgrade their skills to one of four levels of paramedic training. Large centers, such as Toronto, have had the funds to cover the training expenses and time for all employees. Other jurisdictions have not. This means that in all emergency services, jobs have become more complex and individuals more highly trained. These changes make the job more interesting and challenging for newly trained individuals, yet they also have the potential to create rifts between new and older workers. Are experience and wisdom acquired on the job still valued, or are older workers viewed as dinosaurs in the organization? One younger emergency responder told us, "If [frontline responders] come up with solutions, we're not listened to, and part of the reason is a generational gap and an educational gap between some management and some of the guys on the road." Is educational upgrading viewed as a benefit and reward or a punishment for being older? One senior paramedic reported the anxiety he experienced when writing recertification exams. "The exams are a stressful thing, because I don't want to embarrass myself in front of my colleagues. That is what everyone is afraid of: the embarrassment of not making it through an exam and having to go through remedial training."

The Culture of Emergency Service Organizations

Cynicism and pessimism is frequently identified within emergency service organizations, and these factors have been found to be related to higher levels of stress and tension in individual workers (Anderson et al., 2002; Dick, 2000). Collective beliefs about pessimism build solidarity within the work group but can serve to undermine a sense of control. When the organization and outside world are viewed too negatively, the sense that one can make a difference or that change can occur becomes severely undermined.

Emergency service organizations often have strong attitudes toward the expression of emotion. In general, there is a denial of emotion and a general tendency to show little caring for others' feelings (Stephens and Long, 1999). The organizational culture of many emergency organizations emphasizes the role of physical and emotional strength and the expectation that when confronted with adversity, individuals remain detached and in control (Dick, 2000). Professional socialization requires that an individual approach tragic circumstances in a personable, yet detached manner (Brown et al., 1999). Individuals frequently disguise their emotions for fear of revealing personal flaws or not measuring up to some image of toughness (Henry, 2004). "Suck it up" becomes the mantra. One police officer spoke about his frustration with this type of organizational culture. "I fought against that for the longest time, when I saw some people having problems and I would actually say, hey this person is having problems. And I'd be told, mind your own business, we'll handle it. And the way they handle it is to forget about it."

Management Support

It has been suggested that the organizational structure of emergency organizations predisposes supervisors and managers to be insensitive to the stresses suffered by line officers (Alexander, 1999). Not surprisingly, then, it is frequently noted that emergency workers report that they feel unsupported by management. Police officers interviewed after the Lockerbie disaster in England in 1988 reported that they felt good about the functioning of their well-integrated team during the disaster but were aggrieved that senior officers did not welcome them back to the organization at the end of the ordeal (Thompson, 1993). A study of Australian police revealed that major organizational stressors emanated from officers' perceptions about the poor quality of supervision they received and the limited extent to which they can rely on superiors (Evans and Coman, 1993). Similarly, in a study of New York police officers, while shift work was identified as the number-one stressor, it was followed closely by inadequate support from the department, excessive discipline, and inadequate support by supervisors (Violanti and Aron, 1994). Other studies concur that police generally view their work environment to be unsupportive and that others within the organization, both supervisors and coworkers, have very little concern for their well-being (McMurray, 1989). One police officer noted the difficulty regarding support and mentorship for newer employees. "We have platoons operating here with sergeants with 30 years of service who are just looking to retire. I don't blame them for that, but we've got a bunch of young guys running around with guns and they got nowhere to go for direction."

Support from management is one of the primary protective factors in reducing stress and post-traumatic stress reactions in emergency responders (Buunk and Verhoeven, 1991; Regehr et al., 2000). It is therefore gratifying to note that some workers perceived a great deal of support from both their immediate supervisors and from management. "There's one captain here who would just say, 'That bothered me, and here's why,' and then everyone would say something. We're not just emotionless machines out there to suppress fires and save lives that don't get scared or upset, we're not like that." A police officer noted, "The chief is really supportive." Support, when received, is valued immensely.

Colleagues and a Source of Support

When responders encounter a dangerous situation such as an automobile crash, house fire, or shooting, there is no question that having the support of colleagues who can be trusted to be loyal and competent is vitally important. In addition, the structure of work in emergency services frequently focuses on the team. This is particularly true in the fire service, where people may remain with the same group, shift after shift, for several years. It also occurs to a greater or lesser degree in policing, such as within the dive team or the tactical squad. When this is added to the fact that most friends and family who are not in the emergency services are likely to work normal nine-to-five hours, it is not surprising that a great deal of socializing occurs with coworkers outside of work. This is a common phenomenon in occupations with high levels of teamwork, compared to jobs performed more independently (Henry, 2004; Murphy et al., 2002).

The high level of social interaction that is common among emergency responders has both pros and cons. In a study of U.S. firefighters, for instance, reliance on coworkers was identified as both a job strain and a source of job satisfaction. In that study, exercise, use of alcohol, and smoking were all strongly related to the work-group culture and were subsequently related to general health. One problem identified by the researchers was the extent to which alcohol played a role in off-duty "debriefings" (Murphy et al., 2002).

Despite the possible negative aspects of the work-group influence, the social support of peers is central to levels of stress and attitudes toward the job in emergency service professionals. One study examining over 1,700 firefighters and 248 paramedics reported that coworker support had a profound effect on both job satisfaction and work morale, and while the influence of family support was still significant, it had a much smaller influence on these factors (Beaton, Murphy, Pike, and Corneil, 1997). In addition, this same study found that support and conflict both at work and at home were negatively associated with all manner of physical and emotional problems, including cardiovascular, respiratory, neurological, gastrointestinal, muscle tension, depression, and anxiety and anger. That is, higher levels of social support were associated with lower levels of physical and emotional ill health. What always remains unclear from cross-sectional design studies of this type is whether social support protects against all these ailments, whether individuals with problems are less able to maintain social supports, or whether they just perceive that others don't fully appreciate the problems they are dealing with.

While our studies have found that peer support mitigates traumatic stress reactions, it appears that different individuals have different experiences of support from colleagues within the organization. Some find that colleagues are not helpful: "Well, peers are generally not very helpful; there is a real tendency to adopt a macho attitude." Others value the work group as a source of support. "After a situation, guys will talk to each other and they'll get in a group or something and talk about [it], or if we're sitting and having breakfast or coffee, someone will bring it up, and then guys kind of get it in the open." "I guess the biggest support that we've got is here with each other." "We can talk about anything, there is no fear of emotions. We have a great bunch of people here, a really strong bond." " A couple of guys phoned me at home, just to see how I was doing. That was comforting." "I wouldn't go for counseling. If I've got something to talk about, I'll go to my buddies, that is the only place I go to talk about anything." "We really circle the wagons. If one of ours is in trouble, whatever that person needs, they get."

Seeking Help

Organizational structures and culture influence whether responders seek help. While increased numbers of women are joining the professional ranks of firefighters, paramedics, and police, nevertheless emergency service organizations tend to have values and norms generally associated with men. One of these norms is the prohibition of expressed emotion, as discussed above. Associated with this is the discouragement of seeking help. Lower rates of seeking treatment by men in all strata of society cannot be attributed to better physical or emotional health, but rather to a discrepancy between men and women in help-seeking behavior (Möller-Leimkühler, 2002). Seeking help involves social costs, because the seeker appears incompetent, dependent, and inferior to others. This is especially true when the help seeker is male, in a male-oriented occupational role, and when the task is viewed as central to the occupation's competence (Lee, 2002). It has been reported that police officers equate seeking help with not being in control and fear that they will be openly ridiculed for obtaining assistance (McMurray, 1989). To support this view, one police officer in our study stated, "If you talk to other people [about distress] you lose your respect, it's the way they look at you. If you are not liked and respected [by peers] as a police officer, it is a very lonely existence." Consequently, very low percentages of rescue workers actually seek professional assistance (Gibbs, Drummond, and Lachenmeyer, 1993).

Summary

Gist and Woodall (1995, p. 768) write, "While the organization may be argued to hold certain responsibilities to ensure that personnel are adequately prepared, equipped, deployed, and configured for effective response and for ensuring that the impact of equivocal events is effectively addressed in organizational and operational review, individual decisions, actions, patterns, and responses are also highly determinative of adjustment. Preparation in these aspects of performance must interact with organizational preparedness on a daily basis to ensure that both the exceptional stressors inevitable in the occupation and the routine strains of personal and organizational living that define their contexts are kept in a reasonable balance that presents challenge, generates responsiveness, and encourages personal and professional growth."

Thus, the ideal work environment, from a stress perspective, clearly defines the expectations of the job and provides feedback regarding performance but also allows workers the opportunity to creatively and independently approach tasks to be accomplished. This is a challenge in emergency service organizations, where tasks are highly complex, demands are high, and the expectation of accountability to the public and funders is central. In addition, the challenge is to create an organizational environment that encourages support at both a collegial level and between manager/supervisors and frontline responders.

7

HEROES OR VILLAINS?
Public Inquiries

Emergency service workers are often faced with life-threatening and un-controllable situations where quick thinking and reasoned action are re-quired. While for the most part these situations resolve favorably, emer-gency workers are not and cannot be expected to be 100% successful in all cases. People die in fires, in ambulances on their way to the hospital, and in violent incidents requiring police intervention. When these tragic events occur, frequently a postmortem inquiry is held in order to determine whether alternative policies or actions of individuals could have averted disaster. These inquiries take many forms, including public commissions, investi-gations internal to the emergency service organization, and actions initiated through the criminal and civil courts. While the stated goal of postmortem reviews is to protect the public and improve the quality of service, it is pos-sible that they in fact may have the opposite result. Failure to deal with acute trauma situations in a manner others consider optimal may result in professional condemnation, community sanctions, and possible legal ac-tions against emergency workers. This understandably can be extremely stressful and destructive for workers and their organizations. Stemming from the belief that their efforts are not valued, workers may become de-moralized, distanced from the public, and disillusioned with their organi-zations.

Death inquiries have become prominent and powerful political institu-tions. Critics suggest that they are a sociopolitical phenomenon with wide-ranging effects on public policy and service delivery (Hill, 1990). In part, inquiries help society deal with moral panic. The public attention becomes focused on a phenomenon driven not necessarily by an increase in incidence, but instead by a surge in attention. If a child dies in a crowded emergency department, attention becomes focused on the availability of health care resources or on the inexperience or indifference of health care staff, rather than neglectful parents or the painful reality that children continue to die of disease. Inquiries are a means for government to demonstrate concern for an issue and to appease the public (Hill, 1990) without necessarily leading to systemic change or increased funding. Further, inquiries themselves frequently take on a tone of moral righteousness. The motto of the Chief Coroner's Office for Ontario, which conducts public inquiries into deaths of patients in care, reads, "We speak for the dead." This implies that those who disagree with findings or the process by which the inquiry was conducted may perhaps not care for those who have died and their surviving loved ones. All these political factors serve to increase pressures placed on emergency responders, whose actions may be the focus of the inquiry.

To date there is a surprising dearth of research on the impact of postmortem inquiries on emergency service workers. Related research has found that testifying in court is the number-one-ranked stressor among police officers (Evans and Coman, 1993). A study of female physicians determined that threat of malpractice litigation was a primary source of distress in female physicians (Richardson and Burke, 1993). Our study of child welfare workers encountering reviews subsequent to the death of a child describes the devastating impact on both workers and the organization (Regehr, Chau, Leslie, and Howe, 2002). Theoretical and anecdotal articles also point to the stress of reviews of performance. Authors point to the stress experienced by nurses (Koehler, 1992) and police officers (Herrman, 1988) when their actions are scrutinized by the media and the court system and the subsequent undermining of the public's confidence when a member of an occupational group is being investigated (MacDonald, 1996). Anecdotal literature on child protection workers suggests that death inquiries have a devastating impact on morale. Staff become depressed and anxious, work becomes defensive and routinized, resignations are common, and recruitment of new staff is difficult (Hill, 1990; Brunet, 1998). In addition, these inquiries can lead to further consequences, such as civil litigation or criminal charges. Following a coroner's inquest into the death of a child in a hospital, two Canadian nurses were criminally charged "Nurses Charged," 2001). Similarly, internal police investigations frequently lead to compensation claims (Bale, 1990). In this chapter, we discuss the results of two studies we conducted with police, firefighters, and paramedics who had undergone scrutiny in public inquiries. One study in-

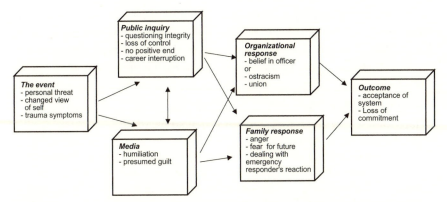

Figure 7.1. Thematic Model of Emergency Responders' Response to Public Inquiries

volved interviews with those who had been through inquiries (Regehr, 2003; Regehr, Goldberg, and Hughes, 2002) and the other involved questionnaires comparing trauma reactions in those who had been through inquiries with those who had not (Regehr, Hill, Goldberg, and Hughes, 2003).

This chapter will discuss factors that contribute to distress experienced as a result of a public inquiry into a rescue operation. We begin with the incident itself, followed by the process and outcomes of the public, the media attention to the issue, and the organizational response. We then look at the impact on both emergency responders and their families. Suggestions made by emergency responders who have undergone inquiries for reducing the stress and distress are then presented. A visual representation of emergency responders' responses to public inquiries is found in figure 7.1.

Replaying the Event: The Critical Incident

Tragic situations, many of which are highly publicized, high-profile occurrences, often lead to postmortem reviews. Firefighters in our studies were subject to inquiries in situations in which elderly nursing home residents or children died in a fire. Paramedics were involved in inquiries where individuals died on their way to the hospital or on the scene. Police events included high-speed chases, shooting of civilians engaged in the commission of a crime, and use of force to subdue individuals who were physically threatening police or injuring another member of the public.

The situation for police officers is somewhat different than that of firefighters and paramedics. Due to the nature of police work, it is often the commission of an act (e.g., shooting someone), rather than the omission of an act (e.g., not saving someone) that results in an inquiry. As one police officer stated, "A police shooting where somebody is killed is probably as traumatic as it gets in police work." One difference is being in a life-threatening situation.

> The last thing I saw was the gun barrel pointed about 3 feet from my face, and a very small weapon, but it looked pretty big at the time . . . my first inclination was to get the hell out of there, but you know you can't, you just can't, that's your job . . . and the physical, your physical environment, all those kinds of things they become blurred, all you look at is here's this guy, and here's the threat which is the weapon, and afterwards I could tell, well I think he may been a bit older, he may have been a bit younger, maybe he had a mustache, and I think that he had close-cropped hair . . . but I could describe the gun to you.

One police officer who was shot during an event described that the unpredictability surrounding a traumatic event was more difficult to cope with than the incident itself. He noted "I think that it bothered me a lot more that time thinking that I came very close, I could have lost my life in that one, and that bothered me more than when I actually got hit by a bullet, and the speed, the trauma of waiting for something to happen."

A second difference is the changed view of self officers experience when they are involved in a shooting incident. One officer described feeling traumatized by the possibility of almost shooting a person: "The biggest thing that bothered me there is the fact that I tried to kill him . . . normal people don't try and kill people." Another stated,

> I tried to kill this guy—now, I've never done that before, never actually tried to kill somebody . . . you know, so that bothered me a lot. And I mean I really got, I got sick, I got really sick to my stomach and I couldn't get rid of the feeling, and there was nothing, like it wouldn't go away, it just wouldn't—I mean I even tried to make myself throw up and it wouldn't go away, so I think it was just in my head that it was making me sick.

Workers involved in events leading to inquiries describe a wide range of symptoms consistent with secondary traumatic reactions in emergency service workers found in other studies (Fullerton et al., 1992; Gibbs et al., 1993; Henry, 2004; Marmar et al., 1999; Regehr et al., 2000). Responders report disturbances of appetite ("I didn't want to eat for a few days") and of sleep ("I couldn't sleep well, my mind was essentially on the call"). They refer to intrusive thoughts when trying to respond to other calls; they report nightmares and flashbacks: "So for a long time after that . . . every time

I closed my eyes what I saw was this guy's face, and it kind of bothered me for a long time."

Involvement in events leading to inquiry causes responders to question their judgment and second-guess their career choice. Emergency responders describe generalized anger directed at colleagues and family members. On the other hand, witnessing the trauma of others causes some people to value their relationships more highly, and creating an urge to "go home and hug the kids." These intense reactions to the event itself provide an important backdrop to any inquiry that follows.

Guilty until Proven Innocent: The Postmortem Review

The disturbing nature of the postmortem review in many ways seems to emanate from the manner in which the process is structured. Depending on the type of review, emergency responders often feel that no protection is afforded to them. In a coroner's inquest as it is organized in Canada, for instance, the rules of evidence are less structured than that in a civil or criminal court. Jury members are permitted to ask questions, and anyone (such as family members of the deceased) can have standing and have lawyers represent them. "It is probably the most horrible experience because you don't have rules of evidence . . . so things like badgering and that kind of thing are allowed," one subject told us. Responders describe the manner in which reviews—whether they are internal to the organization, a coroner's inquest, or a trial—cause them to feel powerless: "It's out of our hands, it's out of our control."

Police officers are often subjected to a greater variety of public inquiry processes than those workers in other emergency service professions. In Ontario, for instance, one form of review encountered by officers is a Civilian Commission on Police Services, a body appointed to review public complaints. Within each police service, there are four additional levels of review and possible discipline: (1) the police chief, (2) the Complaints Bureau, (3) the Internal Investigations Service, and (4) the Police Services. Another form of review is the Special Investigations Unit (SIU), a civilian agency with investigative jurisdiction over all policing in Ontario, covering 68 services and approximately 21,600 officers. Its mandate is to investigate circumstances involving police and civilians that result in serious injury or death. It is therefore possible for a subject officer to be investigated by six different levels of investigative bodies. In addition, some of the officers involved in our study had been criminally charged or civilly sued.

Regardless of the intent of the review, responders feel that it is adversarial in nature and that they are "on the hot seat." One paramedic suggested that "the job of the lawyers is to discredit you." Another felt that the cross-examination process was aimed at "twisting the truth." Several responders suggest that in the quest to find the truth and determine who was to blame, the process tarnished all participants. "Even if you are just presenting evidence, it is as if you are on trial." When the actions of emergency workers are in question, this is intensified. Responders feel that there is an assumption of guilt or wrongdoing throughout the review process. "The way you are treated is that you are already guilty . . . [while members of the public] are innocent until proven guilty."

This has the effect of making participants feel that the review system strips workers of their sense of professionalism. "There was no courtesy, there was no professionalism; it was just a complete joke." This has a profound effect on the emergency responder's sense of personal and professional self. "Your identity is through your work: I'm a police officer, I'm a paramedic, I'm a fireman." "The greatest fear of an emergency health worker is that someone is going to question your abilities to do your job." Further, while undergoing the review process, emergency workers begin to question themselves, even if they believe that they did the right thing and have nothing to hide. "On the stand I was doubting my own mind, and this lawyer was trying to crucify me." "Hindsight is 20/20, you know. You make the best decision at the time, but you say something, and the lawyers twist what you are saying around, and then you get confused and look like an idiot." Responders are concerned about not only themselves in this respect, but also the organizations they work for: "The crown seemed to have a grudge against the ambulance service." "They think that all cops are just gun happy."

Other aspects of the process also create distress. One aspect is the length of time that could be involved in an inquiry. "I was exonerated, the other [person] that was named was exonerated, everything was fine, but, I mean, it took 8 years." Several of the police officers in our study were involved in inquiries that lasted over 10 years. During this time, they experienced significant anxiety about the possible outcomes and about what might be the next thing that they would encounter if they were found not responsible. Civilians not satisfied with the outcome of complaints procedures could initiate court processes. Further, court rulings that were in favor of the officer were frequently appealed. Throughout this time, emergency responders are constantly reminded of the tragic event, at a point when "some things you just want to leave behind you."

In reviews where there was another individual accused of the death, such as in a criminal trial, paramedics and firefighters describe their discomfort in facing the accused. There is also a perception that in the zeal to determine what emergency responders could have done better, attention is deflected from the civilian offender. One paramedic described how the inquiry into the shooting death of a police officer became focused on the ambulance response and not the fact that he was shot dead by a civilian.

Another issue, particularly for paramedics and firefighters, is dealing with a foreign environment and unfamiliar legal jargon. Responders discuss the lack of preparation they receive before attending the inquiry. They are not told about the process of the inquiry, are not given legal advice regarding their rights and responsibilities, and are not given time to prepare. "They hand you the subpoena and then you go." When the organization does have legal representation, responders often feel that the lawyers do not have sufficient knowledge about the organization to be able to adequately represent their issues.

Finally, the outcome of the review process is generally viewed as negative. "There is never a positive outcome." When actions of responders have been questioned, a cloud of suspicion remains. "The investigation never says, 'You did the right thing,' or just something to remove the air of mystery from the whole thing. They just don't. That's sad." "So you never get justice." "In the eyes of the public, all it says is that the cops got away with it again." Further, a common theme is that responders involved in inquiries very frequently are not notified of the outcome. "Was it my fault? Was I partially to blame? Or was I not at fault? I never heard the results." "I know it was not my fault, but still to get that official OK would have meant something."

In the end, some of the firefighters and paramedics and virtually all of the police officers in our study identified that their careers were significantly negatively affected by the fact that they had become tainted. Some had been transferred to less prestigious duties, some were suspended. Others described how they realized that they had now fallen off the promotion list. "[I felt] a lot of anxiety because the effect on my career is unknown. . . . for the last 10 years I've done all of these different things to prepare myself for the next step up in the hierarchy here. . . . so there's a lot of resentment."

Many responders involved in reviews describe feeling like pawns in a larger political process. When civil cases are settled out of court with cash payments, there is a sense that they are not given the opportunity to be vindicated by their day in court. "I'm very aware that the service settles a huge number of lawsuits; if we end up shooting somebody, they end up paying the victim's family, and these are criminals that have actually pulled guns on police officers, and we end up shooting them, and we give the family $100,000."

Are You Guys Really That Bad? The Media and Public Response

Henry (2004) describes the ambivalent relationship that police officers in particular have with the public, in which they are viewed almost simultaneously as oppressors and heroes. This ambivalence is often crystallized in media portrayals of police officers. There is no question that negative media attention has a profound effect on those who suddenly find themselves in an unwelcome and unfavorable limelight. The July 2003 suicide of British government scientist Dr. David Kelly is a clear example of the possible consequences of such a furor. Kelly, an adviser to Britain's Ministry of Defense on chemical and biological warfare, was alleged by the media to have leaked information that a dossier on Iraq's weapons of mass destruction had been altered for political purposes. Six weeks later, Kelly appeared publicly before the Foreign Affairs Committee in a grueling and inconclusive hearing in which he denied his involvement. Questions remained about whether or not he was to be disciplined. The controversy was covered in every national newspaper in Britain and by the foreign press throughout the world. Three days later he was found dead (Blitz, 2003). For Dr. Kelly the public scrutiny and criticism were intolerable. The events called into question the role of the press as investigators and reporters of the news versus creators of the news.

Participants in our study had a great deal to say about the media coverage of the events and the negative impact that this had on them as individuals, on their families, and on the organization. "The biggest problem with media is having parents in another city read what a bad guy their son was." "The media wrote things and said things on the air, and then I get friends and family phoning up and saying, 'Are you guys really that bad?'" People that the responder might run into casually ask about the inquest and question their skills and integrity. Responders suggest that the neighbors pass judgment based on the media coverage. "I wasn't getting a lot of support outside of the organization—in fact, I actually took to not walking in the immediate vicinity of my home, because people assumed I had done something wrong."

The fact that frequently responders view the coverage as biased compounds this problem. "There was a lot of media coverage, and there was one, I still have all the articles, _____ was her name, this media reporter, she hated my guts, every time she walked into the courtroom, she scowled at me and, like, I don't know what I did to her . . . even when the evidence came out that what we did was right, she would put a spin on it to make it look bad."

In the end, two responders described how negative media coverage ceased to have an impact on them. "Fifteen years ago I cared about what the media said. . . . You just get used to it." "The negative media attention, over the year you realize the reason, they are just trying to sell papers. You got no control. That won't change how I feel about people on the street."

Treated as an Outcast: The Organizational Response

A major issue described by responders involved in inquiries is humiliation within the organization. This includes organizational responses in which they are given a change of duties, are transferred to another division, or, in the case of police officers, have their gun taken away. "I was horrified, in that I was taken off [my duties] and the only time you are taken off [duties] in here is a disciplinary issue because you f—ed up. So the implication being that I did something wrong. Did this guy die because I did something wrong? Did I do something wrong? Could I have done something better? None of those questions were asked, [fault was] just implied." Such changes in duties result in gossip within the organization and speculation about who was at fault.

Further, when major events occur, generally organizations conduct an internal review to determine if there has been any wrongdoing. Responders view these reviews as highly stressful and undermining their sense of support. "Then there's the internal review, but I think their main function is so that the organization can cover themselves . . . that's more a stress than a help." "A little thing happens and there is a knee jerk reaction. Everything is blown out of proportion. People are left scattered and destroyed afterwards, regardless of the outcome. Changed attitude to the organization." "In making sure their ass is covered, [the management] forget the human side of things and they forget that there are people working here."

Respondents in our studies repeatedly discussed the lack of management support. Management did not attend the inquiries, and emergency responders were left to fend for themselves. Management questioned the actions of workers. When responders attempted to discuss their concerns and stress, they believed that they were dismissed as complainers. In one case where the organization elected to settle a civil suit, the responder felt betrayed by the organization. The individual was sure that he was in the right, and the choice to settle for the sake of expediency appeared to be an admission of guilt. In another case, despite the fact that the worker was found not responsible in the external inquiry, he still felt that management viewed him as responsible for the tragedy. "The witnesses perjured themselves and still I didn't get support from management. . . . They still wanted to discipline me in the internal accident review committee."

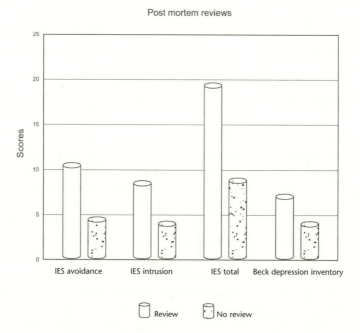

Figure 7.2. Depression and Trauma in Emergency Responders Encountering
Reviews

Picking Yourself Apart: Personal Reactions

Responders describe the stress experienced by both themselves and their
families during the review process. In our study of 264 firefighters and
paramedics, 23.9% of the total sample had been involved in formal reviews
of events. Statistical analysis of post-traumatic stress scores on the Impact
of Event Scale and the Beck Depression Inventory demonstrated that those
involved in inquires reported significantly higher level of post-traumatic
stress and depression than those who had not (Regehr, Hill, Goldberg, and
Hughes, 2003).

Common themes described in interviews include sleeping on days off
and waking throughout the night: "And suddenly I'm sitting on the edge of
the bed, not sure what is going on. Like it was scary, I didn't know what was
going on." The length of time before an inquiry was called adds to the
trauma for some workers. "There is the issue of going to court and having
to relive [the trauma], usually a couple of years down the road just when
you think you have come to terms with it, now all of a sudden you've got
to go to a coroner's inquest or a homicide trial."

Responders indicate that family members comment on their change of
mood and irritability during the review process. Some responders report feel-

ings of isolation as they perceive that they are unable to discuss their concerns with family or colleagues for fear that they may be called as witnesses in the inquiry. They discuss the stress of being questioned during the inquiry and report that they begin to question themselves: "You start to second-guess yourself." "You are your own worst enemy, you're literally picking yourself, picking your activities apart and questioning your own judgment." They are worried about the outcome: "If I lose my job, who will support my family?"

Again because of the nature of inquiries encountered by police, many officers in our study described the enormous impact that the process of public inquiry had on their families. Several officers indicated that relationships ended during the review due to the preoccupation of the subject officer with the trial or the investigation against them. Another issue was the decision to delay having children until they had been cleared, because they feared that they may go to jail and did not want children to experience that. A major issue, however, was the anger and resentment experienced by family members, particularly spouses. Family members often were already stressed by fears for their loved one's safety, the shift work, overtime, and the dedication of their loved one to policing. When the same organization and public to whom these men had devoted their lives questioned their integrity, wives were overcome with anger and resentment. One officer summarized the issues for families as follows:

> First of all you got a husband, somebody you love dearly, that's totally obsessed with his own case rather than dealing with his own family and his own relationship with his own wife, you have the possibility of your husband going to jail, and for police officers nothing brings out more horror than the idea of being stuck in a prison institution, . . . and the inability to control what's happening too, and knowing down deep that you're right, that you did nothing wrong, and seeing the whole system, once again, the anger and frustration with the system really, really comes to the forefront, because how could this be happening? I live in Canada, I didn't do anything wrong, and look what's happening to me.

Emergency responders involved in reviews also worried about family members who had to deal with the reactions of neighbors to the media reports. In the end, even through the workers were exonerated, the cloud of suspicion continued. "Even though the judge says you were acting properly, that does not get fully reported."

Outcomes

Despite the fact that all responders in our study described negative experiences during the inquiry process, several described positive outcomes. A frequently reported positive outcome was the learning derived from the experience. This included how to plan for the attack of opposing counsel, identifying means of documenting and ensuring responders' work was well represented, and then providing this information to new staff.

One positive outcome for some of the responders is recognition for a job well done. Some responders discuss the appreciation they receive from emergency workers in other agencies; others receive thanks from relatives of the victim. "The relative coming up and shaking my hand, there was no question, that was the most positive aspect of it." A paramedic spoke about his sense that the inquiry was listening and trusted his skills, "that gave me confidence." Similarly, many responders identified that the most positive outcome was that they were exonerated. "The only positive thing I think that came out of the inquest was the fact that my partner and I did our jobs properly." Others feel that as a result of their involvement in the inquiry justice has been served through the conviction of a guilty person. One respondent reported feeling good about "contributing to getting these people the punishment they deserved."

System change is another positive outcome. Some responders identify that recommendations made did in fact lead to improved policies and better quality assurance. For instance, one firefighter was pleased that as a result of the inquiry, carbon monoxide detectors are now mandated by law. Recommendations from the inquiry can lead to more resources when they are used in negotiations for increased staffing. Sometimes the positive outcome is policy change in another organization; in one case the reported positive outcome was that a nursing home was closed down.

There are also many themes about long-term negative outcomes of inquiries. These include reduced commitment to the job and the public, increased stress, and increased anger. "You get more perspective, you know, trying to do too many things at once. I was a very energetic [worker], I still am, but this puts it in perspective a little more. . . . I am not going to die of a heart attack when I'm 50 or 55." "Everything is being scrutinized so much more than it used to be. And that's not a bad thing, it's changed, tightened up, and made procedures better, and that is more accountable than it used to be. But the price is, that when things don't go well, there is more accountability for the [workers] that have to pay the price for it. That has added a lot more stress to the job." "[People are] anxious and just angry, probably anger and resentment more than anything, is the ripple effect of everything you go through, it just puts more demands on everybody, there's a lot of pressure."

In general, however, responders believe that the increased accountability and scrutiny is a fact of life that must simply be dealt with. "The public wants us to be accountable and we have to realize that as a group, whether you like it or not. . . . That cat is out of the bag, you're not shoving it back in."

Suggestions for Change

While inquiries may be an inevitable part of the work of the emergency responder, participants in our studies offered many suggestions to reduce the strain they placed on workers. A common theme is education including coaching, information regarding the process, training, role playing, attending reviews, and/or watching testimony on tape. Responders suggest that education regarding the process and watching of tapes should be part of the standard training offered when an individual first begins work with the organization. This could then be upgraded at different stages of an individual's career and include role-playing testimony and attending reviews that may be conducted. Any time someone is called to testify, an immediate education session should be available, again reviewing the process, the possible outcomes and role-playing answers to challenging questions.

Another suggestion for improvement is legal representation for all workers, who are acting not only as defendants, but also as witnesses, as they may be found to be responsible by making self-incriminating statements. Our subjects strongly suggested that the union or management hire lawyers whose sole responsibility in the matter is to represent the specific needs of workers. These lawyers must be knowledgeable about both the unique nature of the inquiry process and the job demands of emergency responders.

Finally, responders recommend proactive support and assistance for both the emergency responder and their families. Support should not be offered only when the person experiences distress, but should be a matter of course. Support for the worker could include a peer attending the inquiry with the worker, a mentor who had been through the process and could offer guidance and support and/or confidential counseling—though many emergency responders are suspicious about counseling and suggest that it could never be confidential in an emergency service organization. As family members often are identified to feel uniquely isolated and distressed, specific counseling programs and perhaps mentor/peer companions consisting of other families who have survived the process could be of use. Families require information not only about the review process but also about common reactions of workers encountering the process and strategies for dealing with media, the public, and the questions from their children.

Summary

When tragic events occur, they rarely end with the tidying of equipment and completion of paperwork. Rather, society has increasingly moved to the process of postmortem inquiries with the goal of identifying errors and avoiding future deaths. While the goals of public accountability and quality assurance are laudable, these inquiries do not come without cost. There is a profound effect on the emergency workers who testify in the inquiries. Police, firefighters, and paramedics identify experiences of feeling unprotected, attacked, and presumed guilty of incompetence or negligence when testifying at a postmortem review. These feelings are intensified by the media attention, which is often sensational and vilifying, and the subsequent public response of suspicion and blame. They are further intensified when workers view the organizational response to be unsupportive. Emergency responders feel that the organization often seems more interested in appearing publicly accountable and avoiding liability than supporting workers. This is particularly important in light of previous research which has suggested that social supports and organizational environment have a significant influence on responses to traumatic events in rescue workers (Alexander and Wells, 1991; Fullerton et al., 1992; Regehr et al., 2000; Weiss et al., 1995). When people feel supported and valued, they experience lower levels of distress. As a consequence, emergency workers report symptoms of intrusion, avoidance, arousal, and self-doubt that begin with the tragic event itself and continue throughout the review process. In the end, several responders are able to identify positive outcomes from the review process, such as new learning, some positive recognition, system change, and especially vindication. Nevertheless, a dominant theme is that of betrayal, anger, and reduced commitment.

Accountability of emergency service workers is a reasonable expectation of the public and society. As a result, death inquiries as a form of achieving this goal are probably here to stay. In order that these inquiries meet their goal of improving service, it is important that organizations provide support for emergency responders participating in these processes. Supports recommended by police, firefighters, and paramedics in our studies include education, legal representation, proactive assistance, attendance at hearings by a peer or mentor, and most importantly signals of support and recognition by management and superior officers. Everyone in the emergency services, as in any other profession, will at times not function at an optimal level and will not always make the best decisions in the heat of the moment. If we focus our efforts on vilifying those who seek to help the public, we cannot expect that they will continue to risk themselves for the safety of others.

8

ARE YOU COMING HOME TONIGHT?

The Impact of Emergency Service Work on Families

The support of family is paramount to reducing the impact of highly stressful work on emergency responders. Yet family members are not immune from the stresses encountered by their loved ones who place themselves in the line of fire. They too are affected by the impact of shift work and unpredictably long hours. They suffer from organizational politics and lack of opportunities for promotion, which would bring more financial resources to the family, along with more regular living and working schedules. They feel the secondary effects of traumatic events through exposure to traumatic material described by their family member and reported in the media. They also experience the trauma on an emotional level, through witnessing and coping with the trauma reactions of the emergency responder. This trauma exposure frequently results in fears and trauma symptoms in family.

The family is not a bottomless resource. Unless the needs of family members are attended to, their ability to support will wither away. While studies on divorce rates among emergency responders differ regarding whether their divorce rates are higher than those in the general public, anecdotal evidence suggests that many senior responders are on their second and third marriages. Responders talk at length about the stresses that the job places on spouses and other family members. They also discuss the importance of family in maintaining a balance in their lives. "[My wife] is easily my best friend in the world. I'm happy to go home to my wife and kids, and that really helps things here on the job."

Married to the Job

The lives of emergency responders, and consequently their families, are fraught with uncertainty and tension. The job competes with the family for time and attention. Shift work in and of itself forces families to accommodate to missed social events and missed children's sports games and concerts. The regular six o'clock dinner of the TV family does not exist in these households. Emergency responders are called upon to work special details or extra shifts. Emergency incidents requiring considerable time and paperwork never occur at the beginning of a shift. Further, emergency responders in our studies, particularly those in policing, describe how family vacation plans can be disrupted by a big case or impending trial. As a result, the spouse of an emergency responder may have to make sacrifices in his or her own career in order to accommodate to the needs of the responder's career and the competing demands of family (Kannady, 1993). Children of emergency responders may feel isolated and abandoned by the absent parent, and there is some evidence that they look exclusively to the other parent (usually the mother) for support (Maslach and Jackson, 1979). As one officer in our study explained: "My wife says she raised the kids, and she did. I wasn't out every night, but it certainly was a few nights a week. I'd mostly be home on weekends, but there's always an excuse. I'm going to do this, do that."

Other factors also interfere with family life. When working on a long and complex case in policing, a sense of competition can arise between the spouse and the actors in the case. For officers in sexual assault squads or special victims units, victims may have access to the officer at all hours of the day and night and when they call to discuss how they are managing, calls can appear to be very personal and intimate to the spouse. For officers working undercover, other challenges arise. One officer talked about the difficulty in readjusting to regular family life after a major undercover drug case. "At 10 or 11 at night, I would go out and walk for 3 hours. It used to drive my wife crazy. 'Where are you going? What are you doing?' I just couldn't sleep. It took me months to get back to routine and to sleeping well."

In addition, the organizational environment can create barriers between the responder and his or her family. In order to protect themselves from the dangers of the job, emergency service workers develop strong ties with colleagues. This cohesiveness and solidarity results in a rigid boundary between the members of the emergency organization and others, including not only the public, but also members of other organizations. Emergency workers do not maintain the professional boundary only when on the job; frequently social activities and social relationships become limited to others in the same profession. This boundary may limit the spouse's sense of connection and accessibility to their loved one and leave them feeling like another outsider (Borum and Philpot, 1993). One responder identified the risks to a marriage in this type of job caused by opportunities for infidelity. "I don't know why guys get married in this profession. There are too many opportunities and guys (and girls) end up cheating. Everyone is running around. Every time I know a marriage has broken up, it's been for another man or woman."

The intensity of the work partner relationship can also produce problems in the family. Particularly among paramedics and police officers, where individuals are paired, these relationships often involve sharing and time together far beyond what is common or even possible in a marriage. One officer described the difficulty that this caused in sexual assault squads. "When you are dealing with victims of sexual assault, they're talking about feelings all the time. If you're dealing with that all the time, the officers start talking about their feelings among the partners. And the two partners develop bonds to each other and consequently they end up breaking up their own marriages. [Management] wants male-female squads. But I'm not sure that is the right thing to do."

The spouse of a firefighter described the interest other women showed toward her husband as a result of the hero image of firefighters. Some expressed envy of her and flirted with her husband at social events. Other women showed up at the fire station with cakes in an attempt to meet a firefighter.

An additional hassle for families is the public scrutiny that they encounter at times. Especially for families living in smaller communities, everyone is aware who the emergency responders are. There may be higher expectations for the behavior of the "cop's kid" and higher visibility for misbehavior. Families can be subject to comments of neighbors when a rescue went badly or a scandal erupts in an organization, and all members of the service become tainted. Responders have reported that families have been subject to accusations of racism or incompetence as a result of media reports. One officer who was involved in a trial heavily covered in the media described the impact on his family. "Some days I'd come home and my daughter would be crying, and she'd say nothing is wrong. Then you'd find out, 'The kids at school are teasing me, that you are a drug dealer.' And I sat down with her and explained what was happening."

The everyday job of an emergency responder is frequently fraught with minor hassles and conflicts. Emergency service organizations tend to be highly structured and organized and allow for little flexibility. This can breed anger and resentment among responders. Much citizen contact involves unlawful or abusive behavior, or people complaining. While this may be most obvious in the work of police officers, our study of paramedics revealed that 70% had been victims of violence on the job (Regehr, Goldberg, and Hughes, 2002). This can result in a sense of emotional exhaustion, a chronic state of physical and emotional depletion resulting from excessive work demands and continuous hassles. Anger, impatience, cynicism, and other negative feelings are frequently expressed at home.

Researchers have demonstrated how job-related stresses experienced in a variety of working environments can be transmitted to other family members once the individual returns home. In general, findings suggest that job stress dampens the quality of marital interactions and causes the other spouse to feel more negatively toward the relationship (Larson and Almeida, 1999; Thompson and Bolger, 1999). One study of police officers, for instance, found that emotional exhaustion and negative affective states of police officers are associated with their spouses' reports of family conflict (Burke, 1993). Another study utilizing physiological measures discovered that on days officers reported higher levels of stress, both the officers and their wives showed greater levels of autonomic arousal during conversations (Roberts and Levenson, 2001). A particularly interesting finding in this study involved cardiovascular and somatic measures. Although greater vascular activity is generally associated with greater somatic or physical activity, Roberts and Levenson found that officers and wives showed greater cardiovascular activity but lower levels of body movement on high-stress days. They hypothesized that lower levels of activity may reflect a freeze-type response associated with intense fear or readiness. In police work this type of vigilance and defensiveness is required to facilitate the quick response required during an incident. They propose that on high-stress days, officers maintain this stance at home and wives similarly take on a defensive stance.

Emergency responders discuss the tremendous dedication they feel toward their jobs. They also discuss the challenge this brings to intimate relationships. "It is hard to find a support person who will put up with the shift work alone, never mind all the other stuff." Experienced workers point to the need for balance. "Although your life is dedicated to the job, the job can't dictate your life."

Trauma Contagion

As we discussed earlier, *trauma contagion* or *secondary trauma* are often experienced by emergency responders who witness the pain and suffering of others. The traumatic experience does not stop there, but continues to ripple outward to encompass other family members. Several research studies have looked at the impact on mental health therapists of working with victims and of repeatedly hearing violent imagery about the atrocities that one human commits against another. It has been found that such exposure can result in experiences of terror, rage, and despair, and symptoms of post-traumatic stress disorder including intrusion, avoidance, dissociation, and sleep disturbance on the part of therapists merely by hearing the stories told by clients (Chrestman, 1995; Figley, 1995a; Kassam-Adams, 1995). In a related area, it was found that researchers doing chart reviews of child maltreatment cases began experiencing symptoms of trauma. Steps had to be taken to protect them from exposure to the traumatic stimuli by limiting their time spent reading the material (Kinard, 1996). If mental health professionals and researchers with specialized training and a support network of other professionals experience this distress, how much greater will the impact be on family members who lack this training and support and who actually love the person who was traumatized?

Family members hear stories of events through direct discussions with their loved one, through overhearing discussions with others, and through reading about events in the paper or seeing them on the news. Casual conversations among emergency responders (as among health care professionals) tend to involve recollections of gruesome details, jokes about dangerous behaviors of perpetrators and victims toward responders, and dangerous near-death situations in which responders are involved. Material brought home to work on may include gruesome pictures or written reports about the events of an incident for the purposes of completion or court preparation. After repeated exposure to graphic imagery of death and destruction, these images may begin intruding on the waking fantasies and dreams of other individuals, such as the family member of a responder (Herman, 1992; McCann and Pearlman, 1990a,b; Horowitz, 1976). It is difficult to shake the image of a child mangled and trapped in the wheel well of a bus, even if you did not see it with your own eyes. Dreams may incorporate your own child in such a horrific situation.

Another aspect for families is dealing with symptoms of the emergency responder who has been exposed. In chapter 2, "All in a Day's Work," we described symptoms of intrusion, arousal, and avoidance experienced by people who encounter traumatic events in the line of duty. Dealing with anger and irritability, sleeplessness, and avoidance of social interactions, all of which may be symptoms of trauma, can be taxing for family members. One firefighter described the negative impact on his family. He would go home after a terrible event and feel angry at family members for having what he perceived to be petty complaints and needs. "Do they not know how lucky they are?" A senior paramedic described how his negative mood was transmitted throughout the household. "Well, my wife noticed I was very grumpy, but if anybody was the best indicator of it all, it was my Jack Russell terrier, who knew I was in such a bad mood he started peeing around the house, and he doesn't do that. Once I started calming down again, he stopped doing it. For a little while there, though, he knew something wasn't right and he was trying to get my attention."

A body of literature looks at the impact of post-traumatic stress experienced by one person on other members of the family. For instance, a study of Bosnian refugee couples found that PTSD symptomatology was the best predictor of marital functioning (Spasojevic, Heffer, and Snyder, 2000). That is, higher rates of trauma symptoms in one family member were related to poorer marital adjustment. Similarly, several studies have focused on the stresses experienced by wives of Vietnam veterans as a result of trying to cope with their husbands' PTSD symptoms (Verboski and Ryan, 1988). In addition to having intrusion symptoms such as flashbacks, nightmares, and sleep disturbances, there is considerable evidence, from both community-based and laboratory studies, that veterans with PTSD have higher levels of anger and hostility and more difficulty managing their anger than do veterans without PTSD and men in the general population (Calhoun et al., 2002; McFall, Wright, Donovan, and Rashkind, 1999). Veterans with PTSD are also found to have less effective coping mechanisms and problem-solving skills (Nezu and Carnevale, 1987). Consequently, veterans with PTSD have been found to have more severe marital problems, parenting problems, and violent behavior in the family (Davidson and Mellor, 2000; Jordan et al., 1992). It is not surprising that these reactions have an impact on family members. Wives of veterans with PTSD report feelings of isolation and loneliness, confusion, being overwhelmed, and having a sense of no control over their lives. While similar studies have not been conducted on the relationship between anger and PTSD in emergency responders, some research has raised concerns about higher rates of violence in police families than in the general population (Lott, 1995).

Of perhaps greatest concern is the impact of parental PTSD on children. The major focus of this research has been children of Holocaust survivors. Symptoms experienced by offspring of Holocaust survivors include depression, mistrust, aggression, hyperalertness, emotional numbing and isolation, and some symptoms directly related to their parents' experiences, such as nightmares of the Holocaust (Solomon, Kotler, and Mikulincer, 1998; Sigal, Silver, Rakoff, and Ellin, 1973; Yehuda, Schmeidler, Wainberg, Binder-Brynes, and Duvdevani, 1998). These individuals have also been found to be less resilient to traumatic events in their own lives and to have higher levels of trauma related to such events as the diagnosis of cancer (Baider et al., 2000) and being exposed to combat (Solomon et al., 1988). Other research has focused on the children of Vietnam veterans. In their study of 1,200 veterans, Jordan and colleagues (1992) found that children of veterans with PTSD were more likely to have behavioral problems, with one third of the group having one child with problems in the clinical range. Further, a similarity between the behavior of fathers with PTSD (especially violent behavior) and their children has been reported (Harkness, 1993; Solomon, Waysman, and Levy, 1992).

Almost no attention has been paid to the impact of this type of secondary trauma on the families of emergency responders. One study, however, investigated the impact of the 1995 Oklahoma City bombing on partners of firefighters. That event resulted in the deaths of 168 people, including 19 children and 1 nurse responder. Rescue and recovery efforts lasted 16 days and involved long hours and unsafe working conditions. Pfefferbaum, North, Bunch, Wilson, and Schorr (2002) interviewed 27 women who were wives of involved firefighters. They found that half the women reported bomb-related PTSD symptoms. In addition, 37% reported permanent changes in their marital relationship and 7% reported temporary changes in the relationship related to the bombing. Clearly this is an area that could benefit from further investigation.

Safety Fears

Immediately after the 2003 crash of the space shuttle Columbia, NASA astronaut Col. Chris Hadfield was interviewed by the press. One reporter asked,

> "As an astronaut how do you prepare yourself and your family for the dangers?"
> "I don't dwell on it. I try to understand the risk as clearly as possible because it is life or death for us. It's different for my wife and children. They have to live with the consequences. My kids know their dad is in a risky profession. My wife and I have been married for 21 years and we discussed the possibility years ago. We get life insurance. It's just part of the relationship."
> "Does a tragedy like this make you re-evaluate your job?"
> "For me no. If there was a shuttle launching tomorrow, I would confidently get onto it. I think we do a tremendous job of providing a safe vehicle to go to space and back. Accidents do happen, but that doesn't mean that people are careless. This is part, unfortunately, of doing business, and for me the business is still infinitely worthwhile." ("Colombia Remembered," 2003, p. 15)

While risk may indeed "just be part of the relationship," it nevertheless has an impact on spouses and families. One spouse of a police officer reported that her husband had told her that if he was ever killed or injured, they would send someone she knew to break the news. She no longer fears every police car coming up the street, just ones where she recognizes the officers. Each time an emergency responder dies in the line of duty, every family of every responder is reminded of the risks. They identify with the grieving spouse and children on the front page of the paper. They fear that one day the flag will be passed to them. One officer described the experience of his wife when he was shot on duty. "My wife was picked up from work by an officer from another division. But she wasn't told what was going on. I was OK so I stayed on scene. She came down to the scene to try to see what was going on. But of course she couldn't get in. It was 6 hours before she knew I was OK."

At times these fears are realized. One study focused on the impact of duty-related death on the surviving children of a dead officer. Williams (1999) describes how these children must deal with not only their own reactions and fears, but also those of people around them. The media attention to the deaths creates images that are etched in the child's mind. These children similarly have fears of losing the other parent, fears of their own death, fears of going to sleep (especially if the death occurred at night), and fears of being unprotected.

Fears for safety spill over from fears for the safety of the police officer, paramedic, or firefighter into concerns for other family members. Emergency responders and their families are well aware of the fragility of life and the danger in everyday activities. Exposure to trauma and suffering challenges an individual's beliefs about the safety of those they love, and they may consequently become hypervigilant about potentially dangerous situations (McCann and Pearlman, 1990b; Resick and Schnicke, 1993a,b; Chrestman, 1995; Stout and Thomas, 1991). While emergency responders may minimize the risk to themselves and control the potential risk through adherence to training and safety standards, they are acutely aware that they are powerless to protect family members from all risks. It is not uncommon for emergency responders to report extreme fears for the safety of their children and strategies to protect them that are beyond that of other families. "I've become very overprotective of my family. I am probably almost paranoid [on] the point of safety because I have seen too many people killed or seriously injured doing common everyday things."

One firefighter described coming home and removing all the hangers from the closet after seeing a child fatally injured by one. He recalls that his wife did not even question why. Another firefighter described cutting his children's food into microscopic pieces so that they would not choke. A police officer noted that his son had never been on a team that he did not coach. He had arrested enough coaches on charges of sexual abuse to be convinced that his son would not be safe. A paramedic stated that after one horrible accident scene, "Personally, I went home and made sure that my kids never had high handlebars on their bikes." While these strategies seem reasonable in the minds of responders who have witnessed the effects of disaster and violence, they may seem to be overcontrolling in the minds of family members who are having their activities restricted. It is important responders work together with their families to assess risk and to ensure that family members do not become resentful. This is one arena where emergency workers must work to control the impact of their traumatic experiences from impinging too heavily on family life.

How Do You Hug a Man of Steel?

While there is no question that the demands of the job and the exposure to tragic and dangerous events have an impact on the families of emergency responders, the influence of the organizational culture on the responder and coping strategies employed by the responder also affect family members. The role of an emergency responder often shifts from mediating civilian disputes to enforcing safety standards and laws, restraining individuals from harming themselves or others, or reviving and rescuing people. Each of these roles requires skills and traits not required in most occupations. These skills include taking control, springing into action, remaining detached, making quick and decisive decisions, and questioning everything. Southworth (1990), a former police officer, notes that the traits and dispositions that make a good emergency responder often do not make a good spouse or parent. He states that not only are emergency responders unaware that they are transferring their professional disposition onto family situations, but when they are aware, they often believe that it is appropriate. Examples of this are limiting behaviors due to safety concerns, issuing orders rather than negotiating family solutions, and investigating whether teenage children are using drugs or alcohol. These problems become particularly pronounced when responders have teenagers who no longer wish to follow rules they see as arbitrarily imposed (Maslach and Jackson, 1979).

Not only are the skills and traits necessary for the job a potential risk for healthy and happy family interactions, but so are the coping strategies employed by emergency responders. Emotional numbing is one of the strategies used by emergency responders to cope with stressful events. As discussed in previous chapters, this approach includes avoiding experiencing the emotional impact of tragic events by consciously minimizing emotions and focusing on the cognitive aspect of the job. Feelings about the event are avoided and efforts are made to avoid seeing the victim in the context of their lives, as this increases the risk of emotional distress in the emergency responder. While this strategy may reduce the risk of traumatic stress symptoms, it does not come without costs. "The downside of my way of dealing with things is the personal side. You start blocking out personal feelings about anything and everyone because you don't want to carry the baggage home with you, but you can't turn it off completely when you go home." Further, as part of this strategy, emergency responders tend not to overtly share the impact of their day with family (although, as noted above, there usually is a spillover). As one responder noted that when he returned from a difficult day on the job he just wanted to be left alone. "Just leave me alone, leave me in a quiet space." In part the rationale for this is to protect family members from hearing about traumatic material; in addition, however, responders often believe that it protects them. The emotional reaction that family members may have to being told about a tragic or dangerous event carries the risk of evoking emotional reactions in the responder. "I try not to tell my wife [about tragic events]. She is very supportive, but she's also a very sensitive type. . . . When something bothers me, whether I'm mad or upset, I just get quiet, and that might not be the nicest thing for her, but that's what I do."

This strategy of emotional numbing has consequences for the responders and for their families. Family members may perceive the police officer, firefighter, or paramedic as emotionally distant and unfeeling. Research has suggested that numbing associated with traumatic stress reactions is significantly associated with negative feelings of family members toward the relationship. In particular, disinterest, detachment and emotional unavailability that characterize emotional numbing may diminish a parent's ability and willingness to seek out, engage in, and enjoy interactions with children, leading to poorer-quality relationships (Ruscio, Weathers, King, and King, 2002).

Not all responders, however, feel the need to numb themselves and project a superhuman image. Some responders in our studies described how they spoke at length with their spouses and found this to be a great support. One officer in particular found it helpful to speak to his wife when he was shot. He found it useful to discuss his feelings about how close he came to death. A paramedic explained, "I always talk about this to my wife, and I think she understands and sympathizes. I think in some ways it may have helped us come a little closer, because it made me more human and less aloof."

Further, in our study many responders noted that they were married to people in the emergency services or medical field and that this made talking about stressful events easier. Responders felt that spouses in similar professions understood the politics and were not frightened or overwhelmed by the details of events.

Suggestions for Family Survival

In the chapters on intervention, we also discuss the importance of programs for families of responders. However, in addition to formal programs and interventions, responders and their families offer many suggestions for making family life easier in trying circumstances.

Work Out Systems to Accommodate Shift Work

Leave lights on at night to welcome home the person on shift and reduce the feelings of isolation. Get an alarm system if you feel frightened to be alone. Communicate through alternate means such as notes, e-mail, and pagers. Plan activities with children that allow time with the parent who works shifts. Special outings can be a good way to reconnect. Spouses should be encouraged to develop independent interests and to attend social events alone if necessary. In addition, because of the unpredictability of schedules in emergency services, it is necessary to develop a system of rain checks for unforeseen occurrences. For instance, are there alternate people who can pick up the children? It is important in this process not to become angry at one another for unavoidable changes but to join together to direct the anger outside the relationship and to find ways to adapt. It is possible, however, that the changes in schedule were not necessary and are ways of avoiding family issues or responsibilities. If this is the case, couples should address those issues.

Establish Decompression Routines

Each person has ways that work best for them to create a space between work and home. Some can change gears while driving home, others need to go for a walk or watch half an hour of TV to wind down. Parents who work in any field report feeling overwhelmed by questions and demands of children who were waiting for the moment of their arrival. In the emergency services, where the stresses of the job may be enormous, and where workers may have had limited contact with their children for several days due to shifts, these feelings of being bombarded can be intensified. It is important for all family members to talk about the best ways for them to deal with stress and have ways to communicate to one another "This is one of those days when I require a decompression period."

Acknowledge Your Own Reactions to Events and Work to Separate Them from Responses to Family Situations

It is important to be aware that while individuals may feel they are hiding their distress related to either everyday hassles or traumatic events, very often family members are aware and affected. The best way to determine if you are under stress is to ask someone who loves you—they are usually a better barometer than you are. When experiencing stress or trauma at work, individuals need to work at not reacting immediately (often therefore overreacting) to situations at home, whether they be the misbehavior of a child, a safety concern, or an annoying behavior of a spouse.

Plan Responses to Questions and Comments from Others

Children and spouses of emergency responders will be questioned about their loved one's work. Negative comments about all police, firefighters, or paramedics will be directed at family members, with the implication that they are somehow responsible. Following a major or highly publicized event, they will be sought out for the "insider's view." Plan responses to common comments or questions. Give enough information to children to make them proud of the work that their parent does.

Establish a System of Supports

As one spouse of an emergency responder stated, "You have a team, we don't." In addition to developing supports of friends and family who can help out in times of disrupted schedules, also ensure that family members are aware of employee assistance and member assistance programs in the responders' organization, where they can turn for information, advice, or support. Trauma response teams, discussed in chapters 10–12, must also work to expand their mandates to include family member support. This frequently requires that additional resources be devoted to the teams as funding and mandates of trauma response teams are almost exclusively devoted to the emergency responders.

Conclusion

The families of emergency responders are arguably the most important resource of not only responders but also emergency service organizations. Family members provide a buffer in times of emotional trauma, they accommodate the needs of responders so that responders can work disruptive schedules and long hours, and they provide a counterbalance to a job where individuals are confronted almost exclusively with the negative side of human nature. Yet families are often the forgotten victims of workplace stress and trauma. Family members deal with trauma contagion, they are confronted with attitudes and behaviors of the responder emanating from the exposures on the job, and they fear for the safety of their loved one. If organizations do not expand their notion of membership to include families and intervention programs do not incorporate family needs, we run the risk of undermining the most important resource of any individual, and therefore of any organization

9

THE CONTINUUM OF INTERVENTIONS I

Doing the Right Job at the Right Time

Adversity and adaptation have been a part of human evolution for hundreds of thousands of years. With every generation there are new developments that offer advantages and disadvantages to our well-being. Fire was a welcome and dangerous development; technologically, the first spear improved our ability to acquire food at the risk of going astray, injuring someone (Hewitt, 1997). Today, new chemicals improve our lifestyle at the risk of creating pollution or toxic waste. As humans we have developed numerous mechanisms to deal with the problems we create or that occur in our environment. Our ancestors learned to travel in small groups for the well-being of the individuals. We developed biobehavioral early warning and emergency action systems, affiliation and cooperation skills, listening and mutual aid skills, the ability to think fast on our feet when required, and at other times to be analytical. Our communication skills developed to signify our ideas, feelings, and immediate and future needs. Our social relationships, skills, and resources create the trajectories to health or health problems.

In this chapter and the next, we focus on important and practical ways to prevent, reduce, or recover from the harm of persistent or extreme stress and adversity. For a moment, consider the image offered in chapter 3 regarding the manner in which theories provide a framework for understanding interventions, much like the blueprint for a home renovation. In the stages of construction, a foundation is made, followed by carpenters framing walls, electricians, plumbers, and later drywall or plaster workers.

One can imagine how frustrating it would be for the walls to be up before electricians or plumbers arrive to knock holes in these new walls to undertake their work. All of the work during a renovation may be done skillfully and expertly, yet it is more important to do the right job at the right time (Ranger, 2003). The right job requires the right resources arriving at the right place in a timely way

In the next two chapters, we propose a continuum of interventions. By *continuum* we are not suggesting a simple linear time frame of pre-, during, and post-event interventions. For training and planning purposes this is useful, however, it does not reflect real-time life as an emergency professional. As we have shown in previous chapters, organizations are continuously meeting numerous challenges. At any time they might be facing a "hiring freeze"; officers may be coping with a shooting event that could become tomorrow's public enquiry; or a passenger with an unknown contagious disease may be arriving in an unexpecting and unprepared city. We use the term *continuum of interventions* to reflect the importance of ongoing and uninterrupted interventions, though the intensity of interventions at any one time must be linked to the health and mental health needs of the emergency responder and the members of responding organizations. Interventions for our purposes are the planned actions to promote well-being and resiliency while preventing or reducing the harm from adversity or advancing the recovery from adversity. We have previously discussed adversities that emergency professionals encounter in their work life which range from daily hassles to the extreme stress of mass violence and disasters. Our first step is to outline principles on which to base interventions.

Principles of Intervention

It is useful to base our interventions on principles that are grounded in the theory, research, and experience of emergency and mental health professionals discussed in the previous chapters. Principles will guide how we understand and work with emergency services professionals facing adversity. Numerous researchers and frontline professionals have completed studies and training manuals highlighting the importance of principles or guidelines for interventions (Norris and Thompson, 1995; Weine et al., 2002; World Health Organization, 2001, 2003). Table 9.1 incorporates and builds on the work of those researchers and writers.

Use a Value-Based Approach in Planning Interventions

We hold many beliefs about our workplace, the world, or ourselves. Our values are a statement about what beliefs are important. Values are often

Table 9.1. Guiding Principles for Interventions

1. Use a Value-Based Approach in Planning Interventions
2. Focus on the Well-Being and Resiliency of Emergency Professionals and Their Families
3. Assess and Plan Interventions in Collaboration with the Emergency Professionals and Their Organization
4. Use a Culturally and Context Appropriate Approach to Interventions
5. Use Interventions Based on the Best Available Research and Consensus-Based Evidence
6. Provide Accessible Interventions at Multiple Levels and Locations
7. Implement Interventions across a Time Continuum So as to Prevent, Prepare for, Reduce, and Recover from the Harm of Adverse Events
8. Build Locally Based and Sustainable Programs to Protect the Current and Future Well-Being of Emergency Professionals

reflected in codes of ethics and professional conduct, and in workplace mission and charter statements. Values will guide our behavior, what we see as resources, our choices, and our priorities. The phrase "above all, do no harm" is a cornerstone value of professional practice. Other commonly held values include respecting the rights and dignity of people, the right to privacy through confidentiality, and the entitlement to safety and security, including food, shelter, and basic health care and education. We also believe in the importance of people feeling a sense of control and choice in determining a course in life.

While personal, organizational, and community values are interrelated and often appear in agreement, there are times when the values of emergency professionals, mental health professionals, and the community may be in conflict. Emergency professionals are expected to serve the public under high-risk conditions. These conditions are changing, mutating, and becoming increasingly complex with the risk of terrorism, the ongoing development of thousands of chemicals for commercial use, and the risk of new contagious diseases. When a community faces situations such as highly contagious diseases or terrorism, community-held values are often challenged. At such times, individual civil liberties and larger public and health safety needs will need to be balanced. It may be necessary to quarantine health professionals, acknowledging that quarantine is a limit on an individual's rights and freedoms, yet is necessary for the public good. Additionally, we would hold values that respect the confidentiality of members of the public or our colleagues. However, knowing a person has been potentially exposed to a contagious disease may require that at some point that person should be named publicly.

During the SARS outbreak in 2003 in Toronto, health professionals were personally at high risk yet continued to serve the public. This dedication creates a duty of reciprocity, in which emergency professionals have the duty to serve the community, and in turn the community and organizations have a reciprocal duty to protect the well-being of professionals (University of Toronto Joint Centre for Bioethics, 2003). Thus, as a society, we should value and support health and safety measures that protect these workers. Reciprocity would be evident when we balance, for example, the need for a public enquiry into the death of a person in care, with the need for a process that is respectful of emergency professionals. At times, however, the best interest of the public and the safety and well-being of emergency responders may be at odds. One potential value conflict is related to the evidence of an increase in alcohol misuse among some emergency professionals following disasters. When does a colleague approach the coworker with a problem, or under what circumstances would one turn to the coworker's supervisor? These are usually uncomfortable interpersonal safety- and value-based decisions. The practical implication of this guideline is that mental health professionals and emergency professionals must have a mechanism in place to review value conflicts and appropriate actions.

Focus on the Well-Being and Resiliency of Emergency Professionals and Their Families

As we have discussed in previous chapters, research has indicated that for the most part, people do not develop post-traumatic stress disorder following extreme, stressful events. This is not to say that people do not feel stress or suffering. Rather, individuals, families, groups, and communities rise to the occasion of traumatic events and mobilize resources to overcome adversity. Stress becomes surmountable because of personal resources such as self-efficacy, as well as communal resources, such as equipment or social support. Resiliency is developed as people face and overcome challenges. From an evolutionary point of view, it makes sense that human beings would be resilient to adversities that occur in our environment. From an intervention perspective, it is useful to keep in mind that trauma is both an individual and a shared event, with stress followed by resiliency as the normal response. Emergency professionals in particular are a resilient group who are less likely to have impaired functioning at home or work following traumatic exposure than are members of the general public. Emergency professionals are well trained, experienced, and self-select these potentially high-stress jobs. Respecting the competency and resiliency of emergency professionals is a key guideline to all interventions (Gist and Lubin, 1999; Violanti, Paton, and Dunning, 2000). Supporting the well-being of the individual, team, and organization is equally important. This often comes through health promotion and prevention programs and efforts supporting the natural recovery of emergency professionals.

This guideline would be evident in the workplace when health promotion and prevention programs exist as the foundation for all other interventions. Three examples of this guideline in action are leadership development, cardiovascular health programs and family support. Healthy organizations develop leaders that are fair, ethical, and conscious of both mental health and material hazards (Shay, 2002). Workplace cardiovascular health programs can promote education and support for healthy lifestyles, such as eating well and physical and emotional wellness throughout the career span. As we outlined in chapter 8, proactively supporting the families of the emergency professionals builds vital social support for both individuals and, indirectly, the larger organization.

Assess and Plan Interventions in Collaboration with the Professionals and Their Organization

In healthy workplaces people look after each other. Securing the genuine commitment and collaboration of all participants and levels of an organization are key factors in the success of the implementation of any intervention. One means of utilizing the knowledge and experience of an organization is the use of peer support teams in planning and implementing interventions. From the onset of the movement to institute post-traumatic support for emergency responders, the use of peer support teams has been an integral component (Mitchell, 1982; Mitchell and Bray, 1990; Robinson and Murdoch, 1991). Greenstone (2000) traces the history of peer support programs in policing and documents the transition, beginning in 1974, of programs from services provided by mental health professionals to services provided by concerned peers. The primary rationale for the use of peer support teams is that members within the organization understand on an intimate basis the job of those they seek to support. In addition, workers with local organizations will be most aware of the network of support, formal or informal leadership, power structures, and how to access resources within the organization. Through tapping the knowledge of peer support teams or key members of the organization, one can gain knowledge of the strengths, history, and issues the emergency professionals have faced. Nevertheless, there are limits and challenges for peer support programs, which we discuss in chapters 11 and 12.

At the same time, collaboration with experienced mental health professionals external to an organization can bring new perspectives, skills, and training that may be useful to organizations facing extreme challenges. When mental health professionals coordinate their efforts with the mechanisms already in place in the organization, the work of peers is enhanced. Mental health consultants also can help assess the policy, routines, and particularly the "blind spots" that may no longer be serving the well-being of the organization. Every service seeks to build on past experiences to update and upgrade equipment and skills such as to deal with emerging chemical, biological, radiological/nuclear, and explosive (CBRNE) incidents and their physical and psychological risks. An excellent example of merging previous knowledge and new flexible approaches occurred following the destruction of the Emergency Operations Center (EOC) in New York City. The EOC for New York was located in the 7 World Trade Center building, directly adjacent to the twin towers of the World Trade Center. The terrorist attacks of 9/11 caused the complete collapse of the building and the destruction of the EOC. Within 96 hours, a new EOC was established at a pier in a space twice the size of the original EOC, with twice the agencies represented. Emergency response experts worked creatively with new private and public partners. For example, local university professors and students worked with emergency services to create geographical information systems for planning needs. Communication systems and computers were networked (Kendra and Wachtendorf, 2003). Accommodation and thousands of meals were arranged, along with the opportunity for support for recovery workers. These creative responses to the safety, information, technical, and basic social and emotional needs occurred because emergency services worked in partnership with familiar and new partners, including mental health professionals.

Use a Culturally and Context Appropriate Approach to Interventions

An ever-expanding body of literature supports the idea that the experience of trauma and the expression of traumatic response are culturally based (Nader, Dubrow, and Stamm, 1999; Norris, Perilla, Ibañez, and Murphy, 2001; Terheggen, Stroebe, and Kleber, 2001). As discussed in chapters 3 and 6, emergency service organizations have norms about decision making, safety priorities, how problems are faced, validated, or disenfranchised. There are typically norms regarding how emotions may be expressed and the rituals that assist a group to grieve the loss of a colleague. The cultural context includes spiritual beliefs, which may be expressed within the organization informally or formally, as in organizations with a chaplain. Norms in the organization around the importance of balancing work with family and life will also influence coping strategies following trauma and subsequently should direct the planning of post-trauma interventions.

Mental health professionals and peers must appreciate that any work in an emergency service organization is a cross-cultural experience. A support peer or mental health worker brings his or her own history and background and needs to be aware of and respect the individual and organizational culture he or she is working within. The collective history of any group—in particular, histories of trauma and violence, oppression, the accepted forms of emotional expression, and whether the culture values individuation or collectivism—will influence how trauma will be perceived and managed. It is important to understand an organization's cultural idioms of stress. That is, how do people express their distress, and what are the preferred (and accepted) ways to resolve and cope with life problems? For instance, emergency service professionals, as we have discussed, frequently use coping strategies that focus on cognitive mastery and rely less on emotional abreaction. Post-event interventions aimed at emotional release may be counterproductive and appropriately resisted. It is important to consider the history of the organization, the roots of the organization in the community, and past experiences of distress or disasters. What are the age groups represented, and at what stage of their career are the individuals? What is the gender and racial mix of the group? Within every community and organization there are also the issues of politics and power. While there may be formal organizational charts that reflect the chain of command, there is always an informal authority and power structure of individuals in groups within an organization. As part of this assessment one must consider the relationship between frontline staff, management, and unions. When a mental health professional enters an organization following a traumatic event with preconceived views of what problems will be encountered and the appropriate remedies, this most likely reflects the cultural beliefs of that professional. Disregard for the culture and context will result in interventions that will not be relevant to the situation at hand and can in fact make situations worse. At the heart of many interventions and communication problems is a misunderstanding of the workplace culture.

Use Interventions Based on the Best Available Research and Consensus-Based Evidence

As we discuss extensively in chapter 13, it is the ethical obligation of all mental health professionals and peer support professionals who are providing stress- and trauma-related services to ensure that their interventions are not harmful to those they are attempting to help and are based on the best available information regarding efficacy. In reviewing the discussions in chapter 13, you will note that an obvious challenge is that there are no universally proven interventions for all extremely stressful events. Nevertheless, there are many good approaches to consider, including the principles outlined in this chapter,. In the coming sections we will discuss specific interventions. What is most important, however, is choosing an intervention through a thoughtful decision-making process that considers both the evidence of effectiveness and the context, in which you plan to apply it, rather than relying on preconceived ideas or prepackaged interventions. It is recommended that as the field of interventions is changing it is useful to develop

- a network of professionals and peers willing to share their experiences
- a plan for attending conferences and reviewing the literature for new findings
- a willingness to modify intervention strategies based on new experiences or information
- a follow-up plan with the participants of any intervention
- a plan for evaluating the effectiveness of your own interventions.

Even when interventions are proven, there are still issues of being feasible and politically acceptable to an organization. In the coming section we will talk about organization development and its role in developing healthy interventions for staff. As research informs our practice, mental health professionals and peers are encouraged to remain committed, flexible, and curious about the needs of the people in the context in which problems occur, and how even tried and true practices may need to be modified and adapted to best meet the needs of the group. Lastly this principle requires us to monitor and evaluate the relevance and effectiveness of the principles themselves.

Provide Accessible Interventions at Multiple Levels and Locations

This principle highlights the importance of interventions being available and accessible to emergency service personnel. Accessibility includes choosing the locations in and outside of the workplace and using many mediums such as print and digital formats and internet based forms of information. Accessibility also requires that the interventions match the needs of the potential participants. Norris and Thompson (1995) and Stokols (1992) have discussed three types of intervention, targeting universal, selective, and indicated populations. *Universal interventions* are for everyone who is exposed to a particular form of adversity and who is currently not showing any health problems, though they may in the future. Typically these interventions involve health education and support to adapt or accommodate to environmental stressors. This approach would include prevention efforts to build resources in the broader community. In emergency service organizations, universal interventions include providing fitness and heart health and stress reduction programs for all staff, including new recruits in the initial training period. *Selective interventions* are more intensive attempts to promote protective processes for individuals or groups who are at higher risk

because of greater vulnerability or exposure to extreme stress. Examples include post–shooting incident peer teams to support officers and families,
peer and mental health education and support sessions for recovery workers in the transition from lengthy human remains recovery to regular duty,
or regular health screenings for firefighters and paramedics involved in
toxic-chemical fire scenes. *Indicated interventions* promote treatment for
individuals and groups experiencing significant levels of distress or symptoms. Such programs can include treatment through employee and family
assistance programs and substance abuse programs (for examples, see Bennett, Reynolds, and Lehman, 2003; Strecher, Wang, Derry, Wildenhaus,
and Johnson, 2002; Rollnick, Mason, and Butler, 1999).

The above suggests that interventions for a service, teams or stations, or
individuals may be simultaneously occurring, on multiple levels, in a large
organization. For instance, the death of a firefighter or a police officer in
the line of duty is a personal loss to those who knew and worked with the
individual, as well as a loss to the community of local and distant emergency professional groups.

Implement Interventions across a Time Continuum So as to Prevent, Prepare for, Reduce, and Recover from the Harm of Adverse Events

In public health three stages of prevention are considered. *Primary prevention* attempts to reduce the incidence of new health problems in a population. The aim is to lower the risk of the population as a whole by reducing
vulnerability factors while building resiliency and resources. Primary prevention examples include developing a system of regulations that limit risk
exposures to harmful chemicals and a set of training sessions to reduce risk
of contacting contagious diseases. *Secondary prevention* is aimed at the early
stages following a potentially traumatizing event and targets groups that are
at increased risk. Secondary prevention entails the planning of emergency
measures such as access to food, shelter, and psychological support services
immediately following a traumatic event. *Tertiary prevention* looks at improving and sustaining health after the event has occurred and distress or
damage has taken place. The goal would be to reduce the duration of the
problems or distress and improve the quality of life. Long-term or tertiary
strategies will involve the renewal of lost resources, treatment, and support
for individuals who are recovering from health and mental-health problems.
The timely and ongoing replenishment of resources is vital to diminishing
the distress individuals or organizations may feel (Hobfoll, 2002). People
adapt well or learn to adapt well when they have the social, emotional, and
economic resources and the opportunities for healthy work (Quick and Tetrick, 2003; Repetti, Taylor, and Seeman, 2002). We suggest throughout this
book that resilient people cope because they have developed flexible problem-

solving and health-seeking behaviors and have the necessary resources to cope with adversity as it happens. In practice primary, secondary and tertiary prevention may overlap and be integrated with the universal, selected, and indicated intervention approaches discussed above. This principle leads us to sustainable interventions as seen in the last principle.

Build Locally Based and Sustainable Programs to Protect the Current and Future Well-Being of Emergency Professionals

Resources need to be built for the long term in a manner that is not detrimental to other organizations and communities. This requires training, finances, skills, and other resources to be developed in an organizational climate that supports workplace health. One of the best ways to pursue this principle is the development of proactive occupational health and safety policies, internal supports such as peer support teams, and external resources such as employee and family assistance programs. The principles outlined point to the importance of not limiting support services to "critical incidents" or "traumatic events." As useful as such interventions may be, they do not build the a broader base of knowledge and skills at the front line and leadership levels to address the daily hassles and accumulation of stress discussed in chapter 6. We believe that health issues and risks need to be addressed through an organizational culture and leadership that is aware of and works to support professionals throughout the lifespan of their careers, from recruitment through retirement. The health needs of professionals will change through their careers and work experience. We are advocating for systems of workplace health programs that protect and promote well-being whether one is a rookie, veteran, or retired from the force. Indirectly these efforts support emergency professionals in other key life roles as spouse, parent, and grandparent.

Advocating for workplace health and safety policies and supports for workers may be a politically more difficult intervention than arranging a one-time stress management workshop, yet the former may offer more lasting gains for an organization and community. As discussed in chapter 6 "Help or Hindrance?", there is mounting evidence that organizational level interventions can be significantly related to protecting the well-being of employees and reducing health risks later in life. These are steps to protect the investment made in training our increasingly specialized and skilled emergency workers. The issue of sustainable development is of worldwide concern and is a discussion beyond the scope of this book; nevertheless, organizations should consider how their policies, resources, and interventions contribute to the health of the current and next generation of emergency workers, families, and communities.

The Continuum of Interventions

Earlier chapters focused on *why* we would intervene and now we discuss *what* to do, *when, where* and with *whom*. The continuum of interventions, as we conceptualize it, falls along these four dimensions of what, when, where and who as reflected in figure 9.1. These dimensions are in keeping with those of numerous other researchers (e.g., Norris and Thompson, 1995). The first dimension is the type of interventions, which range from 'big picture' actions such as workplace consultation and policy development to health promotion through education and training to assessments, referrals and treatment interventions. The second dimension is the timing of the intervention, such as promoting good health prior to the occurrence of the next traumatic event, actions to minimize health risks and distress during the crisis phase of an event, or following up with highly distressed individuals or organizations affected by an event. The third dimension is the setting or location of the intervention, such as at a management meeting, a fire hall group meeting, or a rest area near the scene of a disaster. The fourth dimension considers which participants to work with such as individual emergency professionals and their families, a work group of administrative support staff, or the organization as a whole. In chapters 3 and 6 we introduced interventions for families and for those facing public inquiries. This chapter focuses on interventions that support organizational, team, and individual health with a focus on health promotion and preven-

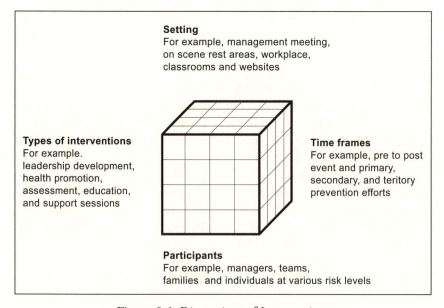

Figure 9.1. Dimensions of Interventions

tion of stress-related problems. Chapter 10 will focus on interventions related to traumatic or extremely stressful events.

Interventions attempt to protect and enhance individual, organizational, and community well-being and resilience, while reducing current vulnerability and harm in a manner that safeguards healthy conditions for the current and next generation of emergency professionals. These goals require a broad range of health, social, economic, and political actions. The range of interventions includes organizational and leadership development, team health promotion and prevention programs, assessing and monitoring the work environment, psychological first aid, crisis intervention, peer support, referral and follow-up, community and workplace outreach, family support, consultation, medical and mental health assessment, referrals, educational and support groups treatment, research and evaluation. In our principles we discussed the importance of many levels and locations for intervention for individuals, group/familial, organizational, and broader public policy initiatives. Typically the time continuum regarding a single isolated incident begins prior to a traumatic event, both in terms of prevention through stress reduction and resiliency building and in planning for services in the event of a traumatic occurrence; continues through the crisis phase of the event; and includes follow-up treatment of individuals managing extreme stress and trauma. As we have discussed, incidents in real time are not isolated from other stressful events that are ongoing or occur during or soon after the identified incident.

Promoting Health and Preventing Stress at the Organizational Level

We begin with prevention at the organizational level for two reasons. First, in our experience, no matter how attractive interventions for individuals or groups of individuals may be, they are not likely to be feasible or well-implemented unless politically supported and culturally appropriate for a given organization. Second, as discussed in chapters 3 and 6, emergency service organizations, like all organizations, have a direct influence on the health and well-being of their employees. Thus, if interventions do not begin at the organizational level, the chances that they will effectively reduce distress and enhance health are limited. A key dynamic for understanding organizations is how change in the organization has been managed and supported.

Watzlawick, Weakland, and Fisch (1974) suggest that there are two levels of change within organizations, first-order change and second-order change. When we try to improve on the things that we are already doing (doing more, faster, sooner, or better) we are undertaking first-order change to improve the efficiency or effectiveness of existing routines or procedures. Second-order change moves the action into a systemic level. Adding new equipment, such as purchasing a new ambulance or fire truck, can be a necessary first-order change. Improving the health of the public by teaching CPR and adding smoke detectors to homes is a second-order change. When we face a health issue or problem, the challenge is to consider whether action needs to be taken at the first or second order. Stress management education for employees can be a useful first-order change aimed at helping people develop strategies to deal with difficult situations. However, at times, individualizing the problem can backfire and create higher degrees of stress and resentment among workers. Ignoring second-order change opportunities, such as destigmatizing stress and trauma responses, may be counterproductive.

With the recent focus on group or individual interventions, less attention has generally been paid to organizational theory and change as a way of supporting the health and well-being of employees, particularly regarding traumatic stress. As we learned in the chapter on emergency service organizations, many emergency health professionals not only face a number of 'critical incidents' they also experience a great number of routine challenges and hassles in their day-to-day work. These routine challenges lead to heightened experiences of stress and render people more vulnerable when a traumatic event is encountered.

An organization can begin to address and consider changes to improve the overall well-being of their employees. At the outset, however, it must be acknowledged that large-scale organizational change is difficult. Developing new innovations in an organization challenges the organization's sense of competency and sense of clarity in its purpose. An organization's identity is related to its hierarchy, structures, and roles. Seeking to make significant individual or systemic changes often requires shifts in structures and roles and, at times, a reordering of the hierarchy. In order for change to occur, the organization and its members must come to appreciate that the risks associated with not changing or adapting are greater than those associated with changing. The challenge of making changes is reflected in responses such as "What is wrong with the way we do things now?" or "We have tried that before, and it never worked." These challenges may be particularly pronounced in organizations that deal with trauma-related issues on a daily basis and in the victims and families who have faced a loss of control with an unpredictable, overwhelming event. Building support to make these changes is vital at all levels within an organization. Helping people overcome any sense of incompetence, confusion, and conflict is vital in laying the groundwork for future interventions (Evans, 1996).

Making the Way for Healthy Change for
Organizations and Individuals

Before beginning any preventative intervention program, it is important to be aware that individuals and organizations may be ambivalent about a change given the multiple demands. The tendency to be cautious and fixed in proven routines has been observed for decades. Over 50 years ago, Lewin (1951) identified three stages of change: (1) unfreezing old behaviors, (2) learning new behaviors or practices, and (3) stabilizing (or, in Lewin's term, refreezing) the new behaviors. Other models for understanding change at both the individual and organizational level include social cognitive theory (Bandura, 1997), the health belief model (Janz and Becker, 1984), stages of change (Prochaska, Norcross, and Diclemente, 1994), theory of reasoned action (Fishbein and Ajzen, 1975) and the information processing model (McGuire, 1973). It is beyond the scope of this book to review all the models of change but we will highlight factors that promote healthy change.

Sometimes it seems easier to avoid or deny a problem, particularly if the disadvantages, such as time or costs seem larger than the perceived advantages to the change. For example mental health issues may not seem significant until the sick and disability insurance costs become significantly higher. Most change models suggest there are three important points to consider: a person or organization's attitude to considering a change, the perceived importance of change and the competency to make the change and behave differently. One of the best approaches for ensuring that interventions and change strategies meet the expectations and needs of staff members, is through staff participation in the planning for change and the implementation process. There are many ways and levels in which participation can occur, from attending a meeting in which staff members are informed of new policy or practices, to having frontline staff be given the time and resources to meaningfully engage in developing and implementing a new health policy and practice. Although this is a complex topic in itself, we would like to at least acknowledge the challenges of an emergency services system with regard to limited financial resources and increasing public accountability. These dynamics are further influenced by whether the organization is public, private, or a combination of both.

The collaboration of staff is critical when beginning with an organizational assessment to better understand the resources and needs of the people within the organization. Evans (1996) suggests that further understanding of an organization can take place by looking at six aspects of organizational life: the occupational conditions, roles, and expectations; organizational politics; history; stressors; finances; and overall organizational culture. Adapting Heaney's (2003) suggestions with our principles raises several useful questions:

- What strengths and strains appear in the employees?
- What are the various physical social and organizational conditions that are potential protectors or sources of stress? .
- What is the history of stress and strengths in the organization? Are stresses related to short-term or long-term conditions?
- What are the leadership and frontline perceptions of the protective or stressful conditions?
- How accessible are support resources, and how widespread is the stress?
- What are the previous efforts to change or modify the sources of stress?
- How is the resiliency of the personnel being enhanced or their vulnerability being reduced or modified?

In our experience, exploring these questions requires courage on the part of a team or an organization. During our work with organizations we may ask the above questions in informal team meetings, focus groups, surveys and action methods. Action methods are interactive and concrete approaches to exploring organizational structure and processes (White, 2002). One example of this can be implemented after establishing a trusting working relationship with a team or management group. At a team meeting we may ask team members to create a live organizational chart in the room. Participants organize themselves in the room according to the organizational structure, with missing people and positions acknowledged. We may then ask the group to create the organizational chart according to a time continuum, reflecting what the organization looked like 6 months ago, 1 year ago, or 5 years ago. It is often interesting to observe the number of organizational changes regarding leadership, work roles, and functions or people over a relatively short span of time. It is informative for the participants and for us to see the range of and changing, formal and informal leadership, knowledge, skills and authority in any group or organization. These exercises are often a good learning opportunity to consider both the obvious and the subtle transitions and structures in a group. It also may lead to a discussion of how changes promote resiliency or resentment. How losses are acknowledged and managed within the organization affects the change process. One interesting example was a team that felt they had experienced a particularly stressful year but had not understood the full extent of their losses. Through the exercise it became clear that many of the team members, senior and experienced coworkers, had left through retirement, relocation, and work-related death. Most of the group had felt the changes and loss yet had not recognized the extent and depth of the losses because of the growing demands of the work.

An organization we know began to collaborate with the local health department to distribute information on heart health after the death of a colleague due to heart disease. Over time the information grew to educational sessions, an expansion of inter-organizational recreational sports teams and change to lower fat meals in the cafeteria. This happened slowly as the organization began to recognize the disadvantages of not supporting health programs and just leaving health to personal choice. Attitudes became receptive to changes as the group began to support healthier eating and fitness. Interestingly the initial efforts did not add any financial cost to the organization and later as the attitudes changed, organizational money was found to support new health programs.

Most of us have been in a meeting where we soon realized that not much will be changing despite a presentation to the group about organizational change. At times our own attitude may prevent us from seeing and supporting opportunities to promote healthy change. There are several keys to effectively facilitating change in organizations that are not involved in health promotion and prevention programs, such as supporting professionals and families during public inquiries, healthy heart and low risk diet, or alcohol drinking education programs. New programs are considered and implemented when a few staff 'get behind' and show a positive attitude towards a new program or action, when the program or new behaviors are seen as a priority, and the skills and resources exist to undertake the new program of behavior. The good news is that there are many useful strategies to develop the skills or confidence to undertake new health policies and behaviors. These strategies include assessing and modifying workplace barriers that interfere with healthy work practices; raising awareness of the true costs and benefits of health practices; providing training and information to develop the knowledge and skills for a healthy workplace and lifestyle; building peer support for progressive occupational health policy and practice; reducing the stigma of addressing mental health issues and most importantly starting with a very small commitment to an plan of action, building momentum, and achieving small successes (Thesenvitz, Hershfield, and Chirrey, 2003). We would briefly note that a significant barrier to promoting healthy workplaces is that organizational development, occupational health, and trauma-related research and interventions are undertaken by a number of sciences, disciplines, researchers and front-line health professionals. Closing the gap between the different disciplines and between researchers, clinicians, and emergency professionals is critical to improving the relevance and effectiveness of our interventions.

Health Promotion and Stress Reduction Interventions at the Individual Level

There are numerous health promotion and prevention strategies in this chapter. We suggest that individuals can organize these and other valuable interventions according to three approaches to dealing with stressful issues: (1) actions to influence or modify the source of stress; (2) actions to modify or change the way one defines the problem; (3) actions to modify or change one's reaction to the stresses (Hoath and Bober, 2000; Pearlin and Schooler, 1978; Quillian-Wolver and Wolver, 2003).

Influencing or modifying the source of stress includes many actions: (1) learning the skills required to network and to advocate for change in the organization; (2) promoting team training to effectively cope with extreme stress of emerging dangers such as CBRNE events; (3) advocating for recognition of potentially high stress public and media events such as public inquiries; (4) supporting effective relationships between the organization, community and media; (5) advocating for reviews of job design and conditions that support long term health; (6) reviewing the clarity of worker roles; (7) advocating for healthy physical conditions, such as ergonomics and the appropriate safety and protective equipment; (8) becoming aware of exposure to dangerous conditions, such as toxic chemicals in the environment; and (9) improving training throughout the career lifespan to promote physical and emotional health (Heaney, 2003).

To change the way in which one defines the problem, one can: (1) become aware of and clarify negative or self-defeating thinking, such as all-or-none thinking and overgeneralization; (2) learn to evaluate the severity of a problem and one's reactions as healthy and indicative of concern; (3) identify whether the problem is a practical issue or evidence of a deeper values conflict between staff and an organization; (4) clarify whether or not the problem is the result of miscommunication or intentional actions; (5) recognize opportunities for positive growth or learning when facing and resolving a problem; and (6) consider whether short-term discomfort is worth long-term gain.

Accepting the situation and reducing the stress can include such actions as: (1) developing and maintaining healthy lifestyles through physical fitness, enjoyable work, and recreational activities; (2) developing good rest and sleep habits; (3) developing relaxation skills such as meditation; (4) building a healthy support network; (5) learning and practicing health awareness skills; (6) developing a range of interpersonal skills, such as communication and conflict resolution, and negotiation and assertiveness skills; (7) seeking out role models when learning new healthy activities and behaviors; and (8) limiting the use of mood-altering drugs, such as using alcohol within safe drinking guidelines.

Although there are a number of potential interventions that could be employed, we know that it is possible to only scratch the surface of multi-level, diverse interventions, so we are selective in discussing promising and practical information, knowing there are ongoing developments in the field. There are numerous preventative education interventions that involve understanding and managing stress and distress following trauma. Traditionally this has involved teaching people how to identify what triggers stress reactions in them, identifying the manifestations of stress and developing techniques for stress management such as guided imagery, deep breathing, and muscle relaxation. We will focus our attention on more recent developments in the field.

Preparing the Ground for Health and Stress Reduction

A useful approach that focuses on the individual's ability to reduce stress related to the workplace is the Mindfulness Based Stress Reduction Program (MBSR), originally developed by Jon Kabat-Zinn (1990) at the University of Massachusetts. The MBSR program provides training through weekly group sessions and daily homework and is offered in several hundred health care settings throughout North America and Europe. Typically it is a program that involves eight weekly 2- to 2 1/2-hour sessions followed by daily homework for the days in between the sessions. In this approach, relaxation and simple stretches are taught in combination with strategies to increase cognitive awareness and cognitive/affective mastery in times of stress.

The first elements of the approach, relaxation, stretching, and meditation, are fairly well known among practitioners who work on stress management. The second major aspect of the approach is cognitive awareness and cognitive/affective mastery. Here, the goal is to improve the awareness of the automatic ways in which the individual responds to the world. He or she can begin to identify unhealthy or self-defeating thoughts. Does the person tend to view most events in a negative light? Does the person tend to personalize each event? For instance, someone might believe, "There are more gruesome accidents because I was on shift." Cognitive awareness provides individuals with the opportunity to learn about themselves through the process of self-observation (Horowitz, 2002). This then allows for the possibility of modifying cognitions in a manner that is less judgmental and less self-critical. As a result of awareness and cognitive reframing of events and reactions, individuals can begin to increase emotional tolerance and regulate affect (Segal, Williams, and Teasdale, 2002). Emotional tolerance involves learning to deal with unpleasant or painful situations. This in turn reduces affective and autonomic arousal. The individual is taught to view the world as manageable and understandable. The approach is consistent with the work of Antonovsky (1979), who postulates that when one retains a sense of control and integrity in the face of catastrophic events, he or she is able to cope more flexibly and moderate the influence of severe stress.

In summary, the MBSR approach aims to return balance to life by helping people to realistically appraise events, to develop confidence in their coping ability, and to avoid moving into automatic pilot at times of stress. MBSR is a means of developing self-awareness and self-observational skills, which in turn lead to improved relational skills and recognizing greater possibility of choices or alternatives to cope. The approach can be used in the context of other educational and therapeutic approaches, such as psycho-education, progressive relaxation, and breath work to overcome high-stress events. As a prevention strategy, it supposes that by providing stress management tools, individuals will be less depleted and possess more coping strategies should they face traumatic events. The relaxation aspects of this strategy have been shown to decrease heart rate and blood pressure and to improve people's responses to a variety of health problems. While Baer (2003), in reviewing the research of the effectiveness of this approach, identifies some methodological flaws, he concludes that there is evidence that it may alleviate a variety of problems. For instance, research has demonstrated that MBSR has significantly reduced anxiety-disorder symptoms and prevented depression relapses (Baer, 2003). Although we are not aware of specific studies of MBSR with emergency professionals, we have incorporated its tools into educational aspects of our work. The comments to date have indicated that professionals believed they have acquired a few additional tools to alleviate distress and the aftermath of working with an accumulation of stresses. Most importantly, they reported an awareness of the "wear and tear" of the work on their minds and bodies, which led to wiser choices in their own self-care. MBSR groups with appropriately trained leaders are increasingly available.

Preparing for Change

Most people resolve health problems on their own. For example, most people reduce or quit smoking or problem drinking without seeking professional help. Motivation results from recognizing a problem, searching for a way to make a healthy change, trying out the new behaviors, learning from the experience as you go and with the support of others staying on the course to health (Miller and Rollnick, 2002). Miller and Rollnick (2002) suggest that self-efficacy and appreciating the balance of pros and cons associated with any change are important dynamics of the change equation. This section briefly introduces three useful and promising ways in which mental health professional and peers can assist in the process of facilitating healthier behavior for both individuals and organizations.

Miller and Rollnick (2002) have stated that ambivalence regarding change can be resolved or dissipated through reducing barriers or "cons" associated with change while enhancing the number of "pros." Their approach is based on the stages of change model in which each stage requires a certain task be completed in order to facilitate the change. In the precontemplation stage, where a person is not even considering change, the task is to have a person heighten their doubt or ambivalence about their health behavior. The person may wish to consider the impact of their substance use on other important people in their lives. In organizations, heightened awareness about the problem is often created through pressure tactics employed by certain members of the organization, such as union members, or by dramatic event that highlights the problem, such as the manner in which SARS highlighted issues regarding infection control in some emergency service organizations in Toronto. In the contemplation stage, a person or organization is beginning to think that there may be need for a change and yet remains ambivalent about the change. The key task is to support resolution of the ambivalence in the direction of a healthy behavioral or organizational change. The issues involved in changing and the consequences of not changing can be reviewed, but ultimately the choice must be made by that individual or organization. In the preparation stage the ambivalence begins to teeter and rest on the choice of making a healthy change. The important task at this stage is to help a person or organization consider the available change options and their relative advantages and to ultimately select an appropriate course of action. In the action stage, which is the process of taking steps to institute change, the goal is to provide support for carrying out the change plans. During the maintenance stage, the challenge is to hold on to the gains that have been made. This involves providing positive feedback about the change and continuously developing strategies to overcome obstacles in maintaining the change.

Miller and Rollnick (2002) outline three types of interventions to facilitate health behavior change in individuals, brief advice, behavioral change counseling and motivational interviewing. The principles may also be relevant to encouraging organizational change. Brief advice is intended to note a health risk, provide information and consider steps to undertake a healthier course. It is useful when someone is asking for information or when a supportive professional has useful information and there is a compelling reason to provide advice. The discussion on alcohol use later in the chapter is an example of this. Behavioral change counseling expands on brief advice in that there is time to build a helping collaborative relationship and use additional interpersonal skill to promote change. Motivational interviewing is a "client centered, directive method for enhancing intrinsic motivation to change by exploring and resolving ambivalence" (Miller and Rollnick, 2002, p. 25). The key ingredient in this approach is not to tell people that they may have a personal problem or what steps they should take. Rather, there are four important principles in facilitating health behavior change through motivational interviewing: (1) express empathy; (2) develop discrepancy; (3) roll with resistance; and (4) support self-efficacy (Miller and Rollnick, 2002).

To *express empathy* is to convey acceptance for a person as they are or an organization as it has developed. Many historical factors led to the current state of affairs. Many adaptations had to be made and many pressures juggled. An essential skill in expressing empathy is reflective listening and seeking to understand the history of this person or place. Few people can move to change unless they believe that the person encouraging change understands how they got here in the first place and the ongoing challenges that they face.

Developing discrepancy is a process in which people are assisted to see how the current individual behavior—or structure or policies of the organization—places them on a trajectory away from important goals or values. No emergency service organization whose aim it is to assist the public wishes to do so at the risk of significantly harming their members. While researchers and teenagers would agree that unsolicited advice or confrontation rarely promote change in another person, Rollnick et al. (2002) suggest that brief advice can be a useful motivational tool in helping to highlight a discrepancy between current policies and behaviors and those which are most conducive to health and well-being. In this context, brief advice typically is short and focuses on a single issue, such as rest or diet, within an opportunistic setting, such as at the time recovery workers leave for home. The goal is to allow people, in a safe and respectful environment, to become aware of the choices they are making and the risk of continuing as they are.

Next, it is important to *roll with resistance*. Arkowitz (2002) suggests reframing resistance as ambivalence, thus using a less judgmental or pejorative term. There is a difference between people who may not want to change and people who may not know how to change. There is a difference between having no incentive or motivation to change versus a lack of knowledge and resources to make healthy changes. The difficulty with change is that it implies unpredictability and uncertainty in one's life. Thus, instead of opposing or confronting people, this approach suggests that a counselor or consultant *support the strengths and self-efficacy* of people involved, so that they believe change is actually possible.

The phrase "ready, willing, and able" describes the heart of the behavior change approach (Miller and Rollnick, 2002). *Able* refers to the confidence to make the change, that is, a belief that the right approach can be found to make a change and that the approach will work. *Willing* refers to the importance of the change in one's life. It reflects the growing discomfort with the degree of discrepancy between the current conditions of life and the preferred goals and values. *Ready* refers to the person wanting the change at this time. Even if one believes in the importance of the change and appears confident, a "yes, but" attitude is a strong indicator of a lack of readiness to change.

The evidence suggests that professionals and peers may be able to help others be "ready, willing, and able" to make a desired change (Miller and Rollnick, 2002). Confidence and goals will be influenced by group norms, which is why we continually recommend supporting both individual and organizational change. For a professional or peer to support another person requires an ability to tolerate uncertainty and be flexible, have a good awareness of one's own thoughts and biases, good affect-tolerance skills, and refraining from jumping in with unwanted advice. Advice may be appropriate to inform or educate a person about options, but it may also disregard a person's previous experiences and life skills.

In summary, motivational interviewing is based on models of psychotherapy and behavioral change and has been influenced by the stages of change model. Naturally, the model takes into account that people may feel ambivalent about change. In fact, it may be an approach best suited to people who are not currently committed to or prepared to change their behavior, such as misusing alcohol or tobacco. Building on the work of Rogers (1957), the model emphasizes a nonjudgmental, empathic, and encouraging stance. It assumes that it is better for the individual or members of the organization to talk more than the counselors or consultants. With training the tools described above are useful for any health professional supporting and facilitating healthy change. Motivational interviewing in particular requires many fine micro skills that require training, practice and counseling experience. These approaches are easily integrated into other treatment approaches.

Behavior Change and Promoting Safe Drinking

Emergency professionals, like the general public, include people who experience substance abuse related problems. There is anecdotal and research evidence indicating that there is increased alcohol use after traumatic events or critical incidents (see chapter 5). Despite these findings we are surprised that little information on alcohol use and specifically on low risk drinking is offered routinely in emergency organizations and specifically post-disaster.

Not all drinking is problematic and a healthy lifestyle may include alcohol consumption that is in keeping with low risk drinking guidelines. The risk of family, health, social, financial, work-related problems, accidents, and injuries would be reduced, however, by following low risk drinking guidelines established for adults. These guidelines do not consider people who are older adults. Further, there are people, who should not drink, even at the low risk level, such as pregnant women, people with existing mental health or health problems, those on many prescribed medications or when one has to have their full attention or coordination to remain safe or keep others safe. It should be noted that some researchers have suggested that the guidelines are too high for it may be healthier to have one or two alcohol free days, further lowering the consumption level for men and women each week. The following are low risk drinking guidelines suggested by the Centre for Addiction and Mental Health (2002):

- Drinking no more than two standard drinks on any day
- Drinking less than 14 drinks each week for men
- Drinking 9 or less drinks each week for women
- Drinking 0 alcohol for those with health problems, pregnant, when participating in activities that require attention, coordination, and skill
- A standard drink equals 12 ounces of beer (5% alcohol), 5 ounces of table wine (12% alcohol), 1.5 ounces of alcohol (40% alcohol) or 3 ounces fortified wine (18% alcohol).

We believe these guidelines should be available to all organizations and professionals particularly after high risk, high stress events. The Centre for Mental Health and Addictions (CAMH) in Toronto has the information available on their web site and in pamphlet form: http://www.camh.net/about_addiction_mental_health/low_risk_drinking_guidelines.html

Given the prevalence of alcohol abuse in the general public, it is likely an emergency professional will encounter a colleague sometime in their career that shows signs of alcohol abuse. A healthy workplace is one where people take care of each other. As a minimum we encourage you to discuss your concerns with professionals, peers or programs that are knowledgeable about alcohol misuse or abuse. Approaching a colleague in difficulty can feel intrusive or that it risks tarnishing a colleague's reputation. We hope colleagues know how to draw the line about their drinking and knows when to seek support. If you choose to approach your colleague, do this with care and compassion and not with anger and blame. It is useful to describe the specific concerns that are worrisome and it is useful to share resources that can be helpful. The goal is to offer supportive listening and care. Be prepared for a range of responses from relief to anger. On the other hand this care may prevent further distress and the support may be a validation that the person is valued. If your concern continues consider seeking additional support and advice from knowledgeable professional and peers. As substance abuse escalates into dependency, even well-trained and usually reliable professionals may not recognize the tipping point at which their drinking is becoming harmful. Some people with substance dependence will not contact resources on their own behalf until there are increasing consequences and at times a crisis resulting from their behavior. If you are concerned about the safety of the person or the performance at work, it is necessary to discuss these issues with workplace supervisors and or professionals. Most organizations have mutual aid and professional support programs that can guide a concerned colleague or manager to respond to this as a health issue and not just a disciplinary issue.

Summary

Typically, organizational-level preventative interventions are aimed at educating individual staff members to change or modify their own behavior. One example of this is requiring people to attend a stress management workshop. The popularity of educational workshops is not surprising, for several reasons. First, the early history of stress theory and research focused on individual responses to stressors in the environment, with the assumption that the experience of stress was the result of individual deficiencies. This assumption, that the roots of stress are an individual matter rather than something influenced by their organization or the environment, has continued to influence organizational practices and strategies for stress reduction. Finally, despite widespread acknowledgement of stress in a workplace, there is still significant stigmatization of those affected. As we discussed earlier, moral or psychological weakness was blamed for trauma reactions in soldiers of the First World War (Copp and McAndrew, 1990). The stigma of health problems, particularly mental health concerns, remains a current dilemma. Educating employees on how to protect their own health and manage stress is useful; however, by over focusing on any one level of intervention we risk mismatching problems and the right intervention strategy—that is, failing do the right job at the right time. When stigma is also addressed through community and organizational efforts, there is a possibility of shifting the norms of a group, to view stress as an issue to face in a nonjudgmental manner.

Interventions related to trauma in the workplace cannot be simple, one-size-fits-all approaches. Rather, trauma response must be viewed as falling on a series of continuums that represent the type of intervention, the timing of intervention, the location or setting of interventions and the range of potential participants. Before any intervention strategy is planned, principles of intervention must be established and agreed upon. In our work, these principles include issues of respect for varied experiences and indigenous knowledge, acknowledgment of the importance of healthy living and working environments, and efforts to sustain programs long after the intervention is over. This requires that we begin at a preventative level aimed at decreasing health risks and stresses and increasing coping ability and trauma management capacity before traumatic events occur. Ideally this involves advocating for risk reduction and health enhancement in the community. In interventions with emergency service workers, it must at least begin at the organizational level. An increasing number of organizations have incorporated programs to promote health and reduce the risk of injury and illnesses. Many important qualities are associated with healthy organizations: (1) fair, respectful, trusting leadership; (2) clear and reliable communication; (3) organizational sensitivity to workplace health on both an individual and an organizational level; (4) clear role expectations and an interest to resolve role ambiguities and conflicts; (5) a good fit between workload demands and resources; (6) a balance between work efforts and rewards; (7) recognition that people develop and have different needs throughout their life spans; (8) meaningful opportunities for employees to participate in workplace health policy and planning; (9) effective communication and conflict-resolution skills; and (10) a broad range of health resources, including occupational health staff, Employee Assistance Programs, and peer-support programs. Types of intervention may target practical work tasks and roles, such as schedules and physical conditions at work, the use of protective equipment, interpersonal communication, and knowledge and skills for the job. Another type of intervention may examine the health and social conditions under which the tasks are performed.

At the individual level of intervention, prevention rests on assisting individuals to identify stresses and the consequences of stress, as well as healthy aspects of their lives. Intervention depends on enhancing the positive forces in people's lives and developing strategies for managing stressful situations more effectively. We must acknowledge, however, that change is difficult for both organizations and individuals. Therefore, various strategies are suggested for assisting organizations and the people within them to work toward healthy changes. With this foundation in place, we move in the next chapter to interventions that may assist at times of extreme stress and trauma.

10

THE CONTINUUM OF INTERVENTIONS II

Interventions for Extreme Stress

In our communities, emergency professionals are asked each day to do the right job at the right time—that is, to save a life or reduce the risk of injury or further harm, and to do it urgently. These highly trained professionals are particularly resilient but not immune to the effects of cumulative or extreme stress. In previous chapters we described the daily interactions between the workplace environment and individual factors that place an emergency professional on a trajectory toward health or health problems. We focused on ways to build strong organizations and support the wellbeing and resilience of professionals before lives are disrupted by extreme stress. In this chapter we will add to the discussion by reviewing a range of interventions for incidents usually perceived as extremely stressful, such as those involving the death of children, injuries to or the death of colleagues, and disasters, particularly those involving mass violence as discussed in chapter 5. These interventions may be primary, secondary, or tertiary prevention for those who are well but may face serious levels of risks, those who have faced extreme stress, and those who are showing signs of distress. Loosely they may be arranged on the timelines of pre-event, during the event, and post-event interventions, although the timelines are not precise about the type of intervention best suited to the specific event and which professionals should receive what intervention. Emergency professionals may be in the post-event stage of managing and infectious disease such as SARS while hearing warnings about a potential terrorist attack and unexpectedly dealing with a massive power failure. So while these interventions are presented in a timeline, it must be recognized that many emergency organizations and their personnel in the world are in several overlapping phases of post-event(s) recovery, in the midst of a current incident, and working to improve pre-event(s) training.

Extreme stress strains and depletes all human beings. Stress- and trauma-related interventions aim to maintain, repair, or restore the well-being of the staff by supporting their resilience and offering additional support and resources when professional personal resources are strained and depleted. Supporting the natural recovery environment—the workplace and the home environment—is a necessary part of a comprehensive range of approaches. This ecological perspective sees healthy, adaptive, and resilient lives in those people able to maintain a positive view of themselves and who possess flexible coping skills to regulate intense reactions and feelings, a willingness to learn or adapt skills throughout a career, the ability to establish and enjoy rewarding interpersonal relationships, and the ability to complete usual tasks of work and home life (Shalev and Ursano, 2003, Pearlman and Saakvitne, 1995). Previously we reviewed part of the continuum of interventions to support these aims: health promotion and prevention through organizational and leadership development; promoting team and individual health and well-being through education, stress reduction, and behavioral change approaches. Now we will focus on selected interventions designed for incidents of extreme stress, and in particular "early interventions" (Litz, 2004; Orner and Schnyder, 2003) which include:

- preparation through education and training
- peer support, referral and follow up
- psychological first aid
- consultation and liaison
- crisis intervention
- risk communication and media relations
- post traumatic stress treatments
- education and support sessions

Preparing for Extreme Stress

Preparation and training begins as all interventions begin, with the establishment of a trusting and respectful working relationship between organizational leaders, front-line professionals, peer support teams, and mental health professionals. Building cooperation between key people within an organization is essential to developing and maintaining supportive programs and resources for the staff. This process requires ongoing attention, as every service and its members encounter multiple competing demands on their resources and time. Without the active support and agreement of the leadership of an organization (or the command center at a disaster site), interventions can be undermined quickly.

Preparation through Education and Training

It is important to gain an understanding of the organization and personnel as it functions prior to an event. The assessment of the education and training to prepare staff should include all levels of management, supervisors, frontline emergency professionals, and administrative personnel. In keeping with the principles in the previous chapter, it is important to develop an understanding of the history of an involved organization, its culture, significant changes in its development, its policies and practices regarding staff health and well-being, and the relationships it has with other organizations. When an organization has mental health consultants and a peer support program in place, much of this information will be known over time. Having a previous history with the organization in terms of building collaboration, coordination, and capacity to deal with health issues is an excellent foundation for future trauma-related interventions. This also ensures that the preparation and planning have included health-related policies and practices within the organization, safety guidelines, stress management training, family education and support, and Employee Assistance Program resources.

An education and training preparation program accomplishes several objectives: it provides information on stressful and potentially traumatic events, normal reactions, and the recovery process; it reviews and expands on healthy and flexible coping approaches to match stressful demands and promote recovery; it builds social support among coworkers; and it reduces barriers to seeking help, such as isolation, stigma, and embarrassment. Education prepares people to be less vulnerable to extreme stress by reducing uncertainty, and helping people to appraise a situation in a way that supports their sense of competency, confidence, and control. Professionals should be aware that all human beings have cognitive and emotional limits as to how much unfamiliar information, danger, and uncertainty can be processed without becoming overwhelmed and distressed. People need support, resources, and time to process intense feelings of loss and distress. The recovery path is affected, as we have discussed, by the event, personal and work history, and the recovery environment—that is, the quality and quantity of organizational and social support. Emergency professionals usually possess excellent coping tools; however, under conditions of extreme or persistent stress, some approaches may create conflicting outcomes. Denial or avoiding discussing uncomfortable feelings may initially be helpful, but if the cost is isolating oneself from family, other difficulties may arise. The education and training for emergency organizations can include the health promotion and wellness programs outlined in the previous chapter. Programs that support healthy organizations and leadership as well as physical, social, and emotional well-being for the frontline staff are the first line of defense against escalating stress. Education would include the characteristics of a disaster or mass emergency and their effects on communities and emergency professionals as outlined in chapter 4.

Peer Support Programs

Peer support programs, and more specifically peer support teams, have formed the core of trauma-related intervention programs for the past several years. Nevertheless, even the early developers of these programs are adamant that they should be viewed as only one component of a more comprehensive range of services (Mitchell and Everly, 2000; Orner and Schnyder, 2003). In the aftermath of the September 11 terrorist attacks, interest in peer support programs has increased, and numerous communities have been working to develop and coordinate peer support teams and critical incident stress management efforts. Indeed, supporting the efforts of peer support teams in their natural environment is one of the best ways to promote health in the workplace. Peer support teams have many advantages, including having indigenous knowledge about the issues faced by the individual workers and the culture and politics of the organization. Peer support programs are also means by which to build capacity and sustainability of knowledge and skills in an organization over time. Peer teams also have challenges in establishing their roles, boundaries, ethics and well-being which require effective team selection, training, support and accountability, as we discuss in chapters 11 and 12.

Ideally, a well-prepared peer program and the availability of mental health consultants are established prior to a major event. Realistically, it is at times of extreme stress that new relationships between organizations, frontline staff, and mental health professionals are often forged. In the early stages of an event it is important to establish clear roles for all personnel, including the mental health professionals. Delineated roles, mutual expectations, and respect for one another's knowledge, values, and experience are necessary prior to any further actions. Peer teams and mental health professionals who are part of an organization typically are expected at a disaster. External teams are also frequently called upon, and few people are surprised by their arrival. It may seem obvious, but it is critical that uninvited peer support programs not go to a disaster scene and offer their services. In the early stages of extreme stress, this support from unknown people is not helpful. Not being part of a coordinated effort and not being familiar with an event or the conditions in rescue effort may jeopardize one's own well-being and that of others at the disaster scene. Depending on the country, trauma-related support efforts might be coordinated through regional or federal agencies. Trauma response teams consisting of peers and/or mental health professionals need to be coordinated within these structures.

It is important to ensure that peer supporters and mental health professionals arriving at a disaster scene are well trained, established, and are willing to be accountable to the command. Regardless of the nature of the team (external or internal), there is a need for team members to begin by observing in order to understand the circumstances of the event and the command structure. Team members must have their own clear guidelines regarding work hours and their roles. Potential health risks need to be addressed, and participants need to be clear about the possibility of dangers so that their involvement in their recovery effort is based on informed consent. We assume that team members' choice not to be involved in some aspects of work is a reflection of their self-awareness and self-regard. For instance, a peer supporter who was a parent of three children under seven chose not to be involved in psychoeducational sessions of recovery workers who were involved in the recovery of bodies of young children. He made a wise choice for himself and for the group. The development, training, and maintenance of peer support and trauma response teams are detailed in chapters 11 and 12.

Interventions during an Event

Psychosocial First Aid

A trauma response team that has established its role and relationship with the command staff has several useful functions in the early phase of a disaster, including establishing rest areas and providing for the basic needs of emergency workers—food, shelter, rest, comfort, and human contact. In addition, team members working in rest areas can provide feedback to the team leaders regarding their observations and assessments of working conditions, particularly dangers. One of the useful services and skills offered by mental health staff or peers under the supervision of mental health professionals in the field is psychosocial first aid, first described by Raphael (1986), which includes:

- ensuring the safety of people from immediate harm
- providing for basic needs such as water, food, warmth, shelter

- helping reduce physiological arousal and support the natural recovery process
- providing comfort, a human presence, and interaction
- offering empathy, listening, and validation
- providing information on resources or useful updates on the status or recovery of coworkers
- identifying ongoing basic needs and next steps of the recovery phase
- linking outside sources of support to the needs of emergency professionals.

These skills are offered on an as-needed basis. It is likely that an emergency professional acting in the role of peer support will primarily be required to provide for basic needs on-site and to engage in casual conversation or work-related information sharing. On-scene everyone is coping to his or her best abilities, and attempts to intrude or lead a person into an unwanted conversation are inappropriate and disrespectful. It is essential that any signs of distress are not defined in medical or mental health terminology. The stress reactions typically experienced during a traumatic event or disaster are a natural part of human beings coping with extreme stress. Nevertheless, at times exhausted individuals will require support to leave the scene. This must be accomplished quietly and respectfully and in a manner that allows the person to save face.

Consultation and Liaison during an Event

One of the most important functions mental health professionals can offer is as consultant and liaison to organizational leaders, peer support teams, and, during mass emergencies and disasters, the Emergency Operation Command Center. One of the more challenging tasks is the management of rescue recovery workers as valuable resources. Determining the hours of work, rotation among intense and dangerous work, and assessing fatigue factors are all critical decisions to be made regarding the safety and well-being of the emergency professionals. Our observation is that overwork and overextending oneself are common, particularly in the early stages of a disaster. In part this is due to the profound dedication of the emergency workers in performing their tasks; in part it is due to a culture that develops in which continuous work becomes the norm and expectation. In certain circumstances, such as during peacekeeping missions described by Lieutenant General Roméo Dallaire, who headed the UN mission in Rwanda, it can be a management strategy to keep people working until they drop, in order to avoid giving people the opportunity to consider the horror that surrounds them (Dallaire, 2003). It is, however, important to establish working norms and rules specific to the conditions of the event, which may have rescue and recovery efforts lasting for months. Physical conditions such as the inclement weather, exposure to toxic materials and other dangers, and the use of protective clothing will all affect the fatigue factor of the workers. Establishing rules regarding when someone must leave the scene not only reduces of risk of injury or accident due to fatigue but also gives permission for rest.

Risk Communication and the Media Relations

Risk communication begins with the recognition of a hazard or danger in the environment. When the public and emergency service professionals face hazards related to disasters and other stress events, they generally respond in a reasonable and civic-minded manner. Effective risk communication can support the typically healthy response to risk and risk management. In extreme events that we have worked on, it is surprising how little attention has been paid to risk communication for emergency professionals and their families. High-profile events that capture media attention, such as technological disasters, terrorist attacks, or epidemic illnesses, have a profound effect on the perception of risk. It is necessary at times to temper sensationalism, correct misinformation, or augment incomplete information.

Risk communication involves recognizing a hazard and then clarifying the risk of exposure, possible harm, and ways to protect against the hazard. The perception of risk may vary among the public, emergency professionals, and scientists. What does it mean when scientists in an urban area state air quality is at an acceptable level? To whom is it acceptable—manufacturers, healthy people who like to drive, or people with asthma? The perception of risk increases when a risk is seen as involuntary, inequitably distributed among groups, not having a beneficial aspect, not being under one's control, or being associated with dreaded adverse or irreversible outcomes (Covello, Peters, Wojtecki, and Hyde, 2001). Even the term *risk* can have multiple meanings, including value judgments about quality of life and the cost of life, and the acceptability of risk will vary among groups. For example, a society would tend to be more concerned about increased risks to children than to adults. In attempts to reduce risk, societies have established wide-ranging regulations regarding peanut butter, lawn darts, driving, seat belts, nuclear energy, guns, and weapons of mass destruction.

Risk communication must be part of a comprehensive intervention plan for emergency service professionals (Sandman, 2001). On disaster sites, we have often heard informal conversations about the risk of exposure to infection, toxic chemicals, or terrorist attacks. Often these conversations are in the context of safety for the emergency responder's family, rather than personal fears. There are three main areas in which risk communications can assist emergency responders to enhance their safety through the use of proper precautions and perform their jobs more effectively.

Provision of information regarding the day-to-day hazards and risks faced by members of their profession and means of self-protection. An example of this was providing ongoing information updates regarding the spread of AIDS and what paramedics and police officers should do when attacked or spit on by someone who claimed to be HIV-positive.

Provision of information regarding the risks encountered at disasters or other extreme stress events. For instance, at Ground Zero, what was the risk caused by airborne substances, and should emergency workers have worn masks? As it stood, some people wore full protective gear, some wore simple paper masks, and some wore no respiratory protection at all.

Delineating the role that emergency services workers can play in risk communication for the public. Many people in the community turn informally to local emergency service workers for information. If workers are unsure about the current state of a health risk, their lack of knowledge and frustration with not knowing can spread panic in the community. Conversely, simple information and safety strategies communicated by emergency workers can have a far-reaching effect.

The risks to the safety and security of the public emergency professionals and their families are important considerations during an extreme event. The concerns and issues raised by emergency professionals need to be addressed as part of an overall intervention strategy. Risk communication can be a part of the routine part of organizational safety and health practices and requires additional steps at specific events such as disasters. The SARS situation in Toronto was a prime example where risk communication was vital. As noted in chapter 4, communications regarding SARS continued to change on an hourly basis as information was gathered regarding the nature of the illness, its mechanism for transmission, and its lethality. Paramedics and hospital workers involved in the first cases worked with limited infection control procedures and thus were quarantined, as were many of their families. As the first deaths were announced through the media, the general public began to panic. Sometime later, when it was revealed that the early deaths occurred in people with other health-related problems, fears subsided, but then were raised again among health care and emergency service workers with the death of the first health care worker. At these times of extreme stress, established, trusting relationships among various levels of an organization and between emergency service organizations are vital. Many of the suggestions in the previous chapter can help build a cohesive, trusting organization.

Demonstrating openness to hearing and clarifying the perceptions of risk and associated feelings of concern is an additional key step to addressing risk issues. Minimizing or avoiding the concerns of front-line staff and/or their families at this stage only serves to undermine future credibility of risk communication efforts. Working collaboratively among organizations, public officials, front-line staff, and the relevant scientific community requires more than exchange of information. Information sharing requires building a common language and a mutual understanding of the issues. A lack of mutual understanding leads to incomplete messages, issues being missed or avoided, or an escalation of conflicts and suspicions.

Emergency service organizations are in the business of risk management on a daily basis and often may be effective in understanding and creating risk communication. At times of extreme events, however, they may benefit from outside consultation from risk communication professionals. When an organization is stretched by extreme events, it is useful to bring in additional resources to assist in developing an accurate understanding of the issues, and to assist in creating a clear and reliable trustworthy message. There are differences in opinion as to how to manage lack of agreement among scientists or leaders. One view is that credibility is enhanced when leaders acknowledge differences or incomplete information and reveal their plans on how they are attempting to address those gaps or differences. This approach suggests that treating frontline staff or the public as capable partners builds respect and trust and the credibility of risk communication efforts. A role for peer support teams and mental health professionals in this effort is to observe and be aware of the risks and hazards developing at a large-scale emergency or disaster. The responsibility of these team members can include forwarding information to their own team leaders, who recycle that information up to key leaders at the scene. In keeping with appropriate boundaries, it is not the role of peer support or mental health professionals to create risk communication messages unless they are specifically delegated to that function.

Many of these issues will be raised and discussed in the media. Organizations typically have key spokespersons who are responsible for addressing and maintaining relationships with the media. At large events, however, it is not uncommon for the media to approach any emergency professional involved in the rescue and recovery work. A discussion of the role of the media at large-scale events is beyond the scope of this chapter. Nevertheless, it is our experience that responding with "No comment" tends not to be an effective response to the media. On the other hand, not every emergency professional should be expected to be a spokesperson. We do believe that every emergency professional should become familiar with the roles of the media and learn to respond in a simple and practical manner. Directing the media to the appropriate people in an organization is a useful skill, as reflected in the following statements: "I am unable to answer that right now, but I know someone in the organization who you can speak to about that issue," and "Thanks for your question and interest, let me give you the name and number of one of my coworkers who can assist you with more information." At times an emergency professional may be asked not about details of the incident but rather for their own specific feelings and reactions to the event. An organization may have its own guidelines around media relations. However, we would also support professionals in knowing that they can respectfully decline to discuss a specific question or issue at the time and refer the media to other resources in the organization. The media can be both valued and vilified at times of extreme stress, as they can be a source of information that can alleviate or escalate concerns or misunderstandings. Establishing an effective working relationship with the media is part of today's emergency service work. Emergency providers should become familiar with the roles of the media and their functions and work toward establishing mutually respectful relationships. At times of extreme stress, the media are actually one of the community's most powerful assets, with the potential to disseminate key safety messages and practical suggestions in an effective manner.

Crisis Intervention

As discussed in chapters 3 and 5, crisis occurs when people experience adversity that exceeds their coping skills and resources. At the time of the crisis, people feel uncertain, and in the moment they are overwhelmed by the challenges of the adversity. There may be a range of physical, emotional, cognitive, and interpersonal signs of distress. Everyone at some point may feel unable to meet the challenges of life. The unexpected loss of a loved one or the accumulation of strain over time may lead any person to temporarily feel a sense of crisis. Emergency service professionals work on a day-to-day basis with people who are experiencing a crisis in their lives. Yet despite the resiliency and experience of emergency professionals, they too at times may experience a sense of uncertainty or unfamiliarity and wonder what the best approach may be to cope with the loss of a colleague or the accumulation of months or years of work stress. People in general, and in particular emergency service professionals, are for the most part able to overcome these crises on their own with the support of family, friends, or coworkers. Feeling temporarily overwhelmed at some point in life is not uncommon, and most people are resilient and find their way through these challenging times. There may be times, however, when the tools of crisis intervention can be useful in supporting a person through a crisis phase of their lives. Effective crisis intervention rests with effective interpersonal communication between the person experiencing the crisis and a peer support or professional responding to the crisis.

While there are many approaches to crisis intervention, an example of a sound approach to crisis intervention is Roberts's stages model of crisis intervention. Crisis intervention is a goal-directed, time-limited intervention aimed at resolving present problems in living (Roberts, 2000). The Roberts model of crisis intervention includes:

- Planning and conducting an assessment, including assessing any risk of harm to the individual or others
- Establishing rapport and demonstrating respect, acceptance, and a nonjudgmental attitude
- Identifying dimensions of the present problem and the precipitating events while using active listening, and validating the emotions and reactions of the individual
- Describing, exploring, and assessing previous coping attempts, the resources, and the coping skills of the person
- Developing and formulating an action plan
- Establishing a follow-up plan and agreement.

This model is intended to support people first in using their own resources and skills as they try to problem-solve their way through the current crisis. The role of the peer support person or mental health professional in crisis intervention is to assist the responder to feel some sense of stability, and renew their sense of self-efficacy as they attempt to resolve their concerns. Crisis intervention also includes supporting the responders to mobilize the resources in his or her network to assist them at this time. In the beginning stages, an individual is asked to simply tell the story of the crisis and what lead to the current circumstances. This provides an opportunity to also learn about significant relationships and any other significant strains, including health problems that may be contributing to the crisis. Discussing the disadvantages and advantages of coping approaches may support the responder in making wiser choices—for example, what are the benefits or disadvantages of having a few extra drinks. One of the important aspects of this assessment is to consider the cultural and contextual factors that influence the meaning of the events for the responder.

The crisis intervention approach assumes that people possess the capability to be competent at managing the strains of life. Under conditions of excessive demands, such as numerous weeks of work in a mass disaster, most professionals' resources will be diminished. The strain of these unusual events may have contributed to the emergency responder's feelings of uncertainty, fatigue, and distress. This is an opportunity to support, validate, and assist someone in using a full range of healthy coping skills to resolve concerns. A focus on the here and now allows people to address their most immediate concerns. A focus on strengths and hope for the future builds confidence and helps mobilize coping skills. It is reasonable to assume that emergency professionals have a high level of functioning, and it is likely that they will soon overcome the challenges that they may face. Nevertheless, a useful follow-up plan is helpful, particularly if there is a peer support program available.

Common Barriers to Effective Support during an Event

In our experience of responding to large-scale disasters, frequently certain conditions limit the effectiveness of interventions. Attending to these issues throughout all phases of mass emergencies and disasters in the preplanning phase or early in the event phase can greatly enhance the quality of services provided.

Logistical barriers often stem from poor coordination and include problems related to transportation, communication, accommodation, food, and opportunities for rest for trauma response team members. Practical matters also include the availability of adequate clothing for the season, protective clothing, and protective devices.

Organizational barriers include work assignments and roles that are unclear. On several occasions we arrived at a disaster site educational session to discover that other peer teams and EAP services had also arrived to offer their services. The need to coordinate and negotiate roles at this time is vital for the well-being of the emergency professionals. At some disasters or ongoing extreme-stress events there may be hundreds of peer supporters and mental health professionals providing services. Managing the workload, hours of service, and days of service is an important organizational task. Keeping track of the intensity of the work and the number of days worked is useful. Providing opportunities for peer support and mental health professionals to review their own work and receive support on an ongoing basis is vital. Establishing the steps and clear expectations or norms at the beginning of their work is essential, including the opportunities for self-care. At one point during a disaster, supporters who went for a run to relieve tension were considered to be avoiding opportunities for work. The discomfort they felt was related to the team not having a norm regarding the importance of self-care.

Technical or clinical barriers include not having the range of skills required to work in a mass event. As skillful as an emergency unit mental health professional may be, working at a disaster scene requires working under very different and at times extreme conditions. The capacity to work in unfamiliar settings, around noise, and under what may appear to be chaotic circumstances is important. Equally important for mental health professionals is to be able to value the importance of providing for basic needs, such as providing juice or water and social conversation as well as providing "treatment." For some people, providing practical support may not feel like meaningful work. Clinically, it is important that professionals and peers respect peoples' coping styles and not disregard the needs of emergency professionals by asking intrusive and probing questions, particularly in the early stages. Clinical errors include having a person exceed their own need to talk, to probe or force emotions they are unwilling to discuss and tolerate, to challenge or interfere with usual coping strategies, and to give advice, lecture, or argue with a person who holds alternate views.

Operating with inadequate knowledge of the circumstances, context, and culture shows a disregard for the responders and their situation. In the course of a disaster, one may come across community volunteers, police, firefighters, forensic investigators, military responders, and medical personnel. Each group has its own culture, and within each culture, every individual will have his or her own unique qualities as well. Assuming that the culture of all emergency services or personnel is the same shows a disregard for the importance of taking time to establish a rapport or working relationship with each group.

Ideological errors include choosing interventions based on one's belief system and biases rather than considering both personal practice wisdom and the research evidence that supports the effectiveness of an intervention. In the field of mental health, addictions, and disaster work, a variety of models and approaches address the health needs of citizens and emergency professionals. A prepackaged service or intervention disregards context and culture. Choosing a single course of action based on ideology, or imposing beliefs about the need for mental health interventions for emergency workers following traumatic events, can be detrimental.

Post-Event Interventions

It is useful in considering specific interventions with individuals following experiences of extreme stress to return to the continuum of traumatic responses found in figure 5.1. Some people will experience a crisis response or acute stress response following exposure to extreme stress events. For these individuals, symptoms may abate within a few days or weeks, but crisis intervention can be useful in assisting them to manage a tough time and mobilize their personal resources. Others may experience acute stress disorder, which while also relatively short-lived, is accompanied by significant trauma symptoms. For these individuals, crisis intervention during the acute phase accompanied by trauma-specific treatments may be useful. Finally, some individuals will develop post-traumatic stress disorder and require more intensive trauma-related treatments.

Symptom-Focused Trauma Treatment

In times of extreme stress, people can experience not only crisis reactions but also symptoms of acute stress disorder, including intrusive thoughts and images and physiological and psychological arousal (see chapter 5). People indicate that they can be plagued with repetitive thoughts about the traumatic event that seem to replay like a tape on an endless loop. Others experience extreme anxiety that they will have flashbacks of the event and will spend a great deal of time avoiding stimuli that may potentially trigger negative reactions—for instance, the paramedic who described an inability to drive into a particular part of town where an event occurred, or the flight attendant who was unable to go anywhere near the airport. These symptoms cause considerable distress, so assisting individuals to gain some type of control over the occurrence of symptoms can be very useful. There is considerable evidence that the use of some simple cognitive-behavioral techniques can be highly effective in reducing stress symptoms (Follette, Ruzek, and Auberg, 1998; Rothbaum and Foa, 1996). Some basic skills can be easily taught to responders for reducing tension and regaining focus at times of extreme stress. These skills include distraction or thought-stopping techniques to reduce focus on repetitive thoughts; rehearsal and positive self-talk; and breathing and relaxation techniques. This section describes some simple techniques that can be used to manage symptoms. Each of these techniques is consistent with the aims of psychosocial first aid and crisis intervention. More intensive treatments that build on these techniques are found below in the section on post-traumatic stress treatment.

Distraction is a technique that builds on avoidance strategies people naturally engage in when dealing with trauma. While it may be argued that one cannot avoid thoughts about the trauma forever, these thoughts are likely to have reduced power to cause distress once the initial crisis period after a traumatic event has passed. Distraction then encourages people to engage in activities that are pleasurable and do not remind them of the event. For instance, if seeing movies is a distraction that responders have used successfully at other times in their lives, they should rent or go to a movie that will not trigger memories of the event. For others, playing hockey or doing something with their children may be a distraction. The key is that the responder is making a conscious decision to choose activities that will be distracting, and thus he or she begins to feel some control over the intrusive thoughts or images. Distraction can be used for a particularly distressing symptom, night terrors. When someone is awakened by a nightmare, they frequently experience not only psychological arousal, but also sweating and a pounding heart. Lying in bed and trying to will oneself back to sleep at these times is futile and can lead to hours awake in which frustration grows.

People experiencing these problems are encouraged to get up from bed and do something distracting and soothing, such as reading, drinking hot chocolate, or watching TV. If the responder is also experiencing repetitive thoughts and images at those times, it is helpful to "get the thought out." This may involve talking into a tape recorder, calling someone who doesn't mind talking in the middle of the night, or writing the thoughts and images down. This process tends to break the cycle of thoughts and allow for rest.

If repetitive thoughts persist and are resistant to simple distraction techniques, *thought-stopping* can be another helpful strategy. In the thought-stopping technique, individuals are encouraged to identify persistent thoughts or images over which they feel they have no control. Following a tragic event, it is common that these thoughts involve self-blame, such as "If I would have done that differently, she would not have died." People experiencing these thoughts are directed to identify what alternate image or thought they may wish to substitute for the disturbing or maladaptive thought. Individuals are then asked to identify an effective way of stopping this thought. For some, it is effective to begin with a step where they set a timer for one minute, during which they will focus on the disturbing thought. When the timer goes off, they must force the negative thought from their mind and replace them with a positive reframing of the situation or positive self-talk. As the responder develops mastery of this technique, he or she can develop more subtle ways of stopping the thoughts, such as shaking his or her head slightly or snapping an elastic band on his or her wrist.

Some people must face difficult situations despite the fact that they cause distress. Assuming that the distress is not immobilizing, simple strategies can be used to assist them in managing the anxiety associated with the task. The technique of rehearsal is illustrated vividly in the urban legend about a famous golfer who envisions a good shot in his mind 1,000 times before actually swinging a club. Similarly, individuals can be encouraged to rehearse events that they negatively anticipate and imagine positive results. For instance, a paramedic can rehearse answering a call and envision himself or herself to be competent in managing the crisis and in control of his or her emotions and the situation. Positive self-talk, in which people assure themselves that they are knowledgeable, competent, and in control, can also help in this situation.

There are two major strategies for dealing with arousal symptoms such as a racing heart, anxiety, or irritability. For some individuals, exercise is the best approach. Putting the excessive energy to positive use yields relief from the intensity of emotions. Other individuals can effectively use relaxation techniques. These techniques generally begin with breathing techniques that may subsequently be augmented by guided imagery or progressive muscle relaxation. Some simple breathing exercises are outlined below.

Breathing: Reducing Tension—Regaining Focus Exercise

Learning a few basic breathing exercises is particularly useful; they can be applied in just about any circumstance. When people are experiencing significant challenges or feeling considerable strain, it is common for their breathing to become rapid. They may even find themselves holding a breath momentarily. These exercises will only take a moment of attention. Staying settled and focused when facing extreme stress with multiple demands is a particularly useful skill. Here are two brief exercises, which can be done while sitting or standing anywhere and anytime, affording a moment to reduce tension and regain focus.

Exercise 1

Begin by just noticing your breathing. Just notice breathing in and breathing out. Breathe slowly and steadily, as air enters and leaves your body. Just for a moment notice how your breath enters and fills your lungs and then how your body can exhale fully to be ready for the next full breath.

Notice whether your breathing involves your abdomen. As your abdomen rises and falls with each breath, it actually allows more oxygen to fully enter and leave your lungs. Just take a moment to be attentive to your breathing and how breathing with your abdomen gives you a fuller and more relaxed breath.

Exercise 2

Using abdominal breathing, one can take any moment as an opportunity for 60 seconds of attention to steady, full breathing. You can begin to simply count 10 cycles of breathing. As a breath enters and then leaves, that is one count, as another breath enters and then leaves, that is two and so on. Another version of this exercise is to go to a higher count, such as 50, or to go for 3 minutes on your watch.

Simply counting up to 10 is a useful way to help settle the body by taking in oxygen. This process sharpens your focus and concentration for a moment. Some emergency professionals do this exercise two or three times routinely each day.

Post-Traumatic Stress Treatment

As we have discussed, people become overwhelmed for a number of reasons related to their individual characteristics and resources, the nature of the event, and the quality of the psycho-social resources following the trauma. Most people recover over time, yet the above circumstances unfold to interfere with the natural recovery process. A person may not have the collections of symptoms that lead to a diagnosis of post-traumatic stress and yet may have significant disruption in his or her life. Alternatively, those with post-traumatic stress disorder, as discussed previously, often have co-occurring physical health problems or depression, and at times experience secondary problems, such as substance abuse, a coping response "gone wrong."

Treatment, or at least a consultation, is indicated when responders experience persistent difficulties in their relationships, changes in their work performance or productivity, withdrawal from usually pleasurable activities, continual symptoms of anxiety or depression, and/or deteriorating health as noted by fatigue, poor sleep, over- or undereating, or persistent aches and pains. A physical health examination is a useful starting point to other psychosocial treatments. Psychotherapy or counseling is offered by accredited professionals such as social workers, psychologists, counselors, and physicians who have been specifically trained in the treatment of trauma-related problems. Not every therapist or counselor is trained or experienced in working with clients with extreme stress-related issues. Referrals or the names of competent professionals may be obtained through an EAP service, family physician, professional associations, or at times through colleagues or friends who have heard of a trusted therapist. Clarifying the experience and the credentials of a therapist is an important step for a person considering therapy. Further, demystifying the process of treatment can be of assistance, as movies and television generally have not portrayed the therapy process accurately or usefully. For instance, the responder may be informed that the relationship between a person and the therapist is as vital to the success of the treatment as are the knowledge and skills of the therapist. A person can expect to feel that the therapist listens and responds in a respectful, empathic, and understanding manner. Thus, if the fit with the therapist does not feel right, it is a good idea to discuss this with the therapist. If the concerns persist, consider another consultation.

Many treatments are available to people experiencing persistent distress associated with trauma-related events (see Solomon and Johnson [2002] for a practical review). *Psychodynamic treatment* focuses on the importance of early life experiences and the manner in which traumatic experiences integrate into one's sense of self. *Hypnotherapy* allows the traumatized responder to express repressed traumatic material and subsequently integrate the traumatic event. While both these therapies are used extensively, to date there are no controlled studies that evaluate the efficacy of psychodynamic treatment or hypnotherapy alone in treating trauma. In the many excellent reviews and meta-analyses of research related to treatment efficacy for traumatized individuals, it is generally acknowledged that only cognitive-behavioral and psychopharmacological methods have been subject to rigorous evaluation with controlled trials (Ehlers and Clark, 2003; Hembree and Foa, 2003; Katz, Pellegrino, Pandya, Ng, and DeLisis, 2002; Solomon and Johnson, 2002). This is not, however, to say these are the only treatments that work. Pharmacological treatment for trauma sufferers has yielded positive results in assisting with symptom management. In particular, selective serotonin reuptake inhibitors (SSRIs) have shown positive results (Albucher and Liberzon, 2001), mood stabilizers have shown promise (Albucher and Liberzon, 2001; Katz et al., 2002), as have beta blockers (Katz et al., 2002). Rothbaum and Foa (1996), Follette, Ruzek, and Abueg (1998), and Harvey, Bryant, and Tarrier (2003) provide extensive overviews of the effectiveness of cognitive-behavioral approaches for post-traumatic stress disorder. They conclude that cognitive-behavioral therapy (CBT) is effective in reducing the severity of PTSD symptoms in individuals who have experienced a wide range of traumatic events and in individuals who suffer from both acute and chronic symptoms. CBT treatment has been demonstrated to have superior effects over supportive treatment in the treatment of PTSD in a number of controlled studies (Bryant, Sackville, Dang, et al., 1999).

Cognitive therapies come in a variety of forms. *Exposure therapy* is based on the notion that the common strategy of avoiding trauma-related memories and cues interferes with emotional processing of the event by reinforcing erroneous cognitions and fears. With the assistance of a trained therapist, responders are encouraged to imagine the traumatic situation and in doing so experience the symptoms that accompany the image. During this imaginal exposure and while recounting the event, individuals are assisted in managing the resulting symptoms through relaxation and breathing techniques. Once they have successfully mastered this, they are encouraged to gradually expose themselves to situations that remind them of the traumatic event and similarly cause distress and again work to manage the symptoms. The theory is that with repeated experiences of exposure and ongoing work on symptom mastery, the distress will habituate. *Stress inoculation training*, based on social learning theory, similarly teaches individuals to manage fear and anxiety through cognitive-behavioral techniques.

Cognitive therapy is based on the theory that each individual develops a set of beliefs about the world and about themselves in the world. These beliefs shape how new situations and information will be interpreted. Thus, an event or situation is viewed as threatening, positive, or benign based on preexisting ideas. For instance, for some individuals, an airplane trip represents an opportunity to see exciting places and thus is viewed very positively; for others it is viewed as potentially fatal. Cognitive therapy assists individuals in identifying trauma-related dysfunctional beliefs that influence response to stimuli and subsequent physiological and psychological distress. The nature and origin of the belief are considered, and evidence that supports or refutes the belief is weighed by the individual. If the belief is indeed dysfunctional, the therapist works to assist the individual to modify it or replace it with a more adaptive belief.

Some researchers have provided evidence that exposure therapy in combination with stress inoculation training or cognitive therapy yields the most positive results (Hembree and Foa, 2003); others have provided evidence that inoculation does not necessarily enhance other cognitive methods and that provided alone, they are equally effective (Harvey et al., 2003; Tarrier et al., 1999b). It is important to note that exposure methods are more selective in the criteria for inclusion and it is suggested that this model of treatment should be used only when a sound therapeutic alliance has been formed and a thorough assessment has been completed (Calhoun and Atkeson, 1991). Individuals in this type of treatment group should have the capacity to tolerate high anxiety arousal, have no active suicidal ideation, no co-morbid substance abuse, and, most importantly, no current life crises (Foy et al., 2000). Thus, if they are equally effective, CBT methods without exposure may yield a lower risk of iatrogenic effects.

Post-Event Education and Support Groups

A range of educational and support groups also called psychosocial educational groups, have been developed and offered for a wide range of illnesses, mental health and substance abuse problems for at least thirty years (Brown, 2004). They have specific purposes or goals, structure and time frames, which differ from ongoing psychotherapy groups. One type of these groups is a crisis debriefing which is usually a single session group offered to emergency responders and others following a shared traumatic event. Generally the purposes of crisis debriefing groups include providing information, education and skill development, sharing common experiences, building support between group members, and developing opportunities for support outside of the group. The purposes can also be described as validating and normalizing people's reactions and the natural course of recovery, educating people about the course of recovery, sharing information about the event, identifying sources of tangible, social or emotional support outside of the group, and reviewing coping skills and their relative advantages and disadvantages (Howard and Goelitz, 2004). The leader needs to be well trained in facilitating groups, and be knowledgeable about group dynamics. They must purposefully use a number of micro skills such as active listening and recognition of verbal and non-verbal communication. Group leaders need to be clear about the content, who the appropriate participants for the designed session are, and what are the benefits of attending the group session.

Crisis debriefing groups can promote a sense of resiliency and efficacy at both the individual and group level. They can provide support when individuals or the group feel depleted after a major event and/or the accumulation of daily hassles. They can empower people with information, skills and support, and reduce stigma, blame and actions that can exacerbate the problem, while promoting the healthy personal and social conditions for recovery (Furr, 2000). These supportive sessions may be particularly helpful when potentially traumatic events have depleted the natural support system in a family, work group or organization.

There is considerable discussion in the trauma field regarding the use of debriefing as an intervention. While there are several positive aspects to debriefing, including the social support, and cognitive-behavioral strategies for adaptive coping, there are concerns, however, that debriefing may not reduce symptoms, and that the exposure to trauma-related stories may actually increase distress. The research regarding the positive and negative aspects of debriefings is reviewed extensively in chapter 13. What is clear is that it is unreasonable to expect that single session psychoeducational support groups can prevent any specific illness or health problem such as depression, PTSD or migraines or diabetes. At this point, however, it is useful to consider how to take the positive aspects of debriefing and modify the techniques that may pose a risk.

Previously, we proposed the following model for educational and support sessions based on the best available empirical evidence of effectiveness (Regehr, 2001). This modified approach to a crisis debriefing model builds on the strengths of models presented by the pioneers and in this area (Raphael, 1986; Mitchell and Everly, 1993) and modifies aspects that may be counterproductive. A similar approach was also described by Ruzek (2002) in his work at the Pentagon following the terrorist attacks.

Introduction
The group begins with a discussion of the purpose of the meeting and an expression of support for the members who have shared a traumatic experience. The group leaders are introduced in order to establish credibility. In addition, ground rules for respectful interactions are discussed.

Shared Understanding
In the CISD model Mitchell and Everly (1993) advise that debriefers collect as much information as possible about the event prior to beginning a debriefing. This is reinforced by Dyregrov (1997), who focuses attention on the prior preparation of the leaders. In addition to this preparation, a brief factual review of the event, as suggested by Everly, Lating, and Mitchell (2000), can be an important tool for creating an alliance between leaders and group members through a shared understanding of the event and expressions of empathy. This component of the debriefing

*could help answer questions regarding the event, fill in gaps in infor-
mation, and therefore assist participants to develop a more comprehensive understanding of what has occurred. Frequently, workers will not
have seen colleagues during the event and have worried about their
safety. This discussion is not meant to be graphic in nature but rather
gives a description of how the event unfolded for each member. Updates,
if any are available, on the state of colleagues who were injured are provided.*

Impact of Experience

*The impact of the experience is discussed, including current emotional,
physical, and cognitive symptoms experienced by participants. In addition, discussion may be held around the impacts on relationships with
family and friends emanating from the experience and subsequent symptoms. Leaders normalize the reactions through education and through
drawing parallels between the experiences of group members.*

Strategies for Coping

*Participants are given an opportunity to discuss their strategies for cop-
ing (both maladaptive and adaptive) and the effectiveness of these strategies for reducing distress. Group members are invited to make suggestions to one another regarding effective symptom management. Leaders
acknowledge the strengths of participants and then present cognitive-
behavioral strategies for managing acute symptoms.*

Mobilizing of Social Supports

*Leaders identify strengths in the interactions between coworkers attend-
ing the debriefing. They are encouraged to continue to support one another. In addition, the group works to identify strategies to engage others
in the personal support network of participants.*

Wrap-Up

*During the wrap-up, participants are thanked for their willingness to en-
gage and share. Strengths are reinforced and opportunities for follow-up
are provided.*

A further caution about the use of crisis debriefing groups is that they must
be placed in the context of a positive working relationship with the organization and its members. Although there is a natural inclination for professionals or peer teams to offer education and support at mass emergencies,
doing so outside of the cooperation of an organization disregards the importance of assessment, effective working relationships, and informed consent. Assessment begins with understanding the event, the people, and the
organization involved, along with the available resources and support. Intervention must be based on this understanding and respectful collabora-

tion with those involved. It is not uncommon to hear stories of debriefing disasters that cause an organization to view the current intervention with suspicion.

Intervention Example—Emergency Workers and Body Recovery

As an example of applying the continuum of interventions to situations of extreme stress, let us consider the case of body recovery following a mass casualty or disaster. Recovery of bodies by emergency professionals is among the most challenging tasks. Several research studies have pointed to the increased levels of traumatic stress and distress in those individuals directly responsible for handling human remains following a disaster when compared to rescue workers with other tasks at the event (McCarroll et al., 1995; McCarroll et al., 1996). Factors associated with increased distress include length of exposure to remains, the gruesomeness of remains, the perceived threat to the emergency worker, and identification with the victim. In addition to the difficulties associated with the task, a number of other factors contribute to increased distress as a result of performing this work, including lack of previous experience or preparation (McCarroll et al., 1996), poor relationships with management, and responders feeling they were not valued for their skills (Thompson, 1993). Increased distress is not necessarily the only outcome of doing this work. Following the Oklahoma City bombing, while individuals who were involved in the recovery of human remains had low levels of post-traumatic stress and depression, there was higher reported use of alcohol in the study by North and colleagues (2002a). Social supports from both family and management have been found to mitigate the trauma responses experienced by emergency workers doing body recovery (McCarroll et al., 1996; Thompson, 1993).

A number of strategies for providing assistance to body recovery workers have been reported that fall along the continuum of pre-event, on-the-scene, and postevent intervention (Ursano et al., 1999). In our experience, the level of preparation, training, and orientation to the work of body recovery varies among emergency service organizations. Pre-event interventions include education regarding the recovery and identification process, and highlighting the meaning and value of this work for surviving family and friends. Focusing not only on the technical aspects of the job, but also on the benefits to others helps reduce the sense of futility associated with work when there is no one left to save.

Prior to working onsite it is important that personnel are briefed as to the nature of the events and conditions of their work environments and human remains. For instance, following the crash of Swiss Air off the coast of Peggy's Cove, one of the tasks to be performed was retrieval of remains from the ocean. Local workers, RCMP, and Transportation Safety Board investigators were recruited to work on a barge 6 kilometers off the coast. A large crane lowered a shovel onto the ocean floor and then dumped an enormous pile onto the barge deck for sorting. One never knew whether this load would hold fish, rocks, parts of the aircraft, personal effects, or body parts. Trauma response team workers were asked to provide short educational sessions to the workers prior to their deployment. In our experience, many workers showed tremendous resistance to these sessions. What quickly became clear was that most of the workers had not been briefed prior to their shift. The greatest assistance was provided by describing the recovery site including the layout of the barge and the crane. Workers crowded around and asked questions as the session became relevant to their immediate needs. There was opportunity to discuss and validate past coping efforts and successes. It was then possible to also approach some of the psychological coping strategies that they might employ both on the scene and after the event. On-scene coping strategies such as cognitive reframing and distancing to avoid overidentification are useful strategies that we have learned from colleagues in the emergency services (see chapter 5).

Organizing the work and rotations of staff is the role of on-site leaders and needs to be considered in the context of larger work conditions and circumstances. In preparation for this work, there needs to be access to rest areas that provide food, shelter, and other basic comfort. Access to supportive peers for the opportunity for contact and general conversation is also useful. Following the event, it is important to recognize and validate the importance of the personnel and their work. Support and educational sessions and the opportunity to discuss reactions and stress reduction techniques are also useful. A brief review of low-risk drinking guidelines may be helpful, given the research on excessive alcohol use as one coping strategy. As previously discussed, low-risk drinking guidelines suggest that drinking levels that may not harm a person's health if they remain at 0 consumption for special populations such as people already with health problems (diabetes, heart conditions); 2 drinks maximum on any day for men and women; and 9 drinks maximum for non-pregnant women weekly and 14 drinks maximium for men weekly. Last, it is vital to establish long-term plans for support. Personnel who have been involved in the difficult work of body recovery should be aware of how they can access information and support for an extended period of time.

Community Work

Discussing ways to building a supportive and cohesive community exceeds the scope of this book, but in many ways it is what this book is about. Healthy communities and healthy workplaces are directly linked to the health status of individuals. Unfortunately, much of the extreme stress that occurs is a result of direct violence or injury between people, or because of neglecting to do something to safeguard the well-being and security of people, as evidenced in mass violence, some technological disasters, and other large-scale emergencies related to human actions. Earlier we noted that well-being is more than the absence of injury or illness. Health seems to follow when communities and workplaces include a sense of fairness, justice, and balance in rewards and efforts, while people feel they can influence their life and community. Judith Herman (1992) notes the importance of people moving from alienation to connection to their community as they recover from trauma. Irishman Brian Keenan was held captive for 4 1/2 years in a suburb of Beirut. (Americans may be more familiar with Terry Anderson, who was held captive at the same time.) Keenan (1993), who endured numerous incidents of beatings, humiliation, and isolation wrote:

> There were many other incidents in this hole in the ground. But each of them was an affirmation of human capacity to overcome despair. I could write at length and try to reveal each of those situations, some hilariously funny, some pathetic, others undignifying and ignoble, but that is not my purpose. For each of these incidents revealed what each and all of us are. We are all made of many parts; no man is singular in the way he lives his life. He only lives it fully in relation to others. (p. 277)

Bishop Tutu reminds us that we have survived and changed as humans because we are civic minded and "built for peace."

11

LAYING THE FOUNDATION
Developing Trauma Response Teams

Trauma response teams are now found within most communities and many emergency service organizations. They provide a range of services to emergency response workers, their organizations, and their communities, and they are now viewed as essential parts of almost every emergency preparedness plan. In order for these teams to be effective, considerable preparation and effort must go into the design of the team, the articulation of team mandates and functions, the selection and training of team members, and the ongoing maintenance and administration of the team. As we have repeatedly stated, the participation of emergency response professionals as integral team members serves to enhance the team significantly. The inclusion of "peers" allows for localized knowledge about the issues faced by emergency service workers and the culture and politics of the organizations in which they work. Including members of the community and organization also builds capacity and promotes the sustainability of knowledge and skills over time.

Deciding on a Team Format

Trauma response teams come in many variations with regard to participating agencies, professional backgrounds of team members, number of team members, and responsibilities of team members. Thus, in determining a team format, a number of questions must be addressed.

Should Membership Be from One Agency or Many Agencies?

Some trauma response teams select members from only one organization. For instance, many police, fire, and paramedic organizations have their own teams that provide services specifically to members of that organization. These teams have the strength of knowing the issues in the organization intimately. Depending on the size of the organization and the team, ideally some members will be known and others unknown to all people in the organization, so a choice can be made by any individual after a traumatic event whether to talk to someone with whom they have or do not have a prior relationship. Other teams function as interagency teams, where members of various response organizations join together to provide service in the event of a traumatic occurrence. The trauma response team that we coordinate at Pearson International Airport in Toronto is such a team. Each member of the team represents an agency that would be involved in a response should a crash occur at Pearson. Thus team members are employees of four fire and emergency services, two policing agencies, the airport authority, air carriers, and first-response hospitals. The strength of this model is that if there is a major event, members of this team can serve to coordinate services of the various agencies and ensure that services are available to all responders without duplication of services or turf wars. Another strength of this model is that it allows representatives from different agencies to obtain a greater understanding of the challenges faced by their colleagues, which will hopefully positively influence interagency rivalry.

What Should Be the Professional Training of Team Members?

Some teams are comprised solely of mental health professionals. This tends to be true of teams provided by contract employee assistance firms that offer services to client organizations. In a local child welfare agency in Toronto, team members are social workers because the "peers" are all in fact mental health workers. Similar team formats are often found in hospitals. In other organizations, such as some fire services, team members are all firefighters and a mental health professional is contracted to join the team in specific situations. In ambulance or police services that employ a psychologist or another mental health professional, frequently the team consists of this one mental health worker and several emergency service professionals. The most commonly discussed team format in the literature is a mix of mental health and emergency service professionals. For instance, the Pearson Team has 6 mental health professionals within the 30-member team.

Who Leads the Team?

It is frequently a political decision regarding who provides the leadership to the team. Depending on the organization, it may be best to have the team headed by a mental health professional within the organization, for instance the organization's psychologist or social worker. In other organizations, pressure for trauma support services has come from the membership, and thus the team will attain greater acceptance if the person in charge is an emergency service professional who may or may not be a member of the union. In the Canadian Armed forces, the trauma response team is headed by the surgeon general, through the Directorate of Health Treatment Services, and finally by the chief social worker, who is responsible for coordinating services. Other models —for instance, that proposed by Robinson and Murdoch (1991)—advocate for a coordinating committee to oversee the program. A peer support team leader and a clinical director then share the responsibilities of team management, training, and direction. At Pearson Airport, the team is jointly led by an administrative director, who is the manager of emergency planning within the airport authority, and a clinical director, who is a mental health worker. Below them in the administrative structure is an administrative committee, comprising representatives from various types of agencies. Regardless of the configuration, the reporting and team deployment structure must be clear and the person leading the team must be in control of team operations.

What Are the Responsibilities of Team Members?

Robinson and Murdoch (1991) describe four major types of peer support teams.

1. *Teams of peers who listen and refer.* These individuals provide an immediate first contact point and then are responsible for ensuring the responder contacting them is provided with appropriate referrals for service. The Royal Canadian Mounted Police Member Assistance Program is one example of this, as is Air Canada's member EAP program.
2. *Teams of peers who provide basic crisis intervention and counseling.* These are again essentially peers who have additional training in counseling. In our experience, these peers may or may not also provide debriefings. Teams that have moved to this model that we have worked with are the Children's Aid Society of Toronto and the Ministry of Natural Resources in Ontario. In this model, individuals within the organization can call anyone from a list of available peer support people and discuss an event that they have encountered on a one-to-one basis. Additional support is available for these people through mental health EAP services contracted by the agency.

3. *Self-help groups comprised of workers who have undergone similar types of events.* Robinson and Murdoch (1991) cite the New York Police Department's self-help groups as an example. Numerous police services have peers involved in a previous shooting incident provide peer support following a shooting.

4. *Critical Incident Stress Debriefing Teams* (CISDs), which perform group debriefings and defusings after a workplace incident. This is the original model proposed by Mitchell and Bray (1990).

What Kind of Support Is Available for the Team?

It is important to assess the support of both management and the membership for any team initiative. Will management support the efforts of the team in terms of resources for training, for travel, for work time and overtime in the provision of services, and for contracting of mental health services if required? Will management support referrals to the team and respect issues of confidentiality? Will management release workers wishing to attend debriefing or defusing services? Are the union and the membership in support of this program, or is the program viewed as a management ploy of some sort? How can an atmosphere of acceptance be created within the organization in order that responders will actually use services? These are all important issues to address prior to launching a team, either within a single organization or as a cooperative effort by many organizations.

Selecting Team Members

Once the format for the team has been established and support has been secured, the next task is selecting team members. In general the goal is to have team members represent a broad number of constituencies. In a multiagency team, that means that people are strategically selected from key organizations. In a single-organization team, people should be selected from different areas of the organization, different levels of the organization, and according to their demographics (e.g., gender representation, minority representation). This, however, must be balanced by carefully considering the individual characteristics of the people applying and their reputations with other people in the organization. That is, team members must be viewed as strong members of the organization (not whiners), good at what they do, and trustworthy. People who are marginalized in the social fabric of the organization will negatively affect the team as a whole and reduce the willingness of others to access services.

Important personal characteristics include the ability to listen to others, a commitment to helping others, and understanding that having difficulty

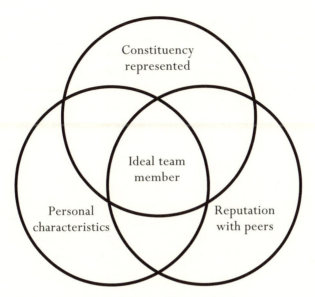

Figure 11.1. Ideal Team Member

dealing with a particular situation does not indicate that someone is weak or unfit (that goes for both emergency responders accessing services and members of the team). In the chapter 9 we described additional qualities such as good tolerance for frustration and ambiguity for those supporting healthy lifestyle change. Team members should be at a stage in their careers where they are comfortable with their expertise in the job of officer, firefighter, or paramedic and are looking for new challenges and learning opportunities. They should also have personal confidence and be self-motivated but not have issues with those in authority. Anger directed toward "those idiots" in management, the union, or others often translates into difficulty with accepting direction within the team. Finally, while sensitivity to the pain of others often comes from having experienced pain oneself, it is important that team members not currently be in the midst of personal or relationship problems. Someone still fighting his way through a bitter divorce or suffering from acute traumatic stress herself will have difficulty separating out his or her own needs and feelings from those presented by responders seeking assistance.

The question then arises of how to screen for all these factors. Some teams, including the team we are involved with at Pearson Airport, rely on interviews and recommendations of other team members. We also require letters of endorsement from supervisors and their organization to ensure full support. In the interviews we ask about the following areas:

- previous experience with trauma teams and/or previous training
- what attracted them to this team
- the types of calls or events that cause stress for members of their organization
- the ways in which members are affected by stress
- the techniques that they are familiar with for dealing with stress
- the characteristics that they think a trauma team member should possess.

Then individuals are presented with a couple of scenarios where peers appear to be having difficulty and asked what they might do in that situation. The interviewers rely on their clinical skills to try to determine who will fit in well with the team and will be best able to perform services. Other teams go beyond interviews and require prospective members to complete psychological testing and background checks (Greenstone, 2000).

Establishing the Commitment of Team Members

Once team members have been selected, a means must be established to ensure ongoing commitment to the team. This is generally done through the process of establishing a psychological contract. A *psychological contract* outlines an individual's beliefs regarding the terms and conditions of a reciprocal exchange agreement (Rousseau, 1989). That is, what does the person believe to be the expectations of him or herself and what does he or she believe will be the rewards of participation? Psychological contracts reduce uncertainty in volunteers regarding what is expected of them, provide the basis by which volunteers can call the team to task if it is not functioning and organized as promised, and provide a basis by which the team can review volunteer participation and performance (Farmer and Fedor, 1999). It is the responsibility of the team leader to clearly identify the expectations of team members at the time team membership is being offered. For instance:

- You are expected to participate in a 3-day training program and subsequently attend bimonthly half-day meetings. We will notify you of meeting times for the entire year in September of that year. We will also undertake to develop training sessions that meet your learning needs and will welcome all suggestions that you make for training opportunities. If more than two training sessions are missed within 1 year, we would like to discuss your continued commitment with you.
- It is expected that you will follow the ethical code of the team, which will be discussed in detail in the training session.

- It is expected that you will be on call and available according to the schedule which will be established, that you provide services in the manner in which we agree as a team, and report back to the team leader regarding your interventions.

Training in Context

There are many excellent training programs on the market that offer 1- to 3-day programs that focus on critical incident stress and debriefings. These programs tend to attract a wide range of individuals from various training backgrounds, including emergency service workers and mental health professionals. Thus they must begin with knowledge that is basic to some audience members and advanced to others. In addition, these training programs usually have large numbers of participants (often well over 100), so they are more didactic in nature, with a small number of excellent and entertaining instructors providing information in a multimedia lecture format. Certificates are generally provided to participants for their attendance. While these larger, well-established training programs provide an important and useful role, training provided to a team working within a particular organization or a team of people from a number of organizations who will jointly provide a service to a community must have a different focus. In addition to imparting information about trauma in the workplace and intervention strategies, other tasks involve: (1) team building in order to ensure that the working relationship between team members is strong and healthy; (2) a discussion of ethical principles that guide the actions of the team; (3) practicing skills with individuals with whom participants will actually be jointly performing service; (4) preparing the ground for ongoing training and consultation; and (5) focusing on the personal experiences of team members and ensuring that they attend to their own self-care needs. The use of digital media and the internet may be promising means of supporting team training and development. Canada's Workplace Health and Public Safety Program (WHPSP) psychosocial emergency response team has made excellent use of the internet for web-based learning and discussion of developments in the field and team protocols.

Adult Learning Theory

Training of this nature must attend to the principles of adult learning theory, because the goal is to present information in a way that will best be assimilated by participants. Adult learning theory, or andragogy, was first introduced in the 1970s and was viewed as a radical departure from traditional pedagogy, where the teacher was viewed as "expert" and the learners as passive recipients of knowledge imparted by the teacher (Knowles, 1972). In contrast, adult learning theory suggests that professionals who enter the learning process have reasonably clear ideas about what they need and want to learn and resist learning in situations in which they are not treated as autonomous individuals. Rather, they respond more favorably if they are involved in the process of determining the learning goals and selecting the most appropriate ways to achieve these goals. Further, adults come to an educational experience with a great deal of knowledge and experience. This means that participants in a training program can be resources for one another, and the trainer acts in the role not only of educator, but also of facilitator. At times the previous learning of participants can be problematic, and if this is the case, the trainer must provide a safe environment where problematic attitudes and behaviors can be appropriately challenged.

As people get older, their views of learning change. While we may be able to convince a child to learn calculus because at some undetermined point in the distant future it will be useful, adults prefer "just in time" learning. That is, adults seek knowledge and skills to deal with situations that they are presently facing. Anyone who has received multiple notices from their children's school regarding the treatment of lice knows that they threw out every piece unread, until the one day their child became infested. In this regard, learning is directed at solving a here-and-now problem with the assistance of others. Theory is useful to the degree that it explains the problem at hand, not for the joy of acquiring more theoretical knowledge.

Team Building

A central goal of the training process for new trauma teams is to build the group of individuals who were selected for their personal skills and traits into a cohesive unit. This evolution is achieved through *group process*, including norms that are developed that govern behavior, the level of cohesion and trust among the members, how conflict emerges and is managed by various team members, and the relationships between particular team members (Corey and Corey, 2002). Individuals attending trauma team training tend to be highly motivated and pleased to have been accepted onto the team. Nevertheless, they are likely to come with some fears regarding their competence in this type of work. Some may have had previous mental health training but are doubtful about their ability to "handle" the nature of emergency service work and the personalities of emergency service workers. Some will be very familiar with emergency service work but are doubtful about their ability to provide emotional assistance to their col-

1. Adults wish to be self-directed and in control of the learning experience.
   - Goals and directions are stated by the learners in terms of what they want to know and what they want to be able to do. This means that the training must be flexible, skipping through parts that are redundant to learners and focusing on topics that are most important to their needs.
   - The competency of people as learners and choice makers for their own lives is recognized and used.
2. Learning must be a collaborative process.
   - Needs are uncovered by mutual sharing and cooperation.
   - People are allowed to make mistakes and not know the answer.
   - Participative decision making is used throughout the learning experience.
3. Previous experience is central to the learning process.
   - The strengths and knowledge of learners must be recognized before needs, gaps and new directions can be examined.
   - Diverse experiences and perspectives are welcomed, valued, and viewed as adding to the learning experience for everyone, including the instructor.
4. Learning outcomes must have meaning for life and professional goals.
   - Trainers must continually draw connections between learning and life experiences of both themselves and the learners.
   - Learning must be related to desired role attainment and not be simply information for information's sake.
5. Learning evolves.
   - Learning experiences promote personal growth as well as professional growth.
   - Personal meanings and emotional reactions shape learning goals.
   - Instructors and learners are involved in mutual discovery and learning.
6. Learning is problem-focused and here-and-now.
   - Adults tend to be much more problem-focused than subject-focused. Thus learning should relate to the specific situations they encounter.
   - Specific situations are then generalized to theory.

Figure 11.2. Principles of Adult Learning Theory

leagues. In the end, most people approaching this type of intensive training are fearful that their inadequacies will be exposed and targeted. This uncertainty and fear can be displayed as mild resistance to certain learning tasks, such as role play; as bravado ("I already know all of this"); or as silence. Members of the team may come with previous relationships with other members and will certainly come with attitudes about the organization or aspect of the organization other team members represent that predispose them to like or not like someone else. The trainer, as the group leader, is therefore responsible for setting the tone and beginning to establish the norms for the group. This tone involves respect for all members of the team and the unique contributions they bring to the group. It also involves displaying personal uncertainties and areas where the trainer can learn from team members. Common norms include:

- commitment to the team and respect for the time of others
- respect for the opinions of others and efforts of others—no one has all the answers
- models of constructive criticism—members are expected to give feedback to one another in nonthreatening and useful ways
- discussion of personal experiences can help the learning process, but self-disclosure should be tempered—this is not a treatment group.

The first group process task of the trainer is to establish trust within the team. The first part of developing trust is establishing that the leader has a clearly defined structure for the group and is able to maintain control over the group process (Reid, 1997). That is, no one member of the group will be able to monopolize or verbally assault another member. The trainer models the group leadership skills of making validating responses to statements or questions raised by team members, accepting challenges, and demonstrating a genuine liking of the members. Team members come to feel that they can express their opinions and concerns without being ridiculed or experiencing disapproval. For those team members who come from highly competitive organizations, this may be a departure from their regular training experiences.

The second major task of the trainer is developing group cohesion within the team. In general, individuals are drawn to any group for three intersecting reasons: (1) the need for affiliation and recognition, (2) the resources and prestige available through group participation, and (3) expectations of the beneficial consequences of participation (Toseland and Rivas, 2001). Cohesive groups recognize the accomplishments of members and support their sense of competence. People are attracted to a team where they feel valued and liked. Second, trauma teams often have a certain prestige of being elite groups of people, so membership enriches the work life of team members and their status within the organization in which they work. Finally, the team must contribute to the ongoing learning and skill base of the team members and provide them with something that helps in daily life, either professionally or personally. The trainer then has the responsibility to generate enthusiasm within the group for the task and to validate the contributions of each member toward achieving the task.

Team Ethics

The final task for the leader in establishing the ground rules and climate of the team is discussing the ethical framework within which the team operates. As stated earlier, team members come with various professional backgrounds and are therefore bound by different ethical codes in their work. The trauma team must have a common ethical stance that includes three main issues: (1) boundaries between team members and those they are assisting, (2) confidentiality of information obtained and the limits of confidentiality, (3) acknowledgment of the limits of competence of each team member and not providing services beyond one's personal level of competence.

Boundaries

Boundaries in helping relationships refers to the spoken and unspoken rules that helpers and those they are helping observe about the physical and emotional limits of their relationship (Roberts and Greene, 2002). People providing support must be adept at breaking down boundaries between themselves and the recipients of help through listening empathically and building trust so the other person is comfortable in sharing their distress. At the same time, they must enforce boundaries in order to protect both themselves and the recipient from enmeshment, provide objective advice, and eventually end the helping part of the relationship (Bacharach, Bamberger, and McKinney, 2000). Maintaining boundaries tends to be relatively clear for mental health professionals. Ethical guidelines for social workers, psychologists, and psychiatrists clearly state that individuals must not engage in dual relationships with clients. That includes personal friendships with clients, business transactions with clients, and, most importantly, sexual relationships with clients and former clients. These prohibitions are based on the concept of fiduciary duties. That is, because professionals have unequal power in comparison to their clients by virtue of their specialized knowledge, clients must trust that professionals are acting in their best interests (Regehr and Antle, 1997). For instance, if our doctor tells us we must have a particular type of surgery, we must trust to some degree that he or she is recommending this for the benefit of our health, not the doctor's bank account. In addition, when we are providing crisis assistance to someone who is feeling very vulnerable, he or she may misinterpret feelings of gratitude for feelings of love and be susceptible to a relationship that is not in his or her best interest. Clearly stated boundaries reduce the risk that a client will misinterpret the intentions of a mental health professional or be vulnerable to exploitation. These boundaries are generally established by clearly defined norms about when and where clients will be met for treatment, the length of treatment sessions, and the behavior of the professional. Obviously from this description, boundaries in peer support relationships in acute trauma situations are not nearly as clear or simple. Trauma team members go on scene, visit people in their place of work, at coffee shops, and potentially in their homes. Hours of assistance can be any length at any time. Nevertheless, trauma team members possess information that the traumatized responder has shared that is likely beyond that of any other person, and therefore they are in a helping role. Thus, they have a similar responsibility to ensure that the responder's vulnerability and gratitude are not exploited. No member of the team should engage in a sexual relationship with someone for whom they have provided services. No member of the team should benefit financially from the gratitude or vulnerability of someone for whom they have provided services.

Confidentiality

Confidentiality is an important aspect of team ethics and assists with maintaining boundaries. The ethical standards that govern all mental health professionals advise that professionals should respect the privacy of clients by holding in strict confidence all information about clients. In trauma teams, the burden of confidentiality is generally understood to extend to all team members, regardless of professional licensure. The rationale for this is self-evident. That is, individuals will be willing to share their fears and concerns only if they are convinced that this will not be communicated to others in the workplace, such as coworkers and management personnel. Disclosure of this personal information could potentially lead to ridicule, lack of trust in the person's ability to perform their job functions, and can even affect chances of promotion. Trauma teams within organizations seek to enhance confidentiality by not recording who attended sessions or what individuals disclosed and by refusing to report back to management about the effects of an incident on any individual.

While confidentiality may be considered the ideal, there are situations where confidentiality cannot be protected. In virtually all jurisdictions in Australia, Canada, the United Kingdom, and the United States, individuals are compelled to breach confidentiality if they are aware of a child that is being abused. In addition, case law in both Canada and the United States has established that information gathered in mental health treatment that leads the treating person to believe that another person is at risk of harm must be disclosed in order to protect the innocent. This concept has a long tradition in the United States, highlighted and clarified by the famous Tarasoff decision in California in 1976. In that case a patient told his treating psychologist that he intended to kill his former girlfriend, Ms. Tarasoff. The therapist, concluding that the patient was dangerous, contacted the campus police but did not warn the intended victim. Ms. Tarasoff was subsequently killed and her family sued the therapist. Despite defense arguments that the duty to warn violated the accepted ethical obligation to maintain confidentiality, the courts ruled in the plaintiff's favor. The court concluded that the confidentiality obligation to a patient ends when public peril begins. This was later codified by amendments to the California civil code (1984), which, due to efforts of the California Psychiatric Association, limited the liability to a "serious threat" against a "reasonably identified victim." While the Tarasoff case and other similar American jurisprudence did not apply to Canadian jurisdictions, it was generally assumed that the reasoning in the case was persuasive and Canadian courts would offer a similar decision should the issue arise. Indeed, 15 years later in the case of Wenden v. Trikha (1991) it was determined that a duty to protect is now owed to third parties under Canadian law when a threat is of a serious nature, and the diagnosis, history, and opportunity to bring the threat to fruition are such that a reasonable therapist would be concerned (Truscott and Cook, 1993; Glancy, Regehr, and Bryant, 1998). Thus, it could be assumed that this obligation would be extended to all members of a trauma team.

The final area where confidentiality may not be maintained is in the situation where disclosure is ordered in a judicial process. Court access to information gathered in a mental health treatment context in order to bolster a criminal case is well established in the United States (People v. Clark, 1990; People v. Wharton, 1991; Menendez v. Superior Court, 1991), although it is somewhat more restricted in Canada (Statutes of Canada, 1997). If individuals are seeking compensation for injuries through civil litigation, their rights to privacy are further reduced. Individuals who initiate legal proceedings that put their treatment, medical condition, or health at issue are viewed as waiving the right to confidentiality and implicitly consenting to the disclosure of confidential information relevant to the action (P. (L. M.) v. F. (D.), 1994). This allows the defendant in a civil action access to information regarding the complainant's care. In addition, treatment records have been ruled to be compellable in custody and access cases (Gibbs v.

Individuals using the services of the team are entitled to strict and complete confidentiality, including anonymity of person and events.

Information regarding an incident will be shared among team members where such sharing of information will be of assistance to the client responder or is necessary for team functioning or supervision.

There are three exceptions to the rule of confidentiality.

1. Life-threatening situations
   - Where an individual is homicidal, suicidal, or is a risk to public safety, such as being physically or mentally unfit to work, such that continuing work would endanger public safety.
   - Should you be aware of a life threatening situation, contact the nearest team mental health professional or physician immediately.
   - Where the individual's continuing to work may endanger public safety, the individual is insisting on returning to work, and a mental health professional is not available to deal with the situation, immediately contact the nearest senior officer.
2. Child abuse
   - Any individual aware of child abuse or suspected child abuse is required by law to contact child protection services.
3. Disclosure is ordered by a court
   - Any team member can be ordered by a judge in civil or criminal court to disclose any or all of the information regarding a client. If an individual should decide to refuse to disclose such information, he or she could then be held in contempt of court.

Figure 11.3. Model Confidentiality Policy

Gibbs, 1985). This has important implications for advising responders that if there is a possibility that they may be involved in court reviews of the incident, they should not disclose information that would jeopardize their case. In light of the complexity of confidentiality issues, trauma teams are urged to develop confidentiality policies that are carefully discussed with all team members.

Limits of Competence

When working on multidisciplinary teams, team members have the opportunity to learn from one another and gain a deeper understanding of the skills and knowledge possessed by other members. At times this can lead to a sense that one has acquired the ability to perform the functions of another profession. For instance, psychologists and social workers may begin making suggestions about medications to clients because they have worked with many clients on medications and have discussed medication issues frequently with doctors. Nevertheless, these professionals continue to lack the in-depth knowledge about biology and biochemistry to allow them to make such recommendations. One psychiatrist once reported that after years of working with police departments, she began intervening in community policing issues, telling people when they were not driving safely and forcing herself not to pull someone over for dangerous driving. Similarly, team members must be clear about their role on the team and not overstep their role by assuming responsibilities beyond their levels of training and competence. One aspect of this is developing the ability to determine when individuals presenting to the team have needs beyond what the team can offer. This is discussed below concerning identifying people in acute need. Team members must be comfortable to discuss situations with one another and to state when they believe that they are dealing with situations at the edge of their competence.

Knowledge Required by Team Members

In general, training programs focus on imparting information about the topics below. These will not be described in detail in this section, as various aspects are covered throughout this book.

- The nature of trauma and traumatic events
- Effects of traumatic events
  - immediate reactions
  - post-event reactions
  - long-term problems
  - functioning of the organization
- Factors affecting the severity of reactions
  - incident factors
  - personal factors
  - organizational factors
- Effects of emergency service work on families
  - family support

- Managing workplace trauma
  - preventative education
  - working with individuals
  - working with groups of people
  - working with the organization
- Protecting team members
  - identifying secondary trauma
  - personal stress management techniques

Skills Building

Developing Listening Skills

While listening appears to be a simple concept that should be possessed by most people by the age of five, listening while engaging in helping others requires different skills than one would use in the average social interaction. In particular, it requires different skills than many responders will have learned for acquiring information from citizens in an emergency context. In providing assistance to others in distress, the term *active listening* is often used, describing a process of absorbing the content of what someone is saying, noting gestures and subtle changes in voice or expression, sensing the underlying message, and gently encouraging him or her to disclose personal and painful information (Corey and Corey, 2002). Active listeners look for recurrent themes in what someone is saying, try to identify what the individual is avoiding saying, and look for inconsistencies between the words, body language, and affect presented (Reid, 1997). Several techniques can be used in this type of listening.

- *Reflecting* is demonstrating to another that you have heard what they said by paraphrasing and repeating back their statements. Obviously, this can become exceedingly annoying if done too often or done verbatim.
- *Clarifying* is checking out whether your perception of what has been said matches with what the person intended to convey.
- *Summarizing* is frequently done after the person has presented a great deal of information, often which has come out in a somewhat disjointed fashion, and the listener creates a two- or three-sentence summary to show that all the information has been absorbed and assimilated.
- *Partializing* is the ability to break the problems presented into discrete parts. "I can see that you are facing many issues at the same time.

Your wife has left you. You are worried about job security, and now you have had this terrible event happen on your last call."

- *Empathizing* can be done either verbally or nonverbally, through body language or facial expressions that demonstrate that the listener understands the affect that the person is conveying. This is not to say, "I know how you feel," but rather, "I can see that makes you feel terrible."
- *Questioning* listeners can prompt people to talk more by asking open-ended questions, such as "What was that like for you?" rather than closed questions that result in yes-and-no answers, like "Did you feel bad?" They can also ask indirect questions, which sound like statements, such as "Being new on the job must have made this tough" instead of "Do you think this was harder because you were new on the job?"

Listeners can also do things that shut down the person who is talking. These include

- bombarding others with questions
- gossiping about others
- storytelling ("Let me tell you what happened to me")
- being judgmental about statements made by the person
- drifting off and/or attending to other things happening around
- pushing too hard ("You have to get this off your chest"; "You must tell me").

Group Leadership Skills

All team members involved in the running of debriefing and defusing groups must develop group leadership skills. The most basic of these skills required in any helping situation, first identified by Carl Rogers (1957), are *warmth, empathy,* and *genuineness.* Added to this, group leaders must, as stated earlier, create an environment of safety where people can take risks, and should model acceptance of others. Group leaders must also, however, maintain control over the group process. They have the responsibility to ensure that one member does not monopolize the group time with his or her own specific needs. Skills that can limit this problem are: (1) drawing linkages between the experience of the person monopolizing and that of others, thereby encouraging someone else to speak; (2) inviting others to comment on their own experiences and whether they are similar or different from that of the speaker; (3) sometimes simply stating, "I am going to stop you there and check with others now." Group leaders must ensure that no member attacks another member or discounts the experiences of others.

Incident factors

- Loss of someone directly known to responder
- Taking personal responsibility for negative outcome of the event in a significant way
- Physical injury of responder that limits activity/career
- Near-death experience for responder

Social support factors

- Prolonged separation from family as a result of incident
- Other recent losses (death of family member/separation)

Organizational/community factors

- Investigation into activities of responder during incident
- Lack of support regarding incident from colleagues, management, and/or union
- Changed duties postincident
- Negative media attention

Personal factors

- Previous mental health problems
- Other health concerns
- Substance abuse/overuse
- History of suicide in personal network
- Family history of mental health problems

Figure 11.4. Factors Increasing Risk of Acute Distress

This often requires direct but calm confrontation of the person behaving in that way and modeling of other responses. In addition, the group leader must at times intervene when the group is spiraling in a negative direction, such as focusing on who did what wrong. Often this can be done by the leader summarizing the concerns and indicating the intention to move the group back to the original task. These types of skills can be practiced through role playing and mock debriefings, after which members can discuss the difficulties they encountered and brainstorm strategies.

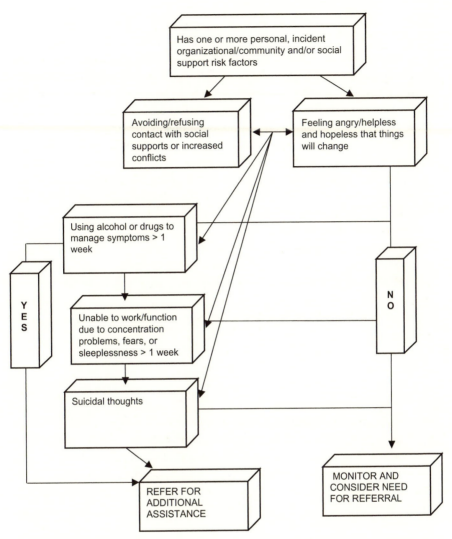

Figure 11.5. Decision Tree for Assessing Need for Referral for Additional Assistance

Identifying People in Acute Need

As we have discussed in various chapters of this book, social, physical, and emotional reactions are common and can reasonably be expected when caring and competent individuals face situations in the line of duty that involve tragedy, loss of life, and/or threats to themselves or their colleagues. Nevertheless, it is a mistake to take the attitude that all reactions are normal and will abate with the assistance of workplace interventions. Members of trauma support teams must be able to differentiate between distressing but not dangerous reactions and those that represent an ongoing threat to the responder's health and well-being. Those members of the team who are mental health professionals undoubtedly possess the knowledge and assessment skills to determine which responders are in particular distress and need additional counseling assistance or referral to another professional. For instance, while suicide remains a relatively rare event (and there is conflicting evidence whether emergency response professionals are at higher or equal risk than members of the general population), individuals in periods of acute distress with access to lethal means are definitely potentially at risk. In addition, if an individual's symptoms are significantly interfering with his or her functioning, a physician can determine whether medication would be of assistance. Team members, perhaps by nature of their training and often by nature of their role, are not expected to conduct full assessments of individuals seeking assistance; however, during the process of informally defusing an event, certainly the team member should be able to identify risk factors and have strategies for suggesting additional assistance.

Summary

Developing and maintaining a trauma response team requires tremendous time and effort. Careful planning must go into determining team structure and membership. Training must be comprehensive and go far beyond simply knowledge about trauma and basic step-by-step guidelines for intervention to include issues related to professionalism and more complex skills. In addition, training does not end after the first intensive training session but continues on, acting as an important means for skill development and team maintenance.

12

KEEPING IT GOING

Team Maintenance

While those individuals who join trauma response teams come with many skills and strengths, generally they are new to this type of work. They are selected either because they offer a wealth of knowledge about emergency service work and its impact on those who do the work or because they are mental health professionals who are experienced in the provision of emergency services. The intensive two- or three-day training offered to new team members is of tremendous benefit. However, in the course of providing mental health and peer support interventions in the context of emergency health, public safety, or disaster work, they will undoubtedly encounter new situations and challenges that will test the limits of their competence and undermine confidence. In addition, the sporadic nature of trauma work and the fact that only a few team members tend to respond to most events means that team members may have few opportunities to practice skills and to maintain contact with other team members. The challenge for team leaders therefore becomes one of continuously developing the skill levels of team members and maintaining commitment and motivation in light of a fluctuating workload. In this chapter we will review several key elements of ongoing team maintenance, including administration of the team, continuous training, ensuring that there are rewards to maintain commitment and motivation, evaluation of team members, and ensuring the safety and self-care of team members so that they do not burn out.

Team Administration

In the preceding chapter we discussed the need to determine the format for the team in terms of the composition and support. This includes the types of incidents that the team envisions it will address and the services that it will provide. In our experience, however, these types of programs evolve, and requests for service vary greatly. This requires ongoing decision making about the scope of services. For instance, should an off-site team that was originally designed to provide service within 48 hours be expected to arrive on the scene within an hour or two of a specific request? Should team members of an agency-specific team provide service to other organizations on request? In general, team members are committed to helping others, and consequently the mandate of the team tends to expand to attempt to meet the needs of everyone. Later, questions may arise about accountability and compensation for team members. For instance, will they get paid for their time away from the job during which they provided service to another agency? Therefore, in setting up a system for ongoing functioning, several issues must be addressed.

How Is the Team Contacted?

Each team must have a system for contact that is widely advertised to managers, who may wish to alert the team of large-scale situations, and to workers, who may wish to contact the team about events that had a particular impact on them. The system for contact should be simple and consistent. There must be one central number or individual to be called, and those calling must get immediate assistance. Teams are certain to fail if people attempting to contact them must repeatedly try numbers until they reach someone or must wait long periods of time for a call back when they feel the situation is urgent. We know that individuals who are distressed experience time delays as hugely prolonged. Ask anyone who has waited for an ambulance or fire truck to arrive, and they will estimate that the 3 1/2-minute wait lasted 20 minutes or more. It is certainly reasonable that on-call responsibilities rotate in order that team members (and their families) do not become burned out by the intrusions on their lives; nevertheless, to service recipients, the process must appear seamless.

How Are Decisions Regarding Service Provision Made?

As stated earlier, requests will inevitably be made of the team that fall outside of the original scope of service. It may be that the first contact person has the ability to make a decision independently about team deployment and will be able to ensure that the employing organization will support any decision made. However, frequently this individual may have to check with others. If this is a single-agency team within a fire department, for example, the team leader may need quick access to the deputy chief in order to authorize the deployment of team members to another county. If the services are being requested by a for-profit organization, compensation of team members may need to be negotiated prior to deployment. Team members may also need to be consulted if the intervention requested requires a change in the mandate. In such situations it is advisable to have in place a small executive committee who can consult quickly and share in the decision making process.

Who Will Go?

It is advisable to have a rotating roster of team members who will have primary responsibility for crisis response. In the absence of a schedule, certain individuals who are known to be available and willing to go at a moment's notice will be called upon repeatedly and will in short order become burned out. In our experience, this also resulted in an overutilization of team leaders, as it was easier to go to a scene in the middle of the night oneself then begin the process of waking others and asking them to go. This results in a tired team leader and a sense of alienation among others who did not get the opportunity to provide service. Expectations for availability during the time one is on call must be clearly stated.

Following Up on Calls

It is vital that a system is in place to follow up on all calls. Generally the first contact person should be responsible for calling the team members who intervened, determining how the intervention went and whether any follow-up is necessary. That is, are referrals required for certain individuals who are acutely distressed? Were there any system problems that interfered with the success of the intervention? Most importantly, this call provides an opportunity for the team member to informally debrief the situation and discuss how responders felt about the situation and the service that they provided. In addition to calling team members, it is important to speak to the original contact person to ensure that they were satisfied with the service provided and deal with any concerns. Brief notes of these calls can be kept in a call log that enhances quality assurance by ensuring follow-up was completed and allowing for discussion among team members.

Keeping Statistics

As we discuss further in chapter 13, "Does It Work?," an essential tool for justifying any program is being able to talk about how many calls were received and what types of services were provided. Thus, while confidentiality regarding the actual events that were debriefed and the actual people

- Referral of information
  — name of caller
  — time of call
  — nature of event
  — nature of request
- Team contact information
  — who contacted
  — time of contact
  — intervention plan
- Follow up with team members
  — types of intervention
  — length of interventions
  — concerns or questions
  — further referrals required
- Follow up with initial caller
  — perceptions of service
  — any outstanding issues to be addressed

Figure 12.1. Call Log

who made use of the service is important, overall utilization numbers are very useful. Teams may elect to conduct an evaluation research study of their program as outlined in chapter 13; however, in the absence of a more comprehensive appraisal, utilization statistics can be simply collected and collated for reporting purposes.

Ongoing Training

In general, teams deal with ongoing training issues by having monthly, bi-monthly, or quarterly team training sessions of either 2-hour, half-day or one-day duration. The timing of meetings is largely dependent on the nature of the team and the distance that team members must travel to attend meetings. These meetings have the joint function of enhancing the cohesion of the team and addressing the learning needs of team members. In keeping with adult learning principles, the members of the team should be involved in determining the content of the training sessions and potentially in the provision of training. The training should be interesting, applicable to either work or life tasks, and (whenever possible) fun.

As the Pearson International Airport team has multiple agencies represented, the ongoing training has included visits to various member organ-

- Time of contact
- Type of caller (supervisor/worker)
- Type of event (multicasualty/personal connection for worker)
- Types of intervention
- Lengths of intervention
- Number of people served
- Nature of follow-up required

Figure 12.2. Utilization Statistics

izations, where team members are given greater insight into the challenges faced and the skills possessed by other professions. For instance, we have witnessed an automobile extrication exercise and have donned fire gear to run up a four-story structure at a fire training center; we have sat on an aircraft while it was secured and entered during a SWAT team exercise and have witnessed a takedown exercise in a SWAT training facility; and we have been in an aircraft training simulator, from which we did an emergency evacuation. In addition, team training involves regular skill updates with role-playing exercises and mock debriefings. Clinical leaders present research updates on the efficacy of interventions and on factors influencing distress. Guest speakers have presented on topics such as the impact of peer debriefing team membership on members' families, the impact of emergency workers' interventions in families following the sudden death of a child, and the work of trauma response teams in remote areas. In addition, team members are invited to discuss recent interventions they have conducted and issues that arose during these interventions. The goal is to keep members engaged, enthusiastic, and committed to the team.

Part of the training involves teamwork exercises and practicing skills. To this end, we frequently present vignettes that encourage the team to work through various issues, as outlined in figure 12.3. Vignettes are often derived from past provincial and federal emergencies (for example, see Transportation Safety Board of Canada reports, found at www.tsb.gc.ca). One such set of vignettes involves large-scale disasters. Team members divide into small groups and are asked to consider being called into one of the situations in the sample vignettes presented below. Then they are asked to consider a number of questions.

- What additional information is required by team members in order to develop an intervention strategy?
- Are there any safety considerations for team members?
- What types of interventions may be offered?

Scenario 1

The area along the Ontario and Manitoba border experienced a warm Ontario spring, droughtlike conditions, and a large number of spring fires. Waterbombers and fire crews assisted with a forest fire in Manitoba near the provincial border.

On June 7 Fire Rangers crews departed northwestern Ontario bound for Manitoba. En route, the 80 firefighters were forced to land on an old, short airstrip. Their plane was damaged and there were a number of injuries. Most pressing, the crews found themselves only 30km from the spreading forest fire. With resources already stretched fighting fires, including fires near two communities, a rescue plan is undertaken. All 80 crew members are rescued, although not before several members' injuries become life-threatening. It appears that all the seriously injured will survive, though many are not likely to return to their careers.

It is now June 20, and our team receives a request to assist crews leaving the fire scene and likely to return. These crews include some 80 firefighters that were rescued only weeks earlier. The team home base will be Kenora, although it is likely that the team will be requested to split up and provide services to several sites near the fire scenes.

Scenario 2

An Emergency Coordination Center in St. Catharine's contacts our team to assist with worker assistance efforts two days after the following incident. Our focus would be with the local emergency response services.

While approaching the locks in St. Catharine's, the vessel Northern Miner, fully loaded with 22,000 tonnes of potash, struck the port side of the upbound tanker Emerald Star, which had just departed the lock. At the time of the collision, both vessels were in the confines of the approach walls to the locks and had increased their speeds: the Agawa Canyon to increase maneuverability, and the Emerald Star to avert collision. The Emerald Star is a tanker with 26 crew. The tanker was filled with 2,800 tonnes of gasoline and 4,400 tonnes of diesel no. 2, bound for Thunder Bay, Ontario. There was a risk of significant pollution, as the vessel has not retained its watertight integrity. Winds have continued for several days from the northwest at 10 to 12 knots.

Figure 12.3. Sample Disaster Scenarios

There is a small fire on Northern Miner that appears to be contained, yet concerns remain. There is extreme tension in the community related to the disaster. The collision has lead to a significant delay to other shipping traffic.

Scenario 3

A Boeing 747-200 was on a cargo flight from Montreal to Anchorage International Airport, Alaska. A second Boeing 747-200 was operating as a scheduled passenger flight from Vancouver International Airport to Frankfurt International Airport, Germany. Both aircraft were cruising at flight level 330 and their planned tracks would converge over Ontario. The minimum distance between the two aircraft was estimated to have been 1.3 nautical miles horizontally while they were at the same altitude. To avoid a collision, each plane was advised to turn right.

The planes passed with an actual separation of approximately 900 feet with minimum required separation being 5 nautical miles, or 2,000 feet. Soon afterward, the Boeing 747 carrying 200 passengers radioed an in-flight emergency near North Bay, and 20 minutes later the airplane crashed. Within a few minutes of the crash, an Ontario Provincial Police (OPP) officer noticed a fire in a forest near the TransCanada pipeline system and identified the location to the OPP dispatcher in North Bay. The pipeline is approximately 1,000 feet to the east of Highway 11. The OPP officer noted that rocks and debris from an explosion had landed on the highway. Initially, the fire was thought to be related to a breach in the pipeline. The fire is found to be the result of the crash. It is now a week after the crash, and our team is approached to provide support in North Bay. Family members are flying in to North Bay. The recovery efforts are hampered by the ongoing high risk of forest fires.

Scenario 4

On January 20 our team was approached by the Health Canada OHSA, to provide support following a train derailment near Sarnia. On January 12 at approximately 1340 (EST), Quebec Northland Railway (QNR) southward freight train No. 402 departed Sarnia,

(continued)

Figure 12.3. Continued

Ontario, for Toronto. The train consisted of 2 locomotives, 38 tank cars loaded with toluene, UN 1294,* 11 boxcars loaded with aluminum products, 1 empty boxcar, and 1 car loaded with steel ingots. The train was approximately 2,700 feet long and weighed 6,600 tons. The operating crew consisted of a conductor and a locomotive engineer. They were familiar with the railway line, the city, and the subdivisions.

At approximately 1400, while the train was rounding a righthand curve, a train-initiated emergency brake application occurred. After conducting the necessary emergency procedures, the crew determined that 29 cars had derailed, commencing with the 13th car behind the locomotives and extending to and including the 41st car. Some liquid spilled and was absorbed into the ground at the north end of the derailment site; a quantity flowed into a creek, which runs parallel to the rail track at the south end of the derailment site, toward a subdivision. Much of the subdivision has been evacuated.

There are numerous local, provincial, and federal emergency response teams present. There are several CIS teams also present, providing services to their organization.

_____

*Toluene, UN 1294, is a colorless flammable liquid with a flashpoint of 4 degrees Celsius (40 degrees Fahrenheit). The lower explosive limit of toluene vapors in a mixture with air is 1.27%. The upper explosive limit for the same mixture is 7%. Toluene is considered to be toxic. It affects the central nervous system and may cause hallucinations, distorted perceptions, and motor activity changes. It has teratogenic and reproductive effects and causes bone marrow changes. Mutations have been reported as a result of exposure. It is also considered to be an eye and skin irritant.

Figure 12.3. Sample Disaster Scenarios (*Continued*)

It is not expected that each event will result in the same intervention plan. Interventions may include on-scene practical assistance for emergency workers, consultation with command about possible employee needs, or offers of follow-up interventions.

Other team training sessions focus on direct intervention and practicing basic interviewing skills in individual defusing situations. First, the basic interviewing skills outlined in the initial training (chapter 11) are reviewed very briefly. These include reflecting, clarifying, empathizing, summarizing, and partializing. Then, using a role-play format, team members take turns in one of three roles: the client, the team member, and the observer. Beginning scripts are provided for the person playing the client and the team member. The observer is expected to provide feedback using the following format: (1) what the person playing the team member did that the observer liked and found useful; (2) what the observer would have done differently in the interaction; and (3) how they would have done it differently. In these three-person groups, we try to mix together mental health professionals and emergency service professionals whenever possible. In this way the mental health professionals also have the opportunity and responsibility to demonstrate their skills. Figure 12.4 contains some sample vignettes for interventions in small communities.

Evaluating Team Members

Evaluation of team members is an important component of ensuring that services provided by the team are of high quality and are consistent with the team's mandate and ethical code. Performance appraisals are well established in the paid workplace and serve three basic functions: (1) to provide employees with feedback about performance; (2) to control or shape employee behavior; (3) to determine merit and financial remuneration (Gabris and Ihrke, 2001). While they are frequently viewed with trepidation by employees and may in fact be demotivators instead of motivators (Boswell and Boudreau, 2000; Deckop and Cirka, 2000; Gabris and Ihrke, 2001), they can nevertheless be imposed by employers by virtue of their power over employees. If members of the trauma intervention team are paid to provide services, a more traditional employee/employer relationship may exist and evaluation may follow a more formal and traditional model. In voluntary organizations, however, the process of evaluation is significantly different. Team leaders must balance the responsibilities of maintaining commitment to the team with the responsibility of evaluating the services provided by team members.

Team members can be evaluated on a number of dimensions. The simplest dimension of performance review is commitment to the team. Does the person attend meetings and make him- or herself available for on-call responsibilities, as was agreed in the original contract? If team members are not meeting these expectations, a discussion needs to be held regarding their conflicting responsibilities and whether the demands of the team fit with other demands in their job and life. This discussion can often be a relief for team members who are feeling guilty about not living up to an original agreement. It can also be an opportunity for the team member to identify how the team is not meeting with their expectations and needs, which may illuminate problems with the team training program or administration.

A second dimension of the evaluation is the intervention skills of the

Person A
Scenario 1—Role: *Emergency worker*
You are the chief of a fire department in a small community. Your crew was called to rescue a group of three cottagers who were in a boat that capsized due to rough weather. Although the fire department is not specifically trained for such rescue work, and it is not the specific responsibility of the department, you feel the department should assist to the best of their ability.

In the stormy weather, all the cottagers are lost in the waves and die. In the process, one firefighter drowns. Everyone blames you for the disaster. You decide to contact the peer support team.

Scenario 2—Role: *Team member*
You have been asked by the local hospital administration to speak to a nurse who lost an infant patient in the emergency room 3 weeks ago. She does not seem able to function since then. Administration is concerned about her, but is most anxious to ensure that it does not continue to affect her work.

Scenario 3—Role: *Observer*

Person B
Scenario 1—Role: *Team member*
You are a team member in the community where a local firefighter has died in a failed water rescue. Your team has offered services to the department, the chief indicated that he would like to see you. He didn't give much information over the phone, but you heard from a friend, whose brother works in the fire department, that they feel the chief should *not* have ordered the water rescue at all.

Scenario 2—Role: *Observer*

Scenario 3—Role: *Emergency responder*
You are a police officer who was called to a crash on the highway. You were first to arrive at the scene. The car was a mess and smoke was coming from the engine. As you pried open the driver's door, you realized that the driver was a friend's son. You managed to free him minutes before the car exploded, but he died on the side of the road from internal injuries.

You have started to drink more since the incident, but you think

Figure 12.4. Sample Intervention Scenarios

you are hiding your distress from everyone else. You are not the type of person who believes in therapy, but a member of the peer support team has dropped by for a chat.

Person C
Scenario 1—Role: *Observer*

Scenario 2—Role: *Emergency worker*
You are a nurse at a small community hospital working in the emergency room in the middle of the night. In your hospital the on-call doctor must be called to the hospital from home in an emergency; it usually takes her about 20 minutes to arrive. Due to budget constraints, there have been staffing cuts and you are alone in the emergency room.

Suddenly a frantic young woman runs into the emergency room holding a tiny child. The mother is screaming incoherently, the baby is not breathing and it seems something is lodged in its throat. You manage to clear the airway, but it is too late and the baby dies in your arms. You are reminded of your own young baby, and now 3 weeks later cannot sleep for fear she will die. You are about to see a peer support team person at the suggestion of your supervisor.

Scenario 3—Role: *Team member*
You are a support team member for a police department. You receive a call from the wife of one of the officers who states that her husband was involved in a fatal rescue attempt. Since then he has been drinking more, is awake at night, and is shouting at her. She asks you to drop in on him for a chat.

Figure 12.4. (Continued)

team member. This is more complex and will depend on the types of services that team members are expected to provide. As we discussed in the previous chapter, trauma team volunteers are selected for a variety of reasons. In part they are selected on the basis of their skills and abilities and in part they are selected on the basis of which constituency they represent. Obviously, those with backgrounds in mental health will be held to a higher standard with regard to intervention skills, as they will be expected to provide more intensive counseling services and provide assessments and consultations for individuals who are highly distressed. Team members with emergency service backgrounds may have difficulty with some of the listening and intervention skills, but nevertheless possess other skills that the team can benefit from, and therefore on the basis of performance appraisal they might be given other responsibilities, such as administration and organization.

Listening and intervention skills can be assessed in a number of ways. First is within the process of team discussions around specific situations. Do team members express empathy for individuals being described, or do they express impatience and disdain? Are team members able to discuss possible interventions at a conceptual level, and do the suggested interventions convey understanding of the possible responses of individuals facing troubling situations? A second way of assessing intervention and listening skills is the process of role playing. Team leaders can watch to see if team members are able to ask open-ended questions and convey warmth or whether they assume an investigative stance and begin bombarding the person with questions in an efficient data-gathering manner. During the role playing, suggestions can be made for altering interviewing and listening styles, and team leaders can observe whether these suggestions are integrated by team members. Another method for evaluating skills is through follow-up discussions after interventions are conducted. If more than one team member is in attendance, each member can be asked to discuss his or her assessment of the intervention. As newer team members are probably paired with those whose skill levels are well established, senior team members can be given the responsibility of mentoring and informally evaluating newer members. In addition, follow-up discussions with initial contact sources who requested the service can provide information that assists in evaluating team members.

A final issue for evaluation is the current emotional state of the team member. At various times team members will have life crises, including marital breakups and the death of loved ones. Emotional responses to these life events can spill into trauma team interventions. At these times, team members should be encouraged to take a break from the team, if this seems most useful to them, or if the team is an important source of support, change the nature of their involvement with the team in order that their issues do not interfere with interventions.

Maintaining Commitment

In a team that relies on voluntary participation of members, it is vital to find means to maintain commitment. Those individuals who volunteer time to a trauma response team tend to be people who are also highly active in other aspects of their work and lives. These are individuals who are already juggling work commitments, family commitments, and other volunteer activities in their communities. Thus, support and appreciation for the time that they give to the team is justified and helps augment their already strong sense of duty and altruism. Studies on facilitating volunteer commitment point to such factors as organizational support, participation in the decision-making process, and respect for the skills and abilities of the volunteers (Farmer and Fedor, 1999; Lucas and Williams, 2000; Reitsma-Street, Maczewski, and Neysmith, 2000). Thus rewards offered by the team must focus on these aspects. In addition, it is important that team leaders remain aware of the psychological contract between the team members and the team and continuously evaluate expectations that volunteers have of the team to ensure that these expectations are being met.

Ongoing training sessions can serve as an excellent motivator for maintaining commitment, as members commonly enjoy the camaraderie, the opportunities to further their skills and knowledge, and the reinforcement that they get from other team members. Initially, these meetings were run in a rather businesslike manner for the Pearson International Airport team. We then realized, however, that team members valued beginning with a social time that allowed for catching up with members from other organizations. In this way, affiliation needs as well as educative needs could be met. It is important to continuously evaluate whether the topics selected for training and education meet with the needs of team members and ensure that team members have input into both the topics and format of training. In addition to training, we have devised other means on the Pearson International Airport team in order to maintain members. We have found these combined methods to be highly effective and to contribute to a strong and loyal team of highly skilled individuals.

- Some team members are selected to participate on a senior administrative committee and participate in decisions regarding services and team administration.
- Letters are regularly sent to management of the members' organizations, thanking the organizations for their continued support and highlighting the contributions of team members.
- Concrete forms of recognition are provided by the team. Team members are given 5-year and 10-year pins for their commitment. Certificates are also presented attesting to the training and years of service. Team pictures appear in local organization newsletters.
- A yearly luncheon or cocktail party for members, and at times their spouses, is also provided.

- Our team has also engaged in joint research projects that have led to presentations and publications in which emergency responders and clinicians share authorship.

Safety for Team Members

At times risk and fears occur due to the unknown hazards associated with the environmental destruction brought on by a disaster. In New York the number of respiratory medical leaves increased five times among NYFD members over the 11 months following the attacks on the World Trade Center (Centers for Disease Control and Prevention, 2000). Several dynamics were involved, including numerous airborne hazards related to both the collapse and the ongoing fires at the site. While at the site, we noticed that some of our mental health colleagues were wearing personal protective equipment and others were not. As we looked around, we noticed that some recovery workers wore respiratory protection and many did not. It raised the importance of clarifying work expectations, recognizing the influence of group behavior, and communicating risk in a proactive manner.

Self-Care for Team Members

While trauma team membership is very rewarding work, team members need to be aware that when they listen to the tragedy and suffering that others have endured or witnessed, it begins to have an impact on them as well. The process of vicarious trauma is discussed in chapters 3 and 13 (Figley, 1995a; McCann and Pearlman, 1990b). Various studies have documented the effects on counselors and others who are exposed to tragic stories. For instance, a study of 70 human rights workers in Kosovo who were responsible for collecting data on human rights violations revealed elevated levels of anxiety in 17.1%, depression in 8.6%, and post-traumatic stress disorder symptoms in 7.1% (Holtz, Salama, Cardoza, and Gotway, 2002). Among lay trauma counselors (or peer support team workers) who had been trained to assist bank employees following bank robberies in South Africa, 10% reported secondary traumatic stress symptoms in the high or extremely high range (Ortlepp and Friedman, 2002). There is some indication that those individuals with professional training in mental health, such as social workers or psychologists, report lower levels of trauma symptoms. For instance, among 67 professional therapists working with perpetrators of sexual abuse in Australia, none had post-traumatic stress symptoms in the clinical range as measured by the revised IES, and 15.4%, 12.5%, and 8.0% reported mild disruptions in the domains of intrusion, avoidance, and hyperarousal, respectively (Steed and Bicknell, 2001). Despite the fact that few trauma counselors may have PTSD, qualitative studies and anecdotal reports demonstrate that the exposure to traumatic material does have a significant impact on these individuals (Iliffe and Steed, 2000; Ortlepp and Friedman, 2002; Regehr and Cadell, 1999; Schauben and Frazier, 1995). Similar to traumatic stress, symptoms of vicarious trauma can include immediate reactions such as intrusive imagery, nightmares, increased fears for the safety of oneself and loved ones, avoidance of violent stimuli in the media, difficulty listening to clients' accounts of events, irritability, and emotional numbing. Longer-term reactions can include emotional and physical depletion, a sense of hopelessness, and a changed worldview in which others are viewed with suspicion and cynicism.

The first step in self-care is developing an awareness of one's own level of stress and distress as a result of working with individuals who have encountered trauma. One way of doing this is seeking the perceptions of caring others, who are likely to view our current level of stress and coping differently than we do. Crisis counselors both with professional mental health training and with emergency service backgrounds are likely to downplay the negative impact of the work and forge on regardless ("It's OK, I'm fine"). Frequently, caring individuals in the lives of counselors are more able to pick up changes in mood and behavior that signify stress and distress. Second, counselors need to acknowledge a personal history of trauma and assess whether this history is affecting their work or their current emotional state (Sexton, 1999). If old wounds are being reopened, counselors must practice what they preach and obtain assistance from others.

It is important for everyone working in this field to establish a support network that can provide consultation, supervision, and debriefing. No one has enough experience to carry the load alone. Trauma support counselors need to take the initiative to contact members of their support network following a difficult intervention (Dane, 2000; Talbot, 1989). In addition, team members and programs must scrutinize the degree of exposure that any one team member has to others in acute need. Finally, team members must attend to their own personal and family needs and ensure that they develop other satisfying aspects of their lives beyond their work and team involvement.

- Practice what you preach.
- Develop an awareness of your personal level of stress and distress (ask the perceptions of caring others).
- Don't try to save the world.
- Identify your personal limits of competence and seek consultation and supervision.
- Establish and use a support network—in addition to support within teams, develop supports with other teams who will not be responding to the same event with whom you can debrief or defuse.
- Attend to your own needs and issues and take a break from the team when dealing with other life challenges.
- Create boundaries between your life and work on the team.
- Advocate for resources that support the trauma team work.
- Have other satisfying elements in your life.

Figure 12.5. Self-Care for Team Members

Summary

It is tempting when developing a trauma support team to invest a great deal of energy into conceptualizing and selling the need for a team, setting up the team, and announcing that the service is now available. However, in our experience the continued functioning of a team is highly dependent on a core of dedicated people who are willing to continue to develop and manage administrative systems, ensure that services are being performed in a timely and competent manner, ensure that team members continue to upgrade skills, and ensure team members maintain positive mental health, both for their own safety and for the safety of those receiving services.

13

DOES IT WORK?

Evaluating the Efficacy of Interventions

In providing any type of mental health service to an individual, a group of individuals, or an organization, it is important to assess whether what we are doing actually works, or, at the very least, doesn't make things worse. Have the group debriefings or individual diffusings met the goal of reducing symptoms and making people generally feel better? Does preventative education reduce the occurrence of distress or change the organizational culture in order to make the workplace more supportive and open to hearing about distress?

Interventions related to workplace trauma have exploded over the past few years and are increasingly becoming a part of everyday language. Whenever a tragedy occurs, reporters rush to interview debriefers who have been called to the scene, seeking comment on how the workers or other affected people are managing. More recently, controversy has arisen about the efficacy of workplace interventions that occur after a disaster, and in particular the crisis debriefing group model. Following the attack on the World Trade Center in September 2001 and in the wake of trauma debriefing teams that descended on the New York area, a group of trauma researchers wrote a letter to the *New York Times* suggesting that the efforts of the debriefers were misguided and that there was no empirical evidence to support their approach.

Developers of crisis debriefing group models, mental health practitioners, and emergency service worker "peers" trained in the model have extolled the virtues of the crisis debriefing model as an intervention strategy,

211

claiming that it achieves remarkable success in terms of reduced trauma symptoms and increased productivity. As a result of the claimed success, the group model has moved beyond use with emergency responders, the original client group, and has been applied to many populations, including teenagers affected by school shootings, bank tellers, and victims of car accidents. Recent reviews of the research, however, have questioned the conclusion that crisis debriefing groups reduce traumatic stress reactions and have expressed concern that debriefing may in fact exacerbate symptoms (Arendt and Elklit, 2001; Bisson, McFarlane, and Rose, 2000; Rose, Bisson, and Wesley, 2003; Raphael, Meldrum, and McFarlane, 1995; van Emmerik, Kamphuis, Huisbosch, and Emmelkamp, 2002). While most practitioners working in this area are quick to point out that the crisis debriefings are only one part of a comprehensive program aimed at reducing the impact of exposure to traumatic events in the workplace, the group debriefings have often become a central part of the training and intervention programs. In particular, it is a central part of the service provided by contracted employee assistance programs.

Crisis group debriefings are certainly not the only type of treatment approach we have recommended in this volume. Rather, we have stressed a continuum of interventions spanning from preventative education and a healthier workplace to individual interventions with acutely distressed individuals to group interventions including crisis debriefings. The research literature's greatest emphasis over the past number of years has been on the crisis debriefing model. In addition, considerable research exists on the efficacy of certain types of interventions with individuals who suffer from PTSD or acute stress disorder. Far less attention has been directed to the preventative education components of intervention programs. This book is not intended to be a review of individual treatments for PTSD, as many excellent review books are available on this topic (Orner and Schnyder, 2003; Foa, Keane, and Friedman, 2000; Follette, Ruzek, and Aubeg, 1998). In general, the findings offer strong support for cognitive behavioral models of intervention, and endorse the use of medication for those who are acutely distressed. This chapter will therefore focus on reviewing the present evidence on crisis debriefings, suggesting ways in which the findings can be applied to other forms of intervention. In reviewing the evidence, we have to be conscious of the fact that crisis debriefings are not unique in proliferating despite limited data to support that they work. This has been a common issue in mental health treatment, and controversy exists over the efficacy of many methods of treatment. Nevertheless, if we are to assert that organizations should invest resources in programs, and if we encourage individuals to attend them, we have an obligation to evaluate our methods and be aware of the work of other researchers evaluating the methods.

Table 13.1. Levels of evidence

Level 1	Meta-analysis or replicated RCT that includes a placebo condition/control group or active comparison condition
Level 2	At least 1 RCT with placebo or active conparison condition
Level 3	Uncontrolled trial with 10 or more subjects
Level 4	Anecdotal case reports

Reprinted from Roberts and Yeager, 2004.

Increasingly it is expected that all intervention programs, regardless of the target of change or the method of intervention, be based on evidence. *Evidence-based practice* is the conscientious, explicit, and judicious use of the best available scientific evidence in professional decision making (Sackett, Richardson, Rosenberg, and Haynes, 1997). More simply defined, it is the use of treatments for which there is sufficiently persuasive evidence to support their effectiveness in attaining the desired outcomes (Rosen, Proctor, and Staudt, 2003). Evidence is generally ranked hierarchically into series of levels according to scientific strength. Various types of intervention will have had the opportunity to be evaluated more frequently and rigorously by virtue of the length of time they have been used and the settings in which they are used. Thus, for newer treatments, only level-4 evidence may be available. In such cases, practitioners should use the method with caution, continue to search for evidence of efficacy, and be prepared to evaluate the efficacy of the method in their own practice (Roberts and Yeager, 2004).

The Efficacy of Crisis Debriefings: Conflicting Evidence

The literature regarding the efficacy of crisis debriefings reports three main types of evidence: (1) anecdotal reports and satisfaction surveys, (2) cross-sectional design studies, and (3) randomized control trials. Each of these is described below, as is research on workplace trauma interventions utilizing the various research methodologies.

Anecdotal Reports and Satisfaction Surveys

Similar to many other new forms of treatment, initial reports of the efficacy of crisis debriefing groups have relied on anecdotal evidence, client satisfaction surveys, and clinical impressions of group leaders. Anecdotal reports refer to case reports or clinical impressions of practitioners providing services. In this type of writing, individual practitioners describe specific debriefings or summarize a series of interventions that they have conducted. They then report their impressions of the process or report statements made by participants regarding the usefulness of the intervention. Lane (1994) described the experiences of group crisis debriefings with nurses in an acute care hospital. She reports that one participant "participated in two debriefings following the incident. She reported them to be extremely helpful" (p. 309). Tehrani and Westlake (1994) similarly described individual debriefings with 500 employees in a postal service in the United Kingdom and reported that "the results looked very promising and are in the process of being evaluated" (p. 258). Armstrong, O'Callahan, and Marmar (1991) report about a group debriefing model with Red Cross personnel, "We believe that the Multiple Stressor Debriefing Model Groups will aid in the reduction of symptom disorders and increase the effectiveness of workers" (p. 592). These types of clinical reports are frequently very powerful, as they describe the acute distress expressed by group participants and the gratitude and relief participants experience as a result of the intervention.

Satisfaction surveys, generally handed out to program participants shortly after the intervention, include questions such as: "Did you find the intervention helpful?" "Did your symptoms decrease as a result of the intervention?" "Did you feel that the group leaders (or educators/therapists) were knowledgeable?" The surveys are then usually collected by the individuals who conducted the interventions, and results are summarized. Burns and Harm (1993) report the results of a survey of 682 emergency room nurses. Thirty-two percent of the nurses had attended crisis debriefings and 88% of those who had attended debriefings found them helpful. Robinson and Mitchell (1993) similarly report that 90% of 288 emergency and hospital workers who attended debriefing groups found them helpful.

A previous study we conducted addressed the issue of crisis debriefings in 164 firefighters in Australia (Regehr and Hill, 2000). In that study the majority of firefighters attending crisis debriefing groups felt that they were at least somewhat beneficial to them personally (86%) and assisted in reducing their level of stress (77%). Figure 13.1 demonstrates the responses to the satisfaction component of the study. This confirmed the findings of prior studies in which participants in crisis debriefing groups responded to interview questions or questionnaires. However, the standardized measures in this study demonstrated a seemingly contradictory picture and suggested that those individuals attending debriefing groups actually had higher rates of depression and traumatic-stress symptoms. This is consistent with the findings of other cross-sectional design studies on crisis debriefing groups for emergency responders.

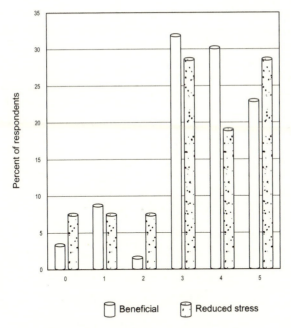

Figure 13.1. Helpfulness of CD groups

Cross-Sectional Design Studies

Cross-sectional design studies are ones in which a group of individuals is surveyed at one point in time regarding their experiences and current state. In studies on crisis debriefings and emergency responders, this means that individuals are generally asked about events they encountered, treatment they received, and their current level of symptoms. In our study, for instance (Regehr and Hill, 2000), firefighters were asked which types of events they had been exposed to, whether they attended debriefings, whether the debriefings were helpful, and what symptoms they were presently experiencing. While, as noted above, most of those attending debriefings indicated that they were helpful, when depressive and post-traumatic stress symptoms were measured utilizing the Beck Depression Inventory (BDI) (Beck and Beamesderfer, 1974) and the Impact of Event Scale (Zilberg, Weiss, and Horowitz, 1982), those individuals who attended debriefing groups had significantly higher scores on the IES intrusion subscale than those exposed to critical events who did not attend debriefings. This means that individuals attending the group debriefing reported higher levels of such symptoms as nightmares, intrusive thoughts, and images of the traumatic event some time after the debriefing occurred. In addition, scores on the BDI and the IES avoidance subscale were higher in the debriefing group, although this

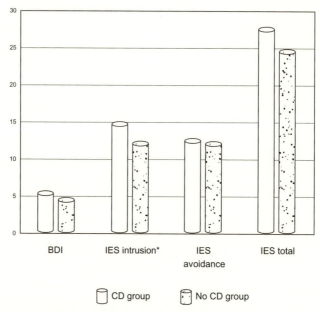

Figure 13.2. PTSD, Depression, and CD Groups
* Significant at p≤ 0.05
BDI: Depression scores as measured by the Beck Depression Inventory
IES intrusion: Scores on the Intrusion Subscale of the Impact of Event Scale
IES avoidance: Scores on the Avoidance Subscale of the Impact of Event Scale
IES total: Trauma symptoms as measured by the total score of the Impact of
Event Scale

did not reach a statistically significant level. Further, there were no significant associations between subjective rating of benefit from crisis debriefing groups and IES or BDI scores. That is, individuals' perceptions
about whether or not they were helped were unrelated to their actual scores
on symptom scales.

Other cross-sectional studies have found similar results. Deahl, Gillhas,
and Thomas (1994), for instance, studied psychological morbidity in British
soldiers who were involved in body-handling duties during the Gulf War and
found no difference in scores on a PTSD scale between soldiers who attended debriefing groups and those who did not. Similarly, Stephens (1997)
reported no difference in PTSD scores for police officers who attended debriefings and those who did not, and Carlier, Lamberts, van Uchelen, and
Gersons (1998) found higher rates of intrusion symptoms at 18 months
among police officers who attended debriefings. McFarlane (1988) compared two groups of firefighters, those attending psychological debriefings
and those who did not, and discovered that while the debriefing group had

lower levels of acute post-traumatic stress, they were more likely to experience delayed reactions. Mathews (1998) looked at the effects of debriefings on 63 direct care psychiatric workers following assaults by community housing residents. Thirty-two of the workers were in an organization where debriefings were available. She found no significant difference in symptoms of post-traumatic stress or work stress, 1 week after the event, between those workers who attended debriefings and those who did not. An interesting finding, however, was that the lowest levels of stress were among workers who had crisis debriefings available to them but chose not to attend.

In a study examining both traumatic stress symptoms and satisfaction with debriefings, Carlier, Voerman, and Gersons (2000) had similar findings to our own. That is, police officers who attended a series of three debriefings felt positively about the experience but had higher rates of post-traumatic stress 1 week after the event than those who did not attend. In a related study, Fullerton, Ursano, Vance, and Wang (2000) evaluated whether individuals who talked about their experiences of disaster informally with friends and colleagues had lower levels of symptoms. Individuals in the study were military personnel who responded to a plane crash in Sioux City, Iowa. Those who talked more about their experiences in the disaster to friends and family had higher rates of intrusion and avoidance symptoms at 2 months following the event. The researchers identified that it was possible that having more symptoms caused people to talk more and not that talking made them worse. However, there was not an association between talking about the event right after it happened (the point at which debriefings generally occur) and symptoms at 2 months afterward. The researchers concluded that this study did not support the idea that talking it out made people feel better.

Randomized Controlled Trials

Experimental design studies using randomized controlled trials (RCTs) are viewed to be the most rigorous form of evaluation when studying the efficacy of programs or interventions. In this type of study, individuals who have a particular problem or illness are randomly assigned to a treatment program or no treatment. Typically in medicine this involves giving some individuals a new medication to treat their problems while the other individuals are given the older, more established medication and/or a placebo. Individuals are usually "blind" to which treatment they are getting, in order to limit the influence of an expectation effect. That is, to control for the fact that in believing that the new treatment will work, individuals may rate themselves as doing better. In evaluating trauma interventions, researchers conducting an RCT will select a group of people who have experienced the same or a similar event and randomly place some in the treatment group.

The remaining individuals will either be given no treatment or placed on a waiting list for treatment at a future time. Standardized measures of symptoms are then given to both the treatment and nontreatment groups at various time periods, and their levels of symptoms are compared. To date, no RCTs have been reported for emergency responders or other work groups regarding single-session crisis debriefings; however, several have been reported for other populations.

Mayou, Ehlers, and Hobbs (2000) randomly assigned road traffic accident victims to psychological debriefing or no-treatment groups. At 4 months post-injury, they reported that the psychological debriefing was ineffective, and at 3 years, the intervention group remained significantly more symptomatic. They concluded that patients who initially had high intrusion and avoidance symptoms remained symptomatic if they received intervention but recovered if they did not receive intervention. Bisson, Jenkins, Alexander, and Bannister (1997) reported that burn victims who received debriefings had significantly higher rates of anxiety, depression, and PTSD 13 months following their injury than burn victims who did not receive debriefings. The authors note, however, that the people who attended the debriefing groups did have higher rates of these problems prior to the intervention (though not significantly) and had suffered more severe injuries.

Two RCT studies are reported of individuals encountering work-related trauma, although neither compare the outcomes of single-session debriefings with no debriefing. Campfield and Hills (2001) compared the effects of immediate (occurring less than 10 hours after the event) and delayed (by more than 48 hours) debriefings on bank tellers involved in a robbery. The number and severity of symptoms did not differ at the time of the debriefing between the two groups. However, at three subsequent intervals, 2 days, 4 days, and 2 weeks, the immediate intervention group had lower levels of symptoms than the delayed-intervention group. This suggests that if debriefing interventions are performed, providing them within the first few hours of the event, before individuals go home and while they are still in the initial stages of arousal, may be more effective. Using a substantially different model of intervention, Gersons and colleagues (2000) designed and tested a 16-week group treatment program for police officers who were already experiencing symptoms of PTSD. Their model, Brief Eclectic Psychotherapy (BEP), incorporates cognitive behavioral strategies such as psychoeducation, homework tasks, guided imagery and cognitive restructuring, and a psychodynamic understanding. Symptoms of traumatic stress were compared at various intervals between the treatment group and waiting-list controls. They report that in the end, the BEP treatment group members were significantly improved with regards to both symptoms and work resumption in comparison to the control group. For these officers, an intensive 16-session program focusing on cognitive behavioral change was useful. Clearly, however, this is substantially different than the single-session model.

A very interesting study by Schnurr and colleagues (2003) reports the results of an RCT conducted with 360 Vietnam veterans with PTSD comparing trauma-focused group treatment with supportive group treatment. Treatment sessions were provided to groups of 6 individuals for 30 weeks, followed by 5 monthly booster sessions. The trauma-focused groups used exposure therapy combined with cognitive restructuring and coping-skills training. Participants in the groups were thus confronted with memories of their own traumatic experiences and were also vicariously exposed to traumatic events described by others. Participants assigned to the other type of group treatment approach received present-focused treatment that avoided traumatic material. In the end, participants in both types of groups had significantly lower PTSD symptoms. However, significantly more people dropped out of the trauma-focused groups—22.8% versus 8.6%—and thus the trauma-focused group had a selection bias. That is, those who were benefiting remained in treatment.

Making Sense of the Disparity in Findings

Satisfaction surveys are somewhat limited in their ability to demonstrate the efficacy of an intervention. First of all, it is difficult to assess whether the fact that people were happy or unhappy with the program or intervention is the same as determining whether it worked or did not work. For instance, a person may feel dissatisfied with their experience in the hospital due to the quality of food, the surroundings, or the temperament of the staff, yet still recover from illness. Similarly, a person may feel good about a treatment program and like his or her therapist, yet the target symptoms—in this case, post-traumatic stress—are not reduced or eliminated.

Cross-sectional design studies also are problematic because we cannot assume causality simply because two factors occur together. For instance, in Holland, there is a higher birth rate in areas that have larger numbers of storks. Despite the affinity with folklore, it is unreasonable to assume that the storks cause babies to be born. Rather, birth rates are higher in rural areas than in urban areas, which unrelatedly also have lower numbers of storks. In considering cross-sectional design studies that assess symptoms of emergency responders and whether they attend crisis debriefing groups, we also need to be cautious about inferring cause and effect. We cannot determine whether findings support the contention of some researchers that exposure to traumatic stimuli in the process of a crisis debriefing group may be iatrogenic, causing those who attend to have higher levels of symptoms (Bisson and Deahl, 1994; Bissonand et al., 1997; Raphael, Meldrum, and McFarlane, 1995), or whether more highly distressed individuals are more likely to attend crisis debriefing groups, and that attendance at the groups simply does not bring the symptoms down to the level experienced by those who do not attend. The RCTs reported to date on crisis debriefings have been conducted on groups other than emergency responders. It may not be appropriate to compare individuals suffering from catastrophic injuries with workers exposed to traumatic events in the line of duty.

Regardless of these limitations, in reviewing research literature on debriefings, Neria and Solomon (1999) conclude that virtually all noncontrolled studies of single-session debriefings point to the effectiveness of debriefings, while the controlled studies at best show no effect and at worst reveal higher vulnerability and increased psychopathology among debriefed subjects. Our study revealed both these findings in the same individuals. That is, people reported feeling better, but had higher rates of symptoms when compared to those who did not attend debriefings. Conversely, there is some evidence that prolonged group treatment programs (16–30 sessions) for those who are mostly acutely distressed are of some benefit. In light of these mixed findings, many questions remain unanswered as yet regarding crisis debriefings. It does seem, however, that the same intervention could simultaneously be helpful in some regards and unhelpful in others. This controversy requires that attention be directed to what aspects of the crisis debriefing model may be helpful and what aspects of the model may be counterproductive.

Enhancing Individual Coping through Crisis Debriefings and Other Interventions

As we have discussed throughout this book, several variables have been identified in the literature as contributing to the intensity and duration of the traumatic stress reactions that crisis debriefings and other post-incident interventions attempt to address. One obvious set of factors is the magnitude of the exposure, the length of exposure, and the number of repeated exposures to traumatic stimuli. But as we have also suggested, people encountering the same event or series of events will not have the same intensity or duration of symptoms. Rather, individual responses are mediated by a variety of individual and organizational factors. One individual variable that contributes to trauma response is the sense of control that an individual has over the environment and over unforeseen stressors (Rotter, 1975). Individuals who, in the face of disaster, manage to retain a belief that they can control outcomes have been found to manage the experience far more effectively than individuals who believed they were controlled by external forces (Gibbs, 1989; Regehr, Cadell, and Jansen, 1999). For instance, it has been demonstrated that firefighters experience difficulty coping and have higher levels of traumatic stress symptoms when they perceive that they have lower levels of control (Bryant and Harvey, 1996; Regehr, Hill, and Glancy 2000).

An important aspect of the crisis debriefing is the psycho-educational component that focuses on regaining control through understanding common reactions to trauma exposure and formulating strategies for symptom management. Cognitive and behavioral strategies discussed in the group session may include the use of exercise to reduce arousal symptoms, acceptance of symptoms as normal and time-limited, reducing reliance on alcohol and drugs during times of high stress, and self-care. Thus, despite the limited nature of the intervention, participants are provided with some tools to increase their sense of control over the recovery process. These types of approaches can also be taught to individuals in educational sessions that occur prior to a traumatic event to prepare them and encourage them to develop healthy stress management strategies. They can also be used on an individual basis with people affected by a particular event or series of events.

Rothbaum and Foa (1996) and Follette, Ruzek, and Abueg (1998) provide extensive overviews of the effectiveness of cognitive-behavioral approaches for post-traumatic stress disorder. They conclude that CBT is effective in reducing the severity of PTSD symptoms in the majority of cases. Similarly, Foy et al. (2000) review six studies of CBT group treatment with trauma survivors (three wait-list control and three single-group pretest/posttest) and indicate that all showed positive outcomes on PTSD symptom measures. Reported effect sizes ranged from 0.33 to 1.09, with a mean of 0.68. Larger treatment effects were reported for avoidance symptoms than intrusion symptoms. In addition, as we noted earlier, there is some evidence that CBT group treatment provided over a longer period of time is of some benefit to such groups as police officers and Vietnam veterans. However, applying these findings on CBT efficacy to single-session debriefings is suspect at best, considering the short duration of this treatment in a crisis debriefing group. One would expect that the results will be more modest than is generally found for CBT and that severe PTSD symptoms will not be ameliorated by the single-session group intervention alone.

Social Support and Crisis Interventions in the Workplace

As we have discussed extensively throughout this book, in addition to individual strengths and vulnerabilities, other external factors such as social supports and the recovery environment have been found to influence responses to traumatic events (Leffler and Dembert, 1998; King, King, Fairbank, Keane, and Adams, 1997; Weiss et al., 1995). While several studies confirm that traumatic events encountered in the line of duty cause stress responses in rescue workers, other researchers have argued that it is organizational stressors that cause the greatest degree of distress in emergency service personnel. For instance, events such as dealing with victims of serious accidents, being attacked by aggressive offenders, or dealing with protesters may cause stress in police officers. However, several large-scale studies in England, Australia, Canada, and the United States have concluded that the greatest source of stress for officers is the police organization itself, with its rules, procedures, communication paths, bureaucratic hierarchy, and management style (Brown and Campbell, 1990; Burke, 1993; Buunk and Peeters, 1994; Coman and Evans, 1991; Hart, Wearing, and Headley, 1995). The outcomes of this stress include high levels of alcoholism, possibly higher suicide rates than that of comparison groups, and a rate of marital problems that is double that of comparison groups (Golembiewski and Kim, 1990). Similarly, ambulance workers involved in body recovery duties following mass disasters in England identified that poor relationships with management, not being valued for their skills, and shift work were the major stressors they encountered (Thompson, 1993).

Not surprisingly, a primary mediating factor of traumatic stress reactions is social support within the organization, particularly from superiors (Buunk and Peeters, 1994; Gibbs et al., 1993; Regehr, Hill, and Glancy, 2000). That is, when people feel supported and valued within their work environment, they experience lower levels of distress. This concept of social support is highly related to the importance of crisis debriefings and other workplace interventions. That is, post-trauma interventions are obvious indicators that an organization supports its workers through the purchase of mental health services and the provision of time to deal with the aftermath of a critical event. The fact that traumatic stress interventions occur at all acts as an acknowledgement that traumatic stress reactions are normal and expected following a tragic event and will be accepted (or at least tolerated) within the organizational culture. Thus, workers who perceive that organizational support is being demonstrated though the interventions are likely to respond positively when asked if the crisis debriefing they attended was helpful. This is compatible with the relatively consistent findings that workers value the debriefing experience (Burns and Harm, 1993; Regehr and Hill, 2000; Robinson and Mitchell, 1993). It may also be consistent with the finding that provision of service within the first 10 hours after a robbery occurred was more useful to bank tellers than interventions that occurred even 2 days later (Campfield and Hills, 2001). That is, people were grateful to have someone to talk to while they were still shocked and acutely upset and before they returned home. However, when considering other factors that may contribute to PTSD symptoms, such as individual vulnerabilities and chronic workplace stressors, it is unlikely that any brief intervention is going to ameliorate symptoms exacerbated by these factors.

Secondary Trauma and Crisis Debriefing Groups

Secondary trauma in mental health professionals working with traumatized individuals is increasingly recognized. Figley (1995) defines secondary traumatic stress as "the natural, consequent behaviors and emotions resulting from *knowledge about* a traumatizing event experienced by a significant other. It is the stress resulting from *helping or wanting to help* a traumatized or suffering person" (p. 10). As a result of this exposure, therapists are reported to experience symptoms that parallel those of individuals suffering the after effects of traumatic experiences. Symptoms include nightmares, intrusive imagery, sleep disturbances, hypervigilance, emotional numbing, and changed worldview (Chrestman, 1995; Regehr and Cadell, 1999). Consequently, several authors speak to the importance of debriefing the debriefers in order to protect their emotional and psychological health (Kahill, 1998; McCann and Pearlman, 1990b; Talbot, Manton, and Dunn, 1992).

McCann and Pearlman (1990a) have offered a theory of vicarious traumatization based on the concept of self-schema theory or constructivist self-development theory. From this perspective, individuals develop mental templates of self and others based on their interactions with the world. While for the most part these are based on personal lived experiences, it is posited that with repeated exposure to traumatic imagery in providing therapy, mental health workers may begin to incorporate an accumulation of clients' traumatic material into their own view of self and the world. The understanding of memory processes subsequent to encountering traumatic events remains speculative for the most part (see Appelbaum, Uyehara, and Elin [1997] for a comprehensive review); nevertheless, it appears possible to incorporate the experiences of others into one's own memory system or schematic structures in situations of high social influence or in times of high emotional intensity (Brewin, 1996; Paris, 1996). In the process of trauma treatment, emotions such as rage, horror, and dismay are often present. Therapists may feel overwhelmed by the emotional state of their clients or by the atrocity of the material presented. At this stage, if they are unable to integrate the material presented into their own cognitive structures, it may be experienced as intrusive thoughts, flashbacks, or dreams, and it can lead to feelings of hopelessness and despair (McCann and Pearlman, 1990b; Horowitz, 1976).

If we accept that vicarious traumatization is possible in therapists, it seems more probable in individuals who have been exposed to a traumatic event. These individuals will more likely be in a state of emotional and psychological vulnerability and may be struggling with symptom management and with making meaning of the experience. A central component of the CISD model described by Everly and colleagues (2000) is the *reaction phase*, where members are encouraged to recount their worst experience during the event, often in graphic detail, in order to allow for cathartic ventilation and emotional abreaction. Dunning (1999) suggests that the traumatized people listening to the graphic descriptions of others' experiences in a group debriefing session may be triggered into the same neurobiological response as they experienced during the traumatic event. In this environment of affective overload, the images described by other members may become incorporated into an individual's trauma set. This conceptualization is extremely useful in our attempts to understand the findings that attendance at crisis debriefings increases risk of PTSD, particularly intrusion symptoms.

In cognitive-behavioral group therapy with trauma victims, participants are frequently encouraged to repeatedly reexperience their own traumatic events and to be exposed vicariously to the experiences of others for the purposes of cognitively processing the traumatic material (Foy et al., 2000). From this perspective, trauma reduction occurs through the process of first reactivating the fear memory and second providing new information that is incompatible with the fear structure so a new memory can be formed (Resick and Schnicke, 1993a,b; Rothbaum, Meadows, Resick, and Foy, 2000). However, it is suggested that this model of treatment be used only when a sound therapeutic alliance has been formed and a thorough assessment has been completed (Calhoun and Atkeson, 1991). This was demonstrated clearly in the trauma-focused group treatment with Vietnam veterans suffering from PTSD described by Schnurr and colleagues (2003). In this instance, care was taken to use the group to create a sense of support and safety for participants prior to and during traumatic exposure. Further, individuals in this type of treatment group should be assessed to have the capacity to tolerate high anxiety arousal, have no active suicidal ideation, no co-morbid substance abuse, and no current life crises (Foy et al., 2000).

Thus while a cognitively based model of treatment incorporating exposure to traumatic imagery has evidence of success in individuals with PTSD, the tested group model differs in several ways from the CISD model. The first important difference is the duration of treatment. Neria and Solomon (1999) posit that the discussion of emotional reactions in the CISD model is "sandwiched between fact finding and cognitive reframing" (p. 316), and that therefore individuals may be given insufficient opportunities to process and place closure on the feelings that are aroused. Second, intervention models that utilize exposure techniques are initiated a considerable time after the traumatic event has occurred, at a time when PTSD symptoms have developed. They are not employed when the person is in the early stages of crisis; then, techniques focus around containment through reducing exposure to further stress and harm. Finally, the nature of crisis debriefings do not allow for prior assessment of the strengths and vulnerabilities of participants. There is no opportunity to assess the ego strengths, prior coping strategies, current social supports, and other concurrent stressors in order to determine the ability of the individual to manage the effects of exposure. In addition, while individuals experiencing acute distress are to be referred for additional individual assistance, the size of the group and the limited time to engage with each member may preclude debriefers' ability to identify those individuals who may experience higher levels of distress. Therefore, the approaches described in therapeutic groups employing cognitive exposure and abreaction do not apply to crisis debriefings, which are aimed at prevention of trauma, not amelioration of entrenched symptoms.

Reviewing the Strengths and Limitations of Crisis Debriefing Groups

In light of the history of equating trauma response with an absence of the "right stuff" to do the job, a considerable strength of the crisis debriefing model is its ability to acknowledge the existence of trauma responses and normalize symptoms. Emergency responders encountering symptoms such as nightmares, intrusive imagery, increased arousal, and irritability may reach the conclusion that they do not possess the psychological attributes required to do the job properly. The crisis debriefing encourages discussion of the aftermath of symptoms and opens the door for further discussions within the group of individuals who have attended.

Organizational stressors and supports have consistently been demonstrated to be major factors mitigating or intensifying traumatic stress reactions (Buunk and Peeters, 1994; Gibbs et al., 1993; Regehr, Hill, and Glancy, 2000). The crisis debriefing both demonstrates support of the workers by management and provides the opportunity to enhance social supports within the work team. By virtue of supporting the program in terms of both time and economic resources, management can often demonstrate their concern for workers. Further, the debriefer can facilitate the process of encouraging mutual aid and support within the work team. He or she can identify characteristics within the team that serve as evidence of the strength of working relationships and mutual support.

An additional strength of the crisis debriefing model is the psychoeducational component. This not only describes possible reactions to

Strengths
- Normalizing of symptoms
- Increasing control of symptoms through education regarding cognitive-behavioral strategies
- Mobilizing of social suports within the organization

Limitations
- Inability to reduce symptoms of PTSD
- Possibility of vicarious traumatization
- Limited opportunities to assess vulnerabilities of participants and risk of PTSD

Figure 13.3. Strengths and Limitations of the CD Model

trauma but also generally includes cognitive-behavioral strategies for symptom management. The introduction of these CBT strategies helps group participants learn alternative strategies to self-medication through alcohol use and can assist them in gaining a sense of control over their reactions. This approach is supported by a large body of literature pointing to the efficacy of this approach in treating PTSD (McCann and Pearlman, 1990a; Resick and Schnicke, 1993a,b; Rothbaum and Foa, 1996).

The major limitations of the crisis debriefing model are the inability to reduce symptoms of PTSD (Bisson and Deahl, 1994; Raphael, et al., 1995) and the possibility of vicarious traumatization of participants. Mental health professionals practicing this model of intervention must not ignore this finding. It appears highly likely that these iatrogenic effects may result from the graphic descriptions of traumatic experiences during the event provided by the various group participants. This information is received by individuals who may already be vulnerable, due to their own traumatic experiences during the event and their own current level of traumatic response. The process of flooding individuals with additional gruesome material may add to their traumatic imagery and symptoms of intrusion. The inability to assess and screen out individuals who may have vulnerabilities such as difficult life histories, concurrent life crises, and co-morbid substance abuse or mental health problems may further increase the risk for some people. As a result, it would appear that debriefers should discontinue encouraging detailed descriptions during the reaction stage.

A review of the literature points to some key elements of intervention that have research support and can be applied to any form of intervention. They can be summarized as follows:

- Workers experience lower levels of arousal and distress when provided with properly timed and accurate information.
- The creation of an organizational climate that supports workers reduces the risk of severe reactions following a traumatic event.
- Teaching workers specific skills to deal with distressing symptoms helps them attain a sense of mastery and feel less out of control.
- The most distressed workers should have the opportunity to access individual services, which may include empirically tested cognitive-behavioral approaches and perhaps medication as required.
- Families and friends continue to be the most important resource for workers, and efforts must be made to ensure that they do not become alienated either due to daily strain or in the aftermath of a traumatic event.

Evaluating Our Own Practice

In providing services to any group of people, we are obligated to attempt to determine that what we are providing not only helps them but certainly does not make them worse. Considering the great gains that have been made in highlighting issues of trauma and distress among emergency workers, it is troubling that claims of success have been so wide sweeping that they have now resulted in a well-publicized backlash that questions the value of all interventions. Thus, those of us providing services must find ways to evaluate our practice so that we can ethically speak with confidence about the benefits of what we are providing. This section of the chapter is intended to do two things: first, to identify some simple steps any team or practitioner can take to ensure that services provided meet with present standards of practice, and second, to provide some beginning guidelines for conducting research into one's own practice.

Ensuring Interventions Meet with Current Practice Standards

Academics and researchers are always quick to vehemently criticize practitioners working in the trenches, for their failure to read the research literature and to integrate new findings into practice. This criticism ignores the context in which practitioners work, where workloads and conflicting expectations continuously rise and people are struggling to keep their heads above water. For mental health professionals, caseloads are high and recording requirements become progressively more demanding as financial accountability increases and the pressure to avoid liability looms. For peer support personnel, the trauma support work provided to colleagues is often an "add-on" or voluntary activity that is not acknowledged or compensated. Criticism is therefore a highly destructive process that pits researchers and practitioners against one another and sets up resistance to hear divergent perspectives. The following suggestions are intended to be less onerous means of meeting the ethical obligation of providing services that are effective and not damaging.

- Develop linkages between teams and/or individual practitioners, so people can share their experiences with interventions, openly discuss what they believe worked and did not work in specific situations, and voice any questions or uncertainties.
- On any team or in a group of practitioners, identify a person or develop a rotating responsibility for watching the literature and reporting new findings back to others. Different individuals may subscribe to various journals or have access to online library services. Establishing a routine where one article is discussed at each meeting helps people who have been trained over a year ago keep up to date.
- Attend conferences that evaluate interventions and report on new ideas in the field.
- Develop contacts with local universities and colleges. This may involve participating with professors or graduate students in research projects. It can also involve providing opportunities for student training. Nothing forces us to think about why we are doing what we are doing more than having a student question our assumptions.
- Be prepared to modify models of intervention based on new experiences or information. All treatments are in a constant state of flux based on emerging data. Only 100 years ago it was discovered that sterilization of surgical equipment reduces infection, causing procedures to change dramatically. Twenty-five years ago we believed that the nagging of mothers caused schizophrenia; we now have biological explanations and hopefully no longer blame mothers.
- Consider designing and implementing your own intervention study that will add to the emerging body of knowledge.

Designing an Intervention Study

In designing an intervention study, it is important to follow standards for good quality research so we do not base our judgments on bad science and in order to ensure findings are not discounted because of methodological flaws. Foa and and colleagues (2000) identify several points for a gold standard in trauma research: (1) clearly defined target symptoms; (2) reliable and valid measures; (3) use of blind evaluators; (4) assessor training; (5) manualized, replicable, specific treatment programs; (6) unbiased assignment to treatment; and (7) treatment adherence. These guidelines refer specifically to the evaluation of an individual or group treatment programs. The discussion that follows will not only include the evaluation of individual or group interventions, but will also be expanded to include the continuum of interventions that may be instituted within an organization.

Defining the Program

When deciding to evaluate a program that is being or has been implemented in any organization, the first important step is clearly defining what the program entails. If we are evaluating a group treatment approach, the group structure and format must be spelled out in specific terms and steps, and we must ensure that all of those individuals who are running the group follow the steps and procedures as outlined. If we are evaluating a comprehensive program that is being implemented in an organization, each aspect of the program must be described. In this way, other practitioners and researchers can have the opportunity to develop the same program in other settings and test whether they obtain the same results. Any shifts away from the planned intervention must be clearly described, as they may be critical to the success or failure of the program.

Selecting Desired Outcomes

The first step in determining whether our intervention works is determining what it is we want the program to address. If we are hoping that employees will be happy with the treatment approach and feel good about what they received, a satisfaction survey may be the approach to take. This could also include questions about whether employees believe that the organization is supportive of their needs and understands the strain experienced by employees when confronted with traumatic events on the job. For instance, in order to convince the company to continue to fund the services, providing evidence that the employees liked it and feel good about the organization for offering it may be sufficient. On the other hand, we may wish to address specific problems with the intervention. These problems may include symptoms of post-traumatic stress, employee absenteeism, productivity losses, or use of disability benefits. The target symptoms we identify for change will then be different. Our measures will subsequently rely on the target symptoms and may include scales that measure post-traumatic stress symptoms, human resource records of absenteeism, or actuarial measures of costs in long-term disability benefits.

Target symptoms	Measures
Satisfaction	Satisfaction survey questions (usually do not have established reliability and validity)
Post-traumatic stress symptoms	Scales with established psychometric properties • Impact of event scale (IES) • Posttraumatic diagnostic scale (PTDS) • Trauma symptom inventory (TSI)
Employee absenteeism Inability to work	Human resource records of employee absences Previously collected data that can be compared before and after establishment of program • Workers' compensation claims • Long-term disability benefits claims • Employee turnover

Figure 13.4. Selecting Target Symptoms and Reliable and Valid Measures

Selecting Outcome Measures

In order to determine whether programs are meeting the established goals, it is important to select measures that reliably and validly address the target symptoms. *Reliability* refers to the dependability of a measure and addresses whether it will give you the same results each time, if what you are measuring does not change. For instance, an object weighed on a scale should weigh the same amount each time. *Reliability* also refers to the degree that the measure can distinguish between different items. Thus, an object twice as heavy as the first item weighed should produce a result on the scale that is twice as high. When researchers seek to determine the reliability of a measure, they are interested in three factors: stability, equivalence, and consistency.

The *stability* of the measure is the degree to which it measures the same thing over time. If we are looking at a scale to measure particular symptoms, the stability of a measure is reported as the test/retest reliability. For instance, an IQ test that is administered at one time should yield more or less the same score when administered again 1 month later. Post-traumatic symptoms, on the other hand, are expected to reduce over time and thus test/retest reliability is not particularly useful. If the measure is something recorded over time, such as employee absenteeism, stability is determined by ensuring that the method of collecting data has remained stable and that definitions of what constitutes absenteeism do not change. For instance, if in the past mental health stress leaves were counted as sick time and now are counted as disability claims, this could be problematic for comparison.

Equivalence reliability is the degree to which two independent measures will produce the same result or the degree to which two independent raters will come up with the same answer (interrater reliability).

The internal *consistency* of items is the degree to which all the items on the scale measure the same concept. The statistic most generally reported for internal consistency is a Cronbach's alpha (α).

Each of these measures of reliability is reported as a number between 0 and 1; the closer the number is to 1, the better the reliability. In general, a reliability of less than 0.7 is unacceptable.

Validity refers to the extent to which a measure actually addresses what we want it to. For instance, even though we have access to great data on absenteeism, does that really address the issue of traumatic stress? Would it be better to try to measure mistakes on the job or willingness to volunteer for difficult duties? Validity of measures such as post-traumatic stress scales is usually addressed by comparing scores on the measure to some other indicator. Post-traumatic stress self-report measures can be tested, for example, by having a mental health professional conduct a clinical interview and determine whether those individuals reporting high levels of symptoms on the test would also qualify for a diagnosis using the standard psychiatric criteria.

Three measures that have been used frequently for assessment of trauma symptoms and have well established psychometric properties are the Impact of Event Scale (IES), the Post-Traumatic Diagnostic Scale (PTDS) and the Trauma Symptom Inventory (TSI).

The Impact of Event Scale (Horowitz et al., 1982) assesses the experience of post-traumatic stress for any specific life event. It extracts dimensions that parallel the defining characteristics of the DSM-IV-TR criteria for PTSD: signs and symptoms of intrusive cognitions and affects together or oscillating with periods of avoidance, denial, or blocking of thoughts and images (American Psychiatric Association, 2002). This scale is reported to have high internal consistency with a Cronbach's alpha of .86 and a test/retest reliability of .87. Scores are classified as low (0–8), medium (9–19), high (20–25), or severe (>26). This scale is probably the most widely used measure in the trauma literature.

The Post-Traumatic Diagnostic Scale (Foa, Cashman, Jaycox, and Perry, 1997) has 17 items corresponding to the three categories of symptoms for PTSD: reexperiencing, arousal, and avoidance. Items are scored for frequency from 0–3. Chronbach alpha is reported as 0.92, and test/retest reliability at 3 weeks was 0.83. When compared with a clinical interview, the SCID, there was 82% agreement.

The Trauma Symptom Inventory (Briere, 1997) contains 100 items and measures both acute and chronic post-traumatic stress symptomatology. As with the other measures, it uses a 4-point severity scale. This scale has been extensively tested on several populations. Internal consistency ratings (α) range from 0.84 to 0.87 on subscales. Scores correlate with independently rated PTSD status, with a specificity of 0.92 and a sensitivity of 0.91.

Reducing Bias

Bias is present in any research project. We may be evaluating a program that we have spent considerable energy developing and implementing. We may be evaluating a program that pays our salary. Our biases determine what we study, how we phrase the questions, whom we include in the study, and what factors we choose to include or ignore. While it is never possible to eliminate bias from a study, the credibility of our research findings is predicated on our ability to limit bias to the greatest degree possible. One way of reducing bias is reporting the results not only on the group in question but also on a comparison group. The ideal method for this is randomly assigning people to one group or another (an RCT). That is, half the people exposed to a trauma are randomly selected for treatment, and the other half are sent home. However, in the real world of applied social research, this is often not possible. We can't just take every second firefighter leaving a scene and send them to a debriefing room. Therefore, often we have a *nonequivalent control group*, a group of people in a comparable situation. For instance, we may have two similar fire services, implement a program in one, and measure the days lost due to sick leave in the two organizations before the program began and again 1 year after it was implemented in the one organization.

Another method of reducing bias is having someone other than a person invested in the program collect and analyze the data. The less these individuals know about which individuals attended the program and which did not, the better. If they have no knowledge, this is referred to as *blind evaluators*. In this way, we are less likely to interpret data in a way that is consistent with our expectations; it allows us to be more open to surprising findings and makes the research findings less open to skepticism. It also requires we be prepared in advance that we may uncover findings that we do not like and that cause us to rethink the program that we are offering.

Be Honest about the Limitations

No research project will be perfect. This is particularly true when the research is being conducted in the real world and not in a laboratory. While we hope that we can randomly assign people to groups, we may not be able to. While we hope for a random sample of the organization, the reality is that we can only get to one shift of people. These limitations do not necessarily discount the value of the study (although at times they may be so significant that they do). What is important is that we honestly discuss the limitations when presenting our findings in written form or in presentations, so that those receiving the information can assess whether the findings make sense for their setting or situation.

Conclusions

The rapid rise of workplace interventions following a traumatic event has meant that new intervention strategies have outpaced the ability to obtain information about the effectiveness. Recent critiques of various intervention strategies and research that has suggested that not all the models of intervention may be of benefit has taken many of those providing service off guard, resulting in a defensive stance. This has been most evident when considering the crisis debriefing model, which has quickly become one of the most popular approaches for dealing with trauma in groups of individuals affected by the same event. From its early days of addressing the needs of military personnel, the model has spread throughout emergency service organizations and health care organizations. It is also now used for victims of large-scale disasters, such as floods and tornados, and in organizations, such as schools where a shooting has occurred. As one watches news reports of tragic events, it is now common to see the debriefing team members interviewed and offering impressions and suggestions for self-care.

While acceptance of mental health needs is a positive step in our society, we as practitioners must ensure that the intervention models we are selecting are likely to be helpful and will not increase morbidity in terms of post-traumatic symptoms. We must be aware of the research conducted into our chosen methods of intervention and attempt to discern how often conflicting data may fit together. Research in the area of workplace trauma interventions is still at an early stage and has not yet clearly delineated which aspects of the programs may be helpful or harmful. It is vitally important that those of us providing service continue to investigate the efficacy of our interventions and be prepared to alter our practices in light of evidence that what we are doing may not result in the optimal outcome.

References

Albucher, R., & Liberzon, I. (2001). Psychopharmacological treatment in PTSD: A critical review. *Journal of Psychiatric Research, 36,* 355–367.

Alexander, C. (1999). Police psychological burnout and trauma. In J. Violanti & D. Paton (Eds.), *Police trauma: The psychological aftermath of civilian combat* (pp. 54–64). Springfield, IL: Charles Thomas.

Alexander, D., & Klein, S. (2001). Ambulance personnel and critical incidents: The impact of accident and emergency work on mental health. *British Journal of Psychiatry, 178*(1), 76–81.

Alexander, D., & Wells, A. (1991). Reactions of police officers to body-handling after a major disaster: A before-and-after comparison. *British Journal of Psychiatry, 159,* 547–555.

American Psychiatric Association. (1980). *Diagnostic and statistical manual of mental disorder* (3rd ed.). Washington, DC: Author.

American Psychiatric Association. (2002). *Diagnostic and statistical manual of mental disorder* (4th ed., text-revision). Washington, DC: Author.

Anderson, G., Litzenberger, R., & Placas, D. (2002). Physical evidence of police stress. *Policing: An International Journal of Police Strategies and Management, 25*(2), 399–420.

Antonovsky, A. (1979). *Health, stress, and coping.* San Francisco: Jossey-Bass.

Appelbaum, P., Uyehara, L., & Elin, M. (1997). *Trauma and memory: Clinical and legal controversies.* New York: Oxford University Press.

Arendt, M., & Elklit, A. (2001). Effectiveness of psychological debriefing. *Acta Psychiatrica Scandinavica, 104,* 423–437.

Arkowitz, H. (2002). Toward an integrative perspective on resistance to change. *Journal of Clinical Psychology, 58*(2), 219–227.

Armstrong, K., O'Callahan, W., & Marmar, C. (1991). Debriefing Red Cross disaster personnel: The multiple stressor debriefing model. *Journal of Traumatic Stress, 4*(4), 581–593.

Auf der Heide, E. (2003). Convergence behavior in disasters. *Annals of Emergency Medicine, 41*(4), 463–466.

Bacharach, S., Bamberger, P., & McKinney, V. (2000). Boundary management tactics and logics of action: The case of peer support providers. *Administrative Science Quarterly, 45,* 704–736.

Baer, R. A. (2003). Mindfulness training as a clinical intervention: A conceptual and empirical overview. *Clinical Psychological: Science and Practice, 10*(2), 125–143.

Baider, L. Peretz, T., Hadani, P., Perry, S., Avarmov, R., & De-Nour, A. (2000). Transmission of response to trauma? Second generation Holocaust survivor's reactions to cancer. *American Journal of Psychiatry, 157*(6), 904–910.

Bale, A. (1990). Medicolegal stress at work. *Behavioral Sciences and the Law, 8,* 399–420.

Bandura, A. (1997). *Self-efficacy: The exercise of control.* New York: W. H. Freeman.

Bankoff, G. (2001). Rendering the world unsafe. Vulnerability as Western discourse. *Disasters, 25*(1), 19–35.

Beaton, R., Murphy, S., Pike, K., & Corneil, W. (1997). Social support and network conflict in firefighters and paramedics. *Western Journal of Nursing Research, 19*(3), 297–313.

Beck, A., & Beamesderfer, A. (1974). Assessment of depression: The depression inventory. In P. Pichot (Ed.), *Psychological measurements in psychopharmacology* (pp. 151–169). Paris: Karger, Basel.

Bell, J. (1995). Traumatic event debriefing: Service delivery designs and the role of social work. *Social Work, 40*(1), 36–43.

Benight, C. C., Ironson, G., Klebe, K., Carver, C. S., Wynings, C., Burnett, K., et al. (1999). Conservation of recourses and coping self-efficacy predicting distress following a natural disaster: A casual model analysis where the environment meets the mind. *Anxiety, Stress, and Coping: An International Journal, 12*(2) 107–126.

Bennett, J., Reynolds, & Lehman, W. (2003). Understanding employee alcohol and other drug use: Toward a multilevel approach. In J. B. Bennett & W. E. K. Lehman (Eds.), *Preventing workplace substance abuse* (pp. 29–56). Washington, DC: American Psychological Association.

Birenbaum, R. (1994). Peacekeeper stress prompts new approaches to mental health issues in the Canadian military. *Canadian Medical Association Journal, 151*(10), 1484–1489.

Bisson, J., & Deahl, M. (1994). Psychological debriefings and prevention of post-traumatic stress: More research is needed. *British Journal of Psychiatry, 165,* 717–720.

Bisson, J., Jenkins, P., Alexander, J., & Bannister, C. (1997). Randomized controlled trial of psychological debriefing for victims of acute burn trauma. *British Journal of Psychiatry, 171,* 78–81.

Bisson, J., McFarlane, A., & Rose, S. (2000). Psychological debriefings. In E. Foa, T. Keane, & M. Friedman (Eds.), *Effective treatments for PTSD: Practice guidelines from the international society for traumatic stress studies* (pp. 317–319). New York: Guilford Press.

Blanchard, E., Hickling, E., Mitnick, N., Taylor, A., Loos, W., & Buckley, T. (1995). The impact of severity of physical injury and perception of life threat in the development of post-traumatic stress disorder in motor vehicle accident victims. *Behavior Research and Therapy, 33*(5), 529–534.

Bleich, A., Gelkopf, M., & Solomon, Z. (2003). Exposure to terrorism, stress-related mental health symptoms, and coping behaviors among a nationally representative sample in Isreal. *JAMA 290*(5), 612–620.

Bliese, P., & Castro, C. (2000). Role clarity, work overload, and organizational support: Multilevel evidence of the importance of support. *Work and Stress, 14*(1), 65–73.

Blitz, J. (2003, August 4). Truth, lies, and what Blair knew. *Macleans,* 23–24.

Borum, R., & Philpot, C. (1993). Therapy with law enforcement couples: Clinical management of the high-risk life-style. *American Journal of Family Therapy, 21*(2), 122–135.

Bosma, H., Peter, R., Siegrist, J., & Marmot, M. (1998). Two alternative job stress models and the risk of coronary heart disease. *American Journal of Public Health,* 88(1), 68–75.

Boswell, W., & Boudreau, J. (2000). Employee satisfaction with performance appraisals and appraisers. *Human Resource Development Quarterly, 11*(3), 283–299.

Bowlby, J. (1979). *The making and breaking of affectional bonds.* London: Tavistock Publications.

Bowman, M. (1999). Individual differences in posttraumatic distress: Problems with the DSM-IV Model, *Canadian Journal of Psychiatry, 44*(2), 21–33.

Bremner, J. D. (2002). *Does stress damage the brain?* New York: W. W. Norton.

Brewin, C. (1996). Scientific status of retrieved memories. *British Journal of Psychiatry, 169,* 131–134.

Brewin, C. (2001). A cognitive neuroscience account of posttraumatic stress disorder and its treatment. *Behavior Research and Therapy, 39,* 373–393.

Brewin, C. R., Andrews, B., & Valentine J. D. (2000). Meta-analysis of risk factors for posttraumatic stress disorder in trauma-exposed adults. *Journal of Consulting and Clinical Psychology, 48*(5), 748–744.

Briere, J. (1997). *Psychological assessment of adult post-traumatic states.* Washington, DC: American Psychological Association.

Briere, J. (2000). Treating adult survivors of severe childhood abuse and neglect: Further development of an integrative model. In J. E. B. Myers et al. (Eds), *The APSAC handbook on child maltreatment* (2nd ed.) (pp. 175–203). Thousand Oaks: Sage Publications.

Briere, J., & Elliott, D. (2000). Prevalence, characteristics, and long-term sequelae of natural disaster exposure in the general population. *Journal of Traumatic Stress, 13*(4), 661–679.

Bronfenbrenner, U. (1979). *The ecology of human development.* Cambridge, MA: Harvard University Press.

Brooks, N., & McKinlay, W. (1992). Mental health consequences of the Lockerbie disaster. *Journal of Traumatic Stress, 5*(4), 527–543.

Brown, N., (2004) Psychoeducational Groups: Process and Practice. Brunner-Routledge

Brown, J. M., & Campbell, E. A. (1990). Sources of occupational stress in police. *Work and Stress, 4*(4), 305–318.

Brown, J., Fielding, J., & Grover, J. (1999) Distinguishing traumatic, vicarious, and routine operational stressor exposure and attendant adverse consequences in a sample of police officers. *Work and Stress, 4,* 312–325.

Brunet, R. (1998). BC's only growth industry: Complaints quadruple against aggressive children and families ministry. *British Columbia Report, 9*(33), 14–17.

Bryant, R., & Harvey, A. (1996). Posttraumatic stress reactions in volunteer fire-fighters. *Journal of Traumatic Stress, 9,* 51–62.

Bryant, R., Sackville, T., Dang, S., et al. (1999). Treating acute stress disorder: An evaluation of cognitive behavioral therapy and supportive counseling techniques. *American Journal of Psychiatry, 156,* 1780–1786.

Burgess, A., & Holstrum, L. (1974). Rape trauma syndrome. *American Journal of Psychiatry, 131*(9), 981–986.

Burke, R. (1993). Work-family stress, conflict, coping, and burnout in police officers. *Stress Medicine, 9,* 171–180.

Burns, C., & Harm, N. (1993). Emergency nurses' perceptions of critical incidents and stress debriefing. *Journal of Emergency Nursing, 19,* 431–436.

Buunk, B., & Peeters, M. (1994). Stress at work, social support, and companionship: Towards an event-contingent recording approach. *Work and Stress, 8*(2), 177–190.

Buunk, B., & Verhoeven, K. (1991). Companionship and support at work: A microanalysis of the stress-reducing features of social interaction. *Basic and Applied Social Psychology, 12*(3), 243–258.

Calhoun, K., & Atkeson, B. (1991). *Treatment of rape victims: Facilitating psychosocial adjustment.* Toronto: Pergamon Press.

Calhoun, P., Bechkham, J., Feldman, M., Barefoot, J., Haney, T., & Bosworth, H. (2002). Partner's ratings of combat veteran's anger. *Journal of Traumatic Stress, 15*(2), 133–136.

Callahan, J. (1998). Crisis theory and crisis intervention in emergencies. In P. M. Kleespies (Ed.), *Emergencies in mental health practice: Evaluation and management* (pp. 22–40). New York: Guilford Press.

CAMH (2003). *Low risk drinking guidelines.* Toronto: Center for Addiction and Mental Health.

Campfield, K., & Hills, A. (2001). Effect of timing of critical incident stress debriefing on posttraumatic symptoms. *Journal of Traumatic Stress, 14,* 327–340.

Cannon, W. B. (1932). *The wisdom of the body.* New York: W. W. Norton.

Caplan, G. (1964). *Principles of preventive psychiatry.* New York: Basic Books.

Carlier, I., Lamberts, R., van Uchelen, A., & Gersons, B. (1998). Disaster-related post-traumatic stress in police officers: A field study of the impact on debriefing. *Stress Medicine, 14,* 143–148.

Carlier, I., Voerman, A., & Gersons, B. (2000). The influence of occupational debriefing on post-traumatic stress symptomology in traumatized police officers. *British Journal of Medical Psychology, 73,* 87–98.

Carr, L. J. (1932). Disaster and the Sequence-Pattern Concept of Change. *American Journal of Sociology, 38*(2), 207–218.

Centers for Disease Control and Prevention (2002). Injuries and illnesses among New York City fire department rescue workers after responding to the World Trade Center attacks. *JAMA, 288*(13), 1581–1584.

Chrestman, K. R. (1995). Secondary exposure to trauma and self-reported distress among therapists. In B. H. Stamm (Ed.), *Secondary traumatic stress: Self-care issues for clinicians, researchers, and educators.* Lutherville, MD: Sidran Press.

Cohen, J. A., Deblinger, E., Mannarino, A. P., & de Avellano, M. A. (2001). The importance of culture in treating abused and neglected children: An empirical review. *Child Maltreatment, 6*(2), 148–157.

Columbia remembered. (2003, February 17). *Macleans,* 15.

Coman, G., & Evans, B. (1991). Stressors facing Australian police in the 1990s. *Police Studies International Review of Police Development, 14*(4), 153–165.

Cone, D. C., Weir, S. D., & Bogucki, S. (2003). Convergent volunteerism. *Annals of Emergency Medicine, 41*(4), 457–462.

Copp, T., & McAndrew, W. (1990). *Battle exhaustion: Soldiers and psychiatrists in the Canadian army, 1939–1945.* Kingston: McGill-Queen's University Press.

Corey, M., & Corey, G. (2002). Groups: Process and practice. Pacific Grove, CA: Brooks/Cole.

Council on Foreign Relations (2003). *Terrorism: Questions and answers.* Retrieved May 3, 2003, from http://www.terrorismanswers.com.

Covello, V. T., Peters, R. G., Wojtecki, J. G., & Hyde, R. C. (2001). Risk communication, the West Nile Epidemics, and bioterrorism: Responding to the communication challenges posed by the intentional or unintentional release of a pathogen in an urban setting. *Journal of Urban Health: Bulletin of the New York Academy of Medicine, 78*(2), 382–391.

Coyne, J., & DeLongis, A. (1986). Going beyond social support: The role of social relationships in adaptation. *Journal of Consulting and Clinical Psychology, 54*(4), 454–460.

Cutter, S. L. (Ed). (2000). *American hazardscapes: The regionalization of hazards and disasters.* Washington, DC: Joseph Henry Press.

Cwikel, J. G., Havenaar, J. M., & Bromet, E. J. (2002). Understanding the psychological and societal response of individuals, groups, authorities, and media to toxic hazards. In J. M. Havennar, J. G. Cwickel, & E. J. Bromet (Eds), *Toxic turmoil: Psychological and societal consequences of ecological disasters* (pp. 39–61). New York: Kluwer Academic/Plenum Publishers.

DaCosta, J. (1871) On the irritable heart: A clinical study of a form of functional cardiac disorder following natural disaster. *American Journal of Medical Sciences, 61,* 17–52.

Dallaire, R. (2003). *Shake Hands with the Devil: The Failure of Humanity in Rwanda.* Toronto: Random House.

Dane, B. (2000). Child welfare workers: An innovative approach for interacting with secondary trauma. *Journal of Social Work Education, 36*(1), 27–38.

Davidson, A., & Mellor, D. (2000). The adjustment of children of Australian Vietnam veterans: Is there evidence for the transgenerational transmission of the effects of war-related trauma? *Australian and New Zealand Journal of Psychiatry, 35,* 345–351.

Davidson, M., & Veno, A. (1980). Stress and the policeman. In C. L. Cooper & J. Marshal (Eds.), *White collar and professional stress.* London: Wiley.

Davis, M. (1983). Measuring individual differences in empathy: Evidence for a multidimensional approach. *Journal of Personality and Social Psychology, 44,* 113–126.

De Jong, J. (2002). Disaster and the selection of public mental health priorities: A perspective from developing countries. In J. M. Havenaar, J. G. Cwikel, & E. J. Bromet (Eds.), *Toxic turmoil: Psychological and societal consequences of ecological disasters* (pp. 237–258). New York: Kluwer Academic/Plenum Publishers.

Deahl, M., Gillhas, A., & Thomas, J. (1994). Psychological sequelae following the Gulf War: Factors associated with subsequent morbidity and the effectiveness of psychological debriefings. *British Journal of Psychiatry, 165*, 60–65.

Deckop, J., & Cirka, C. (2000). The risk and reward of a double-edged sword: Effects of merit pay program on intrinsic motivation. *Nonprofit and Voluntary Sector Quarterly, 29*(3), 400–418.

DePue, R. (1979). Turning inward: The police officer counselor. *FBI Law Enforcement Bulletin, 48*(2), 9.

Dick, P. (2000). The social construction of the meaning of acute stressors: A qualitative study of the personal accounts of police officers using a stress counseling service. *Work and Stress, 14*(3), 226–244.

Dobreva-Martinova, T. (2002, January). *Occupational role stress in the Canadian forces: Its association with individual and organizational well-being.* Unpublished master's thesis, Carleton University, Ottawa, Ontario.

Doka, K. J. (1989). *Disenfranchised grief: New directions, challenges, and strategies for practice.* Champaign, IL: Research Press.

Dreisbach, V. (2003). Post-traumatic stress disorder is an occupational disease eligible for worker's compensation. *Journal of the American Academy of Psychiatry and the Law, 31*(1), 120–123.

Dubos, R. (1980). *Man adapting.* New Haven: Yale University Press.

Dunning, C. (1999). Prevention strategies to reduce police trauma: A paradigm shift. In J. Violanti & D. Paton (Eds.), *Police trauma: The psychological aftermath of civilian combat* (pp. 269–286). Springfield, IL: Charles Thomas.

Dyer, C. L. (2002). Punctuated entropy as culture induced change. The case of the exam Valdez oil spill. In S. M. Hoffman & A. Oliver-Smith (Eds), *Catastrophe and culture.* Santa Fe, NM: School of America Research Press.

Dynes, R. (1994). Community emergency planning: False assumptions and inappropriate analogies. *International Journal of Mass Emergencies and Disasters, 12*(2), 141–158.

Dyregrov, A. (1989). Caring for the helpers in disaster situations: Psychological debriefing. *Disaster Management, 2*, 25–30.

Dyregrov, A. (1997). The process in psychological debriefing. *Journal of Traumatic Stress, 10*, 589–605.

Dyregrov, A., Kristofferson, J., & Gjestad, R. (1996). Volunteer and professional disasterworkers: Similarities and differences in reactions. *Journal of Traumatic Stress, 9*, 541–555.

Ehlers, A., & Clark, D. (2003). Early psychological interventions for adult survivors of trauma: A review. *Biological Psychiatry, 53*, 817–826.

Erlandson, D. A., Harris, E. L., Skipper, B. L., & Allen, S. D. (1993). Doing naturalistic inquiry: A guide to methods. London: SAGE Publications.

Evans, R. (1996). The human side of school change. In *Performance, resistance, and the real-life problems of innovation.* San Francisco: Jossey-Bass.

Evans, R. G., Barer, M. L., & Marmor, T. R. (Eds.). (1994). *Why are some people healthy and others not? The determinants of health of populations.* New York: Aldine de Gruyter.

Evans, B., & Coman, G. (1993). General versus specific measures of occupational stress: An Australian police survey. *Stress Medicine, 9*, 11–20.

Everly, G., Lating, J., & Mitchell, J. (2000). Innovations in group crisis intervention: Critical incident stress debriefing and critical incident stress management. In A. Roberts (Ed.), *Crisis intervention handbook: Assessment, treatment, and research* (pp. 77–97). New York: Oxford University Press.

Fairfax County Fire and Rescue Department v. Mottram, 559 S. E.2d 698 (va. 2002).

Farmer, S., & Fedor, D. (1999). Volunteer participation and withdrawal: A psychological contract perspective on the role of expectations and organizational support. *Nonprofit Management and Leadership, 9*(4), 349–367.

Fielding, N. (1994). The organizational and occupational troubles of community police. *Policing and Society, 4,* 305–322.

Figley, C. (1978). *Stress disorders among Vietnam veterans: Theory, research, and treatment.* New York: Brunner-Mazel.

Figley, C. (1980). *Strangers at home: Vietnam veterans since the war.* New York: Praeger.

Figley, C. (1995a). Compassion fatigue: Towards a new understanding of the costs of caring. In B. Stamm (Ed.), *Secondary traumatic stress: Self-care issues for clinicians, researchers, and educators* (pp. 3–28). Lutherville, MD: Sidran Press.

Figley, C. R. (1995b). *Compassion fatigue: Coping with secondary traumatic stress in those who treat the traumatized.* New York: Brunner/Mazel.

Figley, C. (1999). Police compassion fatigue: Theory, research, assessment, treatment, and prevention. In J. Violanti & D. Paton (Eds.), *Police trauma: The psychological aftermath of civilian combat* (pp. 37–53). Springfield, IL: Charles Thomas.

Fishbein, M., & Ajzen, I. (1975). *Belief, attitude, intention, and behavior: An introduction to theory and research.* Reading, MA: Addison-Wesley.

Fisher, H. W. (1998). *Respond to disaster: Fact versus fiction and its perpetuation* (2nd ed.). Landham, Maryland: University Press of America, Inc.

Fisher, H. W. (2002). Terrorism and 11 September 2001: does the behavior response to disaster model fit? *Disaster Prevention and Management, 11*(2), 123–127.

Flannery, R. B., & Everly, G. S. (2000). Continuing education: Crisis intervention: A review. *International Journal of Emergency Mental Health, 2*(2), 199–125.

Foa, E., Cashman, L., Jaycox, I., & Perry, K. (1997). The validation of a self-report measure of posttraumatic stress disorder: The posttraumatic diagnostic scale. *Psychological Assessment, 9,* 445–451.

Foa, E., Keene, T., & Friedman, M. (2000). *Effective treatments for PTSD.* New York: Guilford Press.

Follette, V., Ruzek, J., & Abueg, F. (1998). *Cognitive-behavioral therapies for trauma.* New York: Guilford Press.

Fontana, A., & Rosenheck, R. (1997). Effectiveness and cost of the inpatient treatment of posttraumatic stress disorder: Comparison of three models of treatment. *American Journal of Psychiatry, 154*(6), 758–765.

Fowlie, J. (2003, July 1). Doctor, paramedic tell of front-line battle against virus. *Globe and Mail,* A12.

Foy, D., Glynn, S., Schnurr, P., Jankowski, M., Wattenberg, M., Weiss, D., et al. (2000). Group therapy. In E. Foa, T. Keane, & M. Friedman (Eds.), *Effective treatments for PTSD: Practice guidelines for the international society for traumatic stress studies* (pp. 155–175). New York: Guilford Press.

Fullerton, C., McCarroll, J., Ursano, R., & Wright, K. (1992). Psychological responses of rescue workers: Fire fighters and trauma. *American Journal of Orthopsychiatry*, 62(3), 371–377.

Fullerton, C., Ursano, R., Vance, K., & Wang, L. (2000). Debriefing following trauma. *Psychiatric Quarterly*, 71, 259–276.

Furr, S. R. (2000). Structuring the group experience: A format for designing psychoeducational groups. *Journal for Specialists in Group Work*, 25(1), 29–49.

Gabris, G., & Ihrke, D. (2001). Does performance appraisal contribute to heightened levels of employee burnout? *Public Personnel Management*, 30(2), 157–172.

Galea, S., Resnick, H., Ahern, J., Gold, J., Bucuvalas, M., Kilpatrick, D., et al. (2002). Posttraumatic stress disorder in Manhattan, New York City, after the September 11th terrorist attacks. *Journal of Urban Health: Bulletin of the New York Academy of Medicine*, 79(3), 340–353.

Galloway, G., & Alphonso, C. (2003, July 1). Nurse's SARS death called poignant. *Globe and Mail*, A12.

Germain, C. B., & Gitterman, A. (1980). *The life model of social work practice*. New York: Columbia University Press.

Gersons, B. (1989). Patterns of PTSD among police officers following a shooting incident: A two-dimensional model and treatment implications. *Journal of Traumatic Stress*, 2, 247–257.

Gersons, B., Berthold, P. R., Carlier, I. V. E., Lamberts, R. D., van der Kolk, B. , A. (2000). Randomized clinical trial of brief eclectic psychotherapy for police officers with posttraumatic stress disorder. *Journal of Traumatic Stress*, 13, 333–347.

Gibbs v. Gibbs. [1985]. 1 W. D. C. P. 6 (Ont. S. C.)

Gibbs, M. (1989). Factors in the victim that mediate between disaster and psychopathology: A review. *Journal of Traumatic Stress*, 2, 489–514.

Gibbs, M., Drummond, J., & Lachenmeyer, J. (1993). Effects of disasters on emergency workers: A review with implications for training and postdisaster interventions. *Journal of Social Behavior and Personality*, 8(5), 189–212.

Gist, R., & Lubin, B. (Eds.). (1999). Response to disaster: Psychological community, and ecological approaches. Philadelphia, PA. Brunner/Mazel.

Gist, R., & Woodall, S. (1995). Occupational stress in contemporary fire service. *Occupational Medicine*, 10(4), 763–787.

Glancy, G., Regehr, C., & Bryant, A. (1998). Confidentiality in crisis: Part I. The duty to inform. *Canadian Journal of Psychiatry*, 43(12), 1001–1005.

Golembiewski, R., & Kim, B. (1990). Burnout in police work: Stressors, strain, and the phase model. *Police Studies*, 13(2), 74–80.

Green, B. L., Krupnick, J. L., Stockton, P., Goodman, L., Corcoran, C., & Petty, R. (2001). Psychological outcome associated with traumatic loss in a sample of young women. *American Behavior Scientist*, 44(5), 817–837.

Greenstone, J. (2000, March/April). Peer support in a municipal police department: Doing what comes naturally. *Forensic Examiner*, 33.

Grossi, G., Theorell, T., Jusisoo, M., & Setterlind, S. (1999). Psychophysiological correlates of organizational change and threat of unemployment among police inspectors. *Integrative Physiological and Behavioral Science*, 34(1), 30–42.

Harkness, L. (1993). Transgenerational transmission of war-related trauma. In J. Wilson & B. Raphael (Eds.), *International handbook of traumatic stress syndromes*. New York: Plenum Publishers.

Hart, P., Wearing, A., & Headley, B. (1995). Police stress and well-being: Integrating personality, coping, and daily work experiences. *Journal of Occupational and Organizational Psychology*, 68, 133–136.

Harvey, A., Bryant, R., & Tarrier, N. (2003). Cognitive behavior therapy for post-traumatic stress disorder. *Clinical Psychology Review*, 23, 501–522.

Havenaar, J. M. (2002). Ecological disaster: A concern for the future by public health aspects of chemical catastrophes. In J. M. Havenaar, J. G. Cwikel, & E. J. Bromet (Eds.), *Toxic turmoil: Psychological and societal consequences of ecological disasters* (pp. 3–18). New York: Kluwer Academic/Plenum Publishers.

Heaney, C. A. (2003). Worksite health interventions. In J. C. Quick & L. E. Tetrick (Eds.), *Handbook of occupational health psychology* (pp. 305–323). Washington, DC: American Psychology Association Press.

Hembree, E., & Foa, E. (2003). Interventions for trauma-related emotional disturbances in adult victims of crime. *Journal of Traumatic Stress*, 16, 187–199.

Hendricks, J. E., & Byers, B. D. (Eds.). (2002). *Crisis intervention in criminal justice/social service* (3rd ed.). Springfield, IL: Charles Thomas.

Henry, V. (2004). *Death Work: Police, Trauma, and the Psychology of Survival*. New York: Oxford University Press.

Henry, V., & King, D. (2004). Public safety and private sector responses to terrorism and weapons of mass destruction. *Brief Treatments and Crisis Intervention*, 4(1) 11-35.

Herman, J. L. (1992). *Trauma and recovery*. New York: Basic Books.

Herrman, J. (1988). Sudden death and the police officer. *Issues in Comprehensive Pediatric Nursing*, 12, 327–332.

Hewitt, K. (1997). *Regions of risks: A geographical introduction to disasters*. Harlow, Essex: Longman.

Hill, M. (1990). The manifest and latent lessons of child abuse inquiries. *British Journal of Social Work*, 20, 197–213.

Hoath, D., and Bober, T. (2000). Sound mind—sound body: Stress management strategies for prosecutors. Unpublished paper.

Hobfoll, S. E. (1989). Conservation of resources: A new attempt of conceptualizing stress. *American Psychologist*, 44(3) 513-524.

Hobfoll, S. E. (2001). The influence of culture, community and the nested-self in the stress process: Advancing conservation of resources theory. *Applied Psychology: An International Review*, 50(3), 337–421.

Hobfoll, S. E. (2002). Social and psychological resources and adaptation. *Review of General Psychology*, 6(4), 307–324.

Hobfoll, S. E., Jackson, A., Hobfoll, I., Pierce, C. A., & Young, S. (2002). The impact of communal-mastery versus self-mastery on emotional outcomes during stressful conditions: A prospective study of Native American women. *American Journal of Community Psychology*, 30(6), 853–872.

Holahan, C. J. (1999). Resource loss, resource gain, and descriptive symptoms: A ten-year model. *Journal of Personality and Social Psychology*, 77(3), 620–629.

Holtz, T., Salama, P., Cordozo, B., & Gotway, C. (2002). Mental health status of human rights workers, Kosovo, June 2000. *Journal of Traumatic Stress*, 15(5), 389–395.

Horowitz, M. (1976). *Stress response syndromes*. New York: Jason Aronson.

Horowitz, M. J. (2002). Self and relational observation. *Journal of Psychotherapy Integration, 12*(2), 115–127.

Horowitz, M., Wilner, N., & Alveraz, W. (1979). Impact of Events Scale: A measure of subjective distress. *Psychosomatic Medicine, 41*, 209–218.

Howard, J. M. and Goelitz, A. (2004). Psycheducation as a response to community disaster. *Brief Treatment and Crisis Intervention, 4*, 1–10.

Hume, D. (1966). *Enquiries concerning the human understanding and concerning principles of morals* (2nd ed.) Oxford, England: Clarendon Press. (Original work published in 1777.)

Iliffe, G., & Steed, L. (2000). Exploring counselors' experience of working with perpetrators and survivors on domestic violence. *Journal of Interpersonal Violence, 15*(4), 393–412.

International Strategy of Disaster Reduction (ISDR). (2002). *Living with risk: A global review of disaster reduction initiatives.* Geneva: United Nations.

Ironson, G., Wynings, C., Schneiderman, N., Baum, A., Rodriguez, M., Greenwood, D., et al. (1997). Posttraumatic stress symptoms, intrusive thoughts, loss, and immune function after Hurricane Andrew. *Psychosomatic Medicine, 59*(2), 128–141.

Janz, N., & Becker, M. (1984). The health belief model: A decade later. *Health Education Quarterly, 11*, 1–47.

Jordan, K., Marmar, C., Fairbank, J., Schlenger, W., Kulka, R., Hough, R., et al. (1992). Problems in families of male Vietnam veterans with posttraumatic stress disorder. *Journal of Consulting and Clinical Psychology, 60*(6), 916–926.

Josephson, R., & Reiser, M. (1990). Officer suicide in the Los Angeles police department: A twelve-year follow-up. *Journal of Police Science and Administration, 17*(3), 227–229.

Kabat-Zinn J. (1990). *Full catastrophe living: Using the wisdom of your body and mind to face stress, pain, and illness.* New York: Delta Books.

Kahill, S. (1998). Interventions for burnout in the helping professions. *Canadian Journal of Counselling Review, 22*(3), 310–342.

Kaniasty, K., & Norris, F. (1999). The experience of disaster: Individuals and communities sharing trauma. In R. Gist & B. Lubin (Eds.), *Response to disaster: Psychosocial, community, and ecological approaches* (pp. 25–62). Philadelphia: Brunner/Mazel.

Kannady, G. (1993). Developing stress resistant police families. *Police Chief, 60*(8), 92–95.

Kant, I. (1949). *Critique of practical reasoning.* (L. W. Beck, Trans). Chicago: University of Chicago Press. (Original work published in 1788.)

Karasek, R., & Theorell, T. (1990). *Health work: Stress, productivity, and the reconstruction of working life.* New York: Basic Books.

Kassam-Adams, N. (1995). The risks of treating sexual trauma: Stress and secondary trauma in psychotherapists. In B. H. Stamm (Ed.), *Secondary traumatic stress: self-care issues for clinicians, researchers, and educators* (pp. 37–50). Lutherville, MD: Sidran Press.

Katz, D., Pellegrino, L., Pandya, A., Ng, A., & DeLisis, L. (2002). Research on psychiatric outcomes and interventions subsequent to disasters: A review of the literature. *Psychiatry Research, 110*, 201–217.

Keane, T. (1993). Symptomology of Vietnam veterans with post-traumatic stress disorder. In J. Davidson & E. Foa (Eds.), *Posttraumatic stress disorder: DSM IV and beyond.* Washington, DC: American Psychiatric Association Press.

Keefe, T. (1976). Empathy: The critical skill. *Social Work, 21,* 10–14.

Keenan, B. (1993). *An Evil Cradling.* London: Random House.

Kendra, J. M., & Wachtendorf, T. (2003). Elements of resilience after the World Trade Center disaster: Reconstituting New York City's Emergency Operations Centre. *Disasters, 27*(1), 37–53.

Kessler, R., Sonnega, A., Bromet, E., Hughes, M., & Nelson, C. (1995). Post-traumatic stress disorder in the national co-morbidity study. *Archives of General Psychiatry, 52,* 1048–1060.

Kinard, E. (1996). Conducting research on child maltreatment: Effects on researchers. *Violence and Victims, 11*(1), 65–69.

King, D. W., King, L. A., Foy, D. W., Keane, T. M., & Fairbank, J. A. (1999). *Journal of Abnormal Psychology, 108*(1), 164–171.

King, L., King, D., Fairbank, J., Keane, T., & Adams, G. (1997). Resilience-recovery factors in post-traumatic stress disorder among female and male Vietnam veterans: Hardiness, postwar social support, and additional stressful life events. *Journal of Personality and Social Psychology, 74*(2) 420–434.

Kirkcaldy, B., Brown, J., & Cooper, C. (1998). The demographics of occupational stress among police superintendents. *Journal of Managerial Psychology, 13*(1–2), 90–101.

Kivimaki, M., Elovainio, M., Vahtera, J., Virtanen, M., & Stansfeld, S. A. (2003). Association between organizational inequity and incidence of psychiatric disorders in female employees. *Psychological Medicine, 33*(2), 319–326.

Knott, T. (2003). *Stress in the workplace.* Alliant University press release. Retrieved May 20, 2003, from http://www.cspp.edu/news/stress.htm.

Knowles, M. (1972). Innovations in teaching styles and approaches based on adult learning. *Journal of Education for Social Work, 8*(2).

Koehler, C. (1992, June). Lawsuit demands coping skills. *American Nurse,* 33.

Kroes, W. (1985). *Society's victim: The police officer.* Springfield, IL: Charles Thomas.

Landeweerd, J., & Boumans, N. (1994). The effect of work dimensions and need for autonomy on nurses' work satisfaction and health. *Journal of Occupational and Organizational Psychology, 67,* 207–217.

Lane, P. (1994). Critical incident stress debriefing for health care workers. *Omega, 28*(4), 301–315.

Larson, R., & Almeida, D. (1999). Emotional transmission in the daily lives of families: A new paradigm for studying family process. *Journal of Marriage and Family, 61,* 5–20.

Lazarus, R. (1966). *Psychological stress and the coping process.* Toronto: McGraw-Hill Book Company.

Lazarus, R., & Folkman, S. (1984). *Stress, appraisal, and coping.* New York: Springer Publishing Company.

Lee, F. (2002) The social costs of seeking help. *Journal of Applied Behavioral Science, 38*(2), 17–35.

Lee, R. T., & Ashforth, B. E. (1996). A meta-analytic examination of the correlates of the three dimensions of job burnout. *Journal of Applied Psychology, 81*(2), 123–133.

Leffler, C., & Dembert, M. (1998). Posttraumatic stress symptoms among U.S. Navy divers recovering TWA Flight 800. *Journal of Nervous and Mental Disorders, 186*(9), 574–577.

Lewin, K. (1951). *Field theory in social science.* New York: Harper.

Lewis, C., Tenzer, M., & Harrison, T. (1999). The heroic response to terror: The case of Oklahoma City. *Public Personnel Management, 28*(4), 617–635.

Liberman, A., Best, S., Metzler, T., Fagan, J., Weiss, D., & Marmar, C. (2002). Routine occupational stress and psychological distress in police. *Policing: An International Journal of Police Strategies and Management, 25*(2), 421–439.

Lifton, R. (1999). *Destroying the world to save it: Aum Shinrikyo, apocalyptic violence, and the new global terrorism.* New York: Henry Holt.

Lindemann, E. (1944). Symptomatology and management of acute grief. *American Journal of Psychiatry, 101,* 141–148.

Litz. B. (ed.) (2004). *Early intervention for trauma and traumatic loss.* New York: Guilford Press.

Litz, B., Gray, M., Bryant, R., and Adler, A. (2002) Early interventions for trauma: Current and future research directions. *Clinical Psychology: Science and Practice, 9,* 112–134.

Loo, R. (1999). Police suicide: The ultimate stress reaction. In J. Violanti & D. Paton (Eds.), *Police trauma: The psychological aftermath of civilian combat* (pp. 241–254). Springfield, IL: Charles Thomas.

Lott, L. (1995). Deadly secrets: Violence in the police family. *FBI Law Enforcement Bulletin, 64*(11), 12–16.

Lucas, T., & Williams, N. (2000). Motivation as a function of volunteer retention. *Australian Journal of Volunteering, 5*(1), 13–21.

Luce, A., Firth-Cozens, J., Midgley, S., & Burges, C. (2002) After the Omagh bomb: Post-traumatic stress disorder in health service staff. *Journal of Traumatic Stress, 15*(1), 27–30.

Lusa, S., Häkkänen, M., Luukkonen, R., & Viikari-Juntura, E. (2002). Perceived physical work capacity, stress, sleep disturbance, and occupational accidents among firefighters during a strike. *Work and Stress, 16*(3), 264–274.

McDonald, A. (1996). Responding to the results of the Beverly Allitt inquiry. *Nursing Times.*

MacKenzie, J. (1916). The soldier's heart and war neurosis: A study in symptomology. *British Medical Journal, 1,* 491–495.

Marmar, C., Weiss, D., Metzler, T., Delucchi, K., Best, S., & Wentworth, K. (1999). Longitudinal course and predictors of continuing distress following critical incident exposure in emergency services personnel. *Journal of Nervous and Mental Disorders, 187*(1), 15–22.

Marmar, C., Weiss, D., Metzler, T., Delucchi, K., Best, S., & Wentworth, K. (1999). Longitudinal course and predictors of continuing distress following critical incident exposure in emergency services personnel. *Journal of Nervous and Mental Disorders, 187*(1), 15–22.

Marzuk, P., Nock, M., Leon, A., Portera, L., & Tardiff, K. (2002). Suicide among New York City police officers, 1977–1996. *American Journal of Psychiatry, 159*(12), 2069–2071.

Maslach, C., & Jackson, S. (1979). Burned-out cops and their families. *Psychology Today,* 59–62.

Maslach, C., & Leiter, M. P. (1997). *The truth about burnout: How organizations cause personal stress and what to do about it.* San Francisco: Jossey-Bass/Pfeiffer.

Mathews, L. (1998). Effect of staff debriefing on post-traumatic stress symptoms after assaults by community housing residents. *Psychiatric Services, 49,* 207–212.

Maunder, R., Hunter, J., Vincent, L., Bennett, J., Peladeau, N., et al. (2003). The immediate psychological and occupational impact of the 2003 SARS outbreak in a teaching hospital. *Canadian Medical Association Journal, 168*(10), 1245–1251.

Mayou, R., Ehlers, A., & Hobbs, M. (2000). Psychological debriefing for road traffic accident victims. *British Journal of Psychiatry, 176,* 589–593.

McCann, L., & Pearlman, L. (1990a). *Psychological trauma and the adult survivor: Theory, therapy, and transformation.* Psychological Stress Series, 21. Philadelphia: Bruner/Mazel.

McCann, L., & Pearlman, L. (1990b). Vicarious traumatization: A framework for understanding the psychological effects of working with victims. *Journal of Traumatic Stress, 3*(1), 131–149.

McCann, L., Sakheim, D., & Abrahamson, D. (1988). Trauma and victimization: A model of psychological adaptation. *Counseling Psychologist, 16*(4), 531-594.

McCarroll, J., Fullerton, C., Ursano, R., & Hermsen, J. (1996). Post-traumatic stress symptoms following forensic dental identification: Mt Carmel, Waco, Texas. *American Journal of Psychiatry, 153*(6), 778–782.

McCarroll, J., Ursano, R., Fullerton, C., Oates, G., Ventis, L., Friedman, H., et al. (1995). Gruesomeness, emotional attachment and personal threat: Dimensions of anticipated stress of body recovery. *Journal of Traumatic Stress, 8*(2), 343–349.

McEwen, B. S. (2000). The neurobiology of stress: From serendipity to clinical relevance. *Brain Research, 886*(1–2), 172–189.

McFall, M., Wright, P., Donovan, D., & Raskind, M. (1999). Multidimensional assessment of anger in Vietnam veterans with post-traumatic stress disorder. *Comprehensive Psychiatry, 40,* 216–220.

McFarlane, A. (1988). The etiology of post-traumatic stress disorder following a natural disaster. *British Journal of Psychiatry, 152,* 116–121.

McFarlane, A. (1990). Vulnerability to posttraumatic stress disorder. In M. Wolf & A. Mosnaim (Eds.), *Posttraumatic stress disorder: Etiology, phenomenology, and treatment* (pp. 3–45). Washington, DC: American Psychiatric Press.

McGuire, W. (1973). Persuasion, resistance, and attitude change. In I. deSola & W. Schramm (Eds.), *Handbook of Communication.* Chicago: Rand-McNally.

McKeown, T. (1979). The role of medicine: Dream, mirage or nemesis? (2nd ed.). Oxford: Basil Blackwell.

McMurray, H. (1989). *Police postassault reactions and the buffering effects of social support.* Ann Arbor, MI: UMI.

Menendez v. Superior Court. (1991). 279 Cal Rptr. 521

Miller, W. R., & Rollnick, S. (Eds.). (2002). *Motivational Interviewing* (2nd ed.). New York: Guilford Press.

Mitchell, J. (1982, Fall). Recovery from rescue. *Response,* 7–10.

Mitchell, J., & Bray, G. (1990). *Emergency services stress: Guidelines for preserving the health and careers of emergency services personnel.* Englewood Cliffs, NJ: Brady.

Mitchell, J., & Everly, G. (1993). *Critical incident stress debriefing.* Ellicot City, MD: Chevron Publishing.

Mitchell, J. T., & Everly, G. S. (2001). *Critical incident stress debriefing: An operations manual for CISD, defusing, and other group crisis intervention services.* Ellicott City, MD: Chevron Publishing.

Moghaddam, F. M. and Marsella, A. J. (Eds) (2003) *Understanding terrorism: Psychosocial roots, consequences and interventions.* Washington, APA Press.

Möller-Leimkühler, A. (2002). Barriers to help-seeking in men: A review of sociocultural and clinical literature with particular reference to depression. *Journal of Affective Disorders, 71,* 1–9.

Mollica, R., McInnes, K., Poole, C., & Tor, S. (1998). Dose-effect relationships of trauma to symptoms of depression and post-traumatic stress disorder among Cambodian survivors of mass violence. *British Journal of Psychiatry, 173,* 482–488.

Monnier, J., Resnick, H. S., Kilpatrick, D. G., & Seals, B. (2002). The relationship between distress and resource loss following rape. *Violence and Victims, 17*(1), 85-92.

Mott, F. (1918). War psychoneurosis: Neurasthenia: The disorders and disabilities of fear. *Lancet, 1,* 127–129.

Murphy, S., Bond, G., Beaton, R., Murphy, J., & Johnson, L. (2002). Lifestyle practices and occupational stressors as predictors of health outcomes in urban firefighters. *International Journal of Stress Management, 9*(4), 311–327.

Nader, K., Dubrow, N., & Stamm, H. (1999). Honoring differences: Cultural issues in the treatment of trauma and loss. Philadelphia: Brunner/Mazel.

National Institute for Occupational Safety and Health (NIOSH). (1999). *Stress at Work.* Retrieved February 10, 2002, from http://www.cdc.gov/niosh/stresswk.html.

Neria, Y., & Solomon, Z. (1999). Prevention of posttraumatic reactions: Debriefing and front line treatment. In P. Saigh & J. Bremner (Eds.), *Posttraumatic stress disorder: A comprehensive text* (pp. 309–324). Toronto: Allyn & Bacon.

Nezu, A., & Carnevale, G. (1987). Interpersonal problem solving and coping reactions of Vietnam veterans with posttraumatic stress disorder. *Journal of Abnormal Psychology, 96*(2), 155–157.

Norris, F. H. (2002). Disasters in urban context. *Journal of Urban Health, 79*(3), 308–314.

Norris, F. H., Friedman, M. J., & Watson. P. J. (2002a). 60,000 disaster victims speak, part 2: Summary and implications of the disaster mental health research. *Psychiatry: Interpersonal and Biological Process, 65*(3), 240–260.

Norris, F. H., Friedman, M. J., Watson, P. J., Byrnie, C. M., Diaz, E., & Kaniasty, K. (2002b). 60,000 disaster victims speak, part 1: An empirical review of the empirical literature, 1981–2001. *Psychiatry: Interpersonal and Biological Process, 65*(3), 207–239.

Norris, F. H., & Kaniasty, K. (1996). Receiving and perceived social support in times of stress: A test of the social support deterioration deterrence model. *Journal of Personality and Social Psychology, 71*(3), 498–511.

Norris, F., Perilla, J., Ibañez, G., & Murphy, A. (2001). Sex differences in symptoms of post-traumatic stress: Does culture play a role? *Journal of Traumatic Stress, 14*(1), 7–28.

Norris, F. H., & Thompson, M. P. (1995). Applying community psychology to the prevention of trauma and traumatic life events. In J. R. Freedy & S. E. Hobfoll (Eds.), *Traumatic stress: From theory to practice* (pp. 49–71). New York: Plenum Publishing.

North, C. S., & Pfefferbaum, B., (2002). Research on the mental health effects of terrorism. *JAMA* 288(5), 633–636.

North, C. S., Tivis, L., McMillen, J. C., Pfefferbaum, B., Cox, J., Spitznagel, E. L., et al. (2002a). Coping, functioning, and adjustment of rescue workers after the Oklahoma City bombing. *Journal of Traumatic Stress, 15*(3), 171–175.

North, C. S., Tivis, L., McMillen, J. C., Pfefferbaum, B., Spitznagel, E. L., Cox, J., et al. (2002b). Psychiatric disorders in rescue workers after the Oklahoma City bombing. *American Journal of Psychiatry, 159*(5), 857–859.

Nurses charged. (2001, November 5). *Macleans*, 16.

Oliver-Smith, A. (1996). Anthropological research on hazards and disaster. *Annual Review of Anthropology, 25*, 303–328.

Oppenheimer, B., & Rothschild, M. (1918). The psychoneurotic factor in the "irritable heart of soldiers." *British Medical Journal, 2*, 29–31.

Orcutt, H. K., Erickson, D. J., & Wolfe, J. (2002). A prospective analysis of trauma exposure: The mediating role of PTSD symptomatology. *Journal of Traumatic Stress, 15*(3), 259–266.

Orner, R., & Schnyder, U. (2003). *Reconstructing early intervention after trauma: Innovations in the care of survivors.* New York: Oxford University Press.

Ortlepp, K., & Friedman, M. (2002). Prevalence and correlates of secondary traumatic stress in workplace lay trauma counselors. *Journal of Traumatic Stress, 15*(3), 213–222.

P. (L. M.) v. F. (D.) (1994). 22 C. C. L. T. (2d) 312 (Ont. Gen. Div.).

Page, H. (1885). *Injury of the spinal cord without apparent legion and nervous shock, in their surgical and medico-legal aspects.* London: J. & A. Church.

Paris, J. (1996). A critical review of recovered memories in psychotherapy, part 2: Trauma and therapy. *Canadian Journal of Psychiatry, 41*(4), 206–210.

Paris, J. (1999). *Nature and nurture in psychiatry: A predisposition stress model of mental disorders.* Washington, DC: American Psychiatric Press.

Patterson, G. (1999). Coping effectiveness and occupational stress in police officers. In J. Violanti & D. Paton (Eds.), *Police trauma: The psychological aftermath of civilian combat* (pp. 214–226). Springfield, IL: Charles Thomas.

Pearlin, L., & Schooler, C. (1978). The structure of coping. *Journal of Health and Social Behavior, 19*, 2–21.

Pearlman, L. A., & Saakvitne, K. W. (1995). *Trauma and the therapist: Countertransference and vicarious traumatization in psychotherapy with incest survivors.* New York: W. W. Norton.

Penn, P., & Bootzin, R. (1990). *Behavioral techniques for enhancing alertness in shift work.* Tucson: University of Arizona Press.

People v. Clark. (1990). 50 Cal.3d.583.

People v. Wharton. (1991). 53 Cal.3d.522.

Perry, R. W., & Lindell, M. K. (2003). Understanding citizen response to disasters with implications for terrorism. *Journal of Contingencies and Crisis Management, 11*(2), 49–60.

Pfefferbaum, B., Doughty, D. E., Reddy, C., Patel, N., Gurwitch, R. H., Nixon, S. J., et al. (2002). Exposure and peritraumatic response as predictors of posttraumatic tress in children following the 1995 Oklahoma City bombing. *Journal of Urban Health: Bulletin of the New York Academy of Medicine,* 79(3), 354–363.

Pfefferbaum, B., North, C., Bunch, K., Wilson, T., & Schorr, J. (2002). The impact of the 1995 Oklahoma City bombing on partners of firefighters. *Journal of Urban Health,* 79, 364–372.

Pisarski, A., Bohle, P., & Callan, V. (2002). Extended shifts in ambulance work: Influences on health. *Stress and Health,* 18, 119–126.

Prezant, D., & Kelly, K. (2002). Recollections of 9/11: Medical officers of the New York City fire department. *JAMA,* 288(13), 1582.

Prochaska, J. O., Norcross, J. C., & Diclemente, C. C. (Eds.). (1994). *Changing for good.* New York: Avon Books.

Quarantelli, E. L. (1950). *Emergencies, disasters, and catastrophes are different phenomena.* Newark, DE: Disaster Research Center, University of Delaware.

Quarantelli, E. L. (Ed.). (1998). *What a disaster? Perspectives on the question.* New York: Routledge.

Quick, J. C., & Tetrick, L. E. (Eds.) (2003). *Handbook of occupational health psychology.* Washington, DC: American Psychology Association Press.

Quillian-Wolver, R. E., & Wolver, M. E. (2003). Stress management at work. In J. C. Quick & L. E. Tetrick (Eds.), *Handbook of occupational health psychology* (pp. 355–375). Washington, DC: American Psychology Association Press.

Ranger, J.G. (2003). Personal communication.

Raphael, B. (1986). *When disaster strikes: A handbook for caring professionals.* London: Unwin Hyman.

Raphael, B., Meldrum, L., & McFarlane, A. (1995). Does debriefing after psychological trauma work? *British Medical Journal,* 310, 1479–1480.

Rees, D. (1995). Work related stress in health service employees. *Journal of Managerial Psychology,* 10(3), 4–11.

Regehr, C. (2001). Crisis debriefings for emergency responders: Reviewing the evidence. *Journal of Brief Treatments and Crisis Intervention,* 1(2), 87–100.

Regehr, C. (2003). Inquiries into deaths in care: Impact on emergency responders. *Australasian Journal of Disaster and Trauma Studies,* 1. http://www.massey.ac .nz/~trauma/info/journal.htm

Regehr, C., & Antle, B. (1997). Coercive influences: Informed consent in court mandated social work practice. *Social Work,* 42(3), 300–306.

Regehr, C., Bryant, A., & Glancy, G. (1997). Confidentiality of treatment for victims of sexual violence. *Social Worker,* 65(3), 137–145.

Regehr, C., & Cadell, S. (1999). Secondary trauma in sexual assault crisis work: Implications for therapists and therapy. *Canadian Social Work,* 1(1), 56–63.

Regehr, C., Cadell, S., & Jansen, K. (1999). Brief reports, perceptions of control, and long-term recovery from rape. *American Journal of Orthopsychiatry,* 69(1), 110–115.

Regehr, C., Chau, S., Leslie, B., & Howe, P. (2002). Inquiries into the deaths of children: Impacts on child welfare workers and their organizations. *Child and Youth Services Review,* 21(12), 885–902.

Regehr, C., & Glancy, G. (1995). Battered woman syndrome defense in the Canadian courts. *Canadian Journal of Psychiatry,* 40(3), 130–135.

Regehr, C., Goldberg, G., & Hughes, J. (2002). Exposure to human tragedy, empathy, and trauma in ambulance paramedics. *American Journal of Orthopsychiatry, 72*(4), 505–513.

Regehr, C., Hemsworth, D., & Hill, J. (2001). Individual predictors of traumatic response: A structural equation model. *Canadian Journal of Psychiatry, 46,* 74–79.

Regehr, C., Hemsworth, D., Leslie, B., Howe, P., & Chau, S. (2004). Predictors of traumatic response in child welfare workers. *Children and Youth Services Review, 26*(4) 331-346.

Regehr, C., & Hill, J. (2000). Evaluating the efficacy of critical incident stress group debriefings. *Social Work with Groups, 23*(2), 69–79.

Regehr, C., Hill, J., & Glancy, G. (2000). Individual predictors of traumatic reactions in firefighters. *Journal of Nervous and Mental Disorders, 188*(6), 333–339.

Regehr, C., Hill, J., Goldberg, G., & Hughes, J. (2003). Postmortem inquiries and trauma responses in paramedics and firefighters. *Journal of Interpersonal Violence, 18*(6), 607–622.

Regehr, C., Hill, J., Knott, T., & Sault, B. (2003). Self-efficacy, social support, and trauma in experienced firefighters and new recruits. *Stress and Health, 19,* 189–193.

Regehr, C., Leslie, B., Howe, P., & Chau, S. (2000). Executive summary of research report: Stressors in child welfare practice. *Journal of the Ontario Association of Children's Aid Societies, 44*(4), 2–4.

Regehr, C., Regehr, G., & Bradford, J. (1998). A model for predicting depression in victims of rape. *Journal of the American Academy of Psychiatry and the Law, 26,* 1–11.

Reid, K. (1997). Social work practice with groups: A clinical perspective. Toronto: Brooks/Cole.

Reitsma-Street, M., Maczewski, M., & Neysmith, S. (2000). Promoting engagement: An organizational study of volunteers in community resource centers for children. *Children and Youth Services Review, 22*(8), 651–678.

Repetti, R. L., Taylor, S. E., & Seeman, T. E. (2002). Risky families: Family social environments and the mental and physical health of offspring. *Psychological Bulletin, 128*(2), 330–336.

Resick, P. A. (2000). *Stress and trauma.* Philadelphia: Taylor & Francis.

Resick, P., & Schnicke, M. (1993a). *Cognitive processing therapy for rape victims: A treatment manual.* Newbury Park, CA: Sage.

Resick, P., & Schnicke, M. (1993b). Cognitive processing therapy for sexual assault victims. *Journal of Consulting and Clinical Psychology, 60,* 748–756.

Resnick, H., Kilpatrick, D., Best, C., & Kramer, T. (1992). Vulnerability-stress factors in development of posttraumatic stress disorder. *Journal of Nervous and Mental Disease, 180*(7), 424–430.

Reza, A., Mercy, J. A., & Krug, E. (2001). Epidemiology of violent deaths in the world. *Injury Prevention, 7,* 104–111.

Richardson, A., & Burke, R. (1993). Occupational stress and work satisfaction among Canadian women physicians. *Psychological Reports, 72,* 811–821.

Roberts, A. R. (2002). Assessment, crisis intervention, and trauma treatment: The integrative ACT intervention model. *Brief Treatment and Crisis Intervention, 2*(1) 1–21.

Roberts, A. R. (Ed.). (2000). *Crisis intervention handbook: Assessment, treatment, and research.* New York: Oxford University Press.

Roberts, A., & Greene, G. (2002). *Social workers' desk reference*. New York: Oxford University Press.

Roberts, A., & Yeager, K. (2004). *Handbook of practice-focused research and evaluation*. New York: Oxford University Press.

Roberts, N., & Levenson, R. (2001). The remains of the workday: Impact of job stress and exhaustion on marital interactions in police couples. *Journal of Marriage and Family, 63*, 1052–1067.

Robinson, R., & Mitchell, J. (1993). Evaluation of psychological debriefings. *Journal of Traumatic Stress, 6*, 367–382.

Robinson, R., & Murdoch, P. (1991). *Guidelines for establishing peer support programs in emergency services*. Melbourne: Waterwheel Press.

Rogers, C. (1957). The necessary and sufficient conditions of therapeutic personality change. *Journal of Consulting Psychology, 21*, 95–103.

Rollnick S., Mason, P., & Butler, C. (1999). *Health behavior change*. London: Churchill Livingstone.

Rollnick, S., Allison, J., Ballasiotes, S., Barth, T., Butler, C. C., & Rose, G. S. (2002). Variations on a theme: Motivational interviewing and its adaptations. In W. R. Miller & S. Rollnick (Eds.), *Motivational Interviewing* (2nd Ed.). New York: Guilford Press.

Rose, S., Bisson, J., & Wessley, S. (2003). Psychological debriefing for preventing post-traumatic stress disorder (PTSD). The Cochrane Library. Retrieved June 5, 2003, from http://www.update-software.com.

Rosen, A., Proctor, E., & Staudt, M. (2003) Targets of change and interventions in social work: An empirically based prototype for developing practice guidelines. *Research on Social Work Practice, 13*(2), 208–233.

Rothbaum, B., & Foa, E. (1996). Cognitive-behavioural therapy for posttraumatic stress disorder. In. B. van der Kolk, A. McFarlane, & L. Weisaeth (Eds.), *Traumatic stress: The effects of overwhelming experience on mind, body, and society* (pp. 491–510). New York: Guilford Press.

Rothbaum, B., Meadows, E., Resick, P., & Foy, D. (2000). Cognitive behavioral therapy. In E. Foa, T. Keane, & M. Friedman (Eds.), *Effective treatments for PTSD: Practice guidelines for the international society for traumatic stress studies* (pp. 60–82). New York: Guilford Press.

Rotter, J. (1975). Some problems and misconceptions related to the construct of internal versus external control of reinforcement. *Journal of Consulting and Clinical Psychology, 43*, 56–67.

Rousseau, D. (1989). Psychological and implied contracts in organizations. *Employee Responsibilities and Rights Journal, 2*(2), 121–139.

Ruscio, A., Weathers, F., King, L., & King, D. (2002). Male war-zone veterans' perceived relationships with their children: The importance of emotional numbing. *Journal of Traumatic Stress, 15*(5), 351–357.

Rutter, M. (1993). Resilience: Some conceptual considerations. *Journal of Adolescent Health, 14*, 626–631.

Rutter, M., Champion, L., Quinton, D., Maughan, B., & Pickles, A. (1995). Understanding individual differences in environmental risk exposure. In P. Moen, G. H. Elder, & K. Luscher (Eds.), *Examining lives in context* (pp. 61–93). Washington, DC: American Psychological Association.

Ruzek, J. I. (2002). Providing "brief education and support" for emergency response workers: An alternative to debriefing. *Military Medicine, 167*(Suppl. 4), 73.

Ryff, C. D., Singer, B. H., & Seltzer, M. M. (2002). Pathways through challenge: Implications for well-being and health. In L. Pulkkinen & A. Caspi (Eds.), *Paths to successful development: Personality in the life course* (pp. 302–330). New York: Cambridge University Press.

Saakvitne, K., & Pearlman, L. (1996). *Transforming the pain: A workbook on vicarious traumatization.* New York: Norton & Co.

Sackett, D., Richardson, W., Rosenberg, W., & Haynes, R. (1997). *Evidence-based medicine.* New York: Churchill Livingston.

Salazar, M. K., & Beaton, R. (2000). Ecological model of occupational stress: Application to urban firefighters. *AAOHN Journal, 48*(10), 470–479.

Sandman, P. M. (2001). *Anthrax, bioterrorism, and risk communication: Guidelines for action.* (2001). Retrieved March 15, 2002, from http://www.psandman.com/col/part1.htm.

Scanlon, T. J. (2002). Helping the other victims of September 11th: Gander uses multiple EOCS to deal with 38 diverted flights. *International Journal of Mass Emergencies and Disasters, 20*(3), 369–398.

Schauben, L., & Frazier, P. (1995). Vicarious trauma: The effects on female counselors of working with sexual violence survivors. *Psychology of Women Quarterly, 19,* 49–54.

Schlenger, W., Caddell, J., Ebert, L., Jordan, K., Rourke, K., Wilson, D., et al. (2002). Psychological reactions to terrorist attacks: Findings from a national survey of American's reactions to September 11, 2001, terrorist attacks. *New England Journal of Medicine, 345,* 1507–1512.

Schnurr, P. P., & Jankowski, M. K. (1999). Physical health and post-traumatic stress disorder: Review and synthesis. *Seminars in Clinical Neuropsychiatry, 4,* 295–304.

Schnurr, P., Friedman, M., Foy, D., Shea, M., Hsieh, F., Lavori, P., et al. (2003). Randomized trial of trauma-focused group therapy for posttraumatic stress disorder: Results from a Department of Veterans Affairs cooperative study. *Archives of General Psychiatry, 60*(5), 481–489.

Segal, Z. V., Williams, J. M. G., & Teasdale, J. D. (2002). *Mindfulness-based cognitive therapy for depression.* New York: Guilford Press.

Selye, H. (1936). A syndrome produced by diverse nocuous agents. *Nature, 138,* 32.

Sewell, J. (1983). The development of a critical life events scale for law enforcement. *Journal of Police Science and Administration, 11*(1), 109–116.

Sewell, J. (1994). The stress of homicide investigations. *Death Studies, 18*(6), 565–582.

Sexton, L. (1999). Vicarious traumatization of counselors and effects on their workplaces. *British Journal of Guidance and Counselling, 27*(3), 393–403.

Shalev, A. (2002). Acute stress reactions in adults. *Society of Biological Psychiatry, 51,* 532–543.

Shalev, A. Y., & Ursano, R. J. (2003). Mapping the multidimensional picture of acute responses to traumatic stress. In R. Orner & U. Schnyder (Eds.), *Reconstructing early intervention after trauma* (pp. 118–129). New York: Oxford University Press.

Shannon, H. (2000). Firm-level organizational practice and work injury. In T. Sullivan (Ed.), *Injury and new world of work* (pp. 140–161). Vancouver & Toronto: UBC Press.

Shay, J. (2002). *Odysseus in America: Combat trauma and the trials of homecoming*. New York: Scribner.

Siegrist, J. (1996). Adverse health effects of high-effort/low-reward conditions. *Journal of Occupational Health Psychology, 1*(1), 27–41.

Siegrist, J., & Peter, R. (2000). The effort- reward imbalance model. *Occupational Medicine, 15*(1), 83–87.

Sigal, J., Silver, S., Rakoff, F., & Ellin, B. (1973). Some second-generation effects of survival of the Nazi persecution. *American Journal of Orthopsychiatry, 43*, 320–327.

Solomon, R., & Horn, J. (1986). Post-shooting trauma reactions: A pilot study. In J. Reece & H. Goldstien (Eds.), *Psychological services for law enforcement* (pp. 383–393). Washington, DC: United States Government Printing Office.

Solomon, S., & Johnson, D. (2002). Psychosocial treatment of posttraumatic stress disorder: A practice friendly review of outcome research. *Psychotherapy in Practice, 58*(8), 947–959.

Solomon, Z., Kotler, M., & Mikulincer, M. (1988). Combat-related post-traumatic stress disorder among second-generation Holocaust survivors: Preliminary findings. *American Journal of Psychiatry, 145*(7), 865–868.

Solomon, Z., Waysman, M., & Levy, G. (1992). From front line to home: A study of secondary traumatization. *Family Process, 31*, 289–302.

Southward, E. (1919). *Shell shock*. Boston: W. M. Leonard.

Southworth, R. (1990). Taking the job home. *FBI Law Enforcement Bulletin, 59*(11), 19–23.

Spasojevic, J., Heffer, R., & Snyder, D. (2000). Effects of posttraumatic stress and acculturation on marital functioning in Bosnian refugee couples. *Journal of Traumatic Stress, 13*(2), 205–217.

Statutes of Canada. (1997). c. 30 [Bill C-46, 1996]. An Act to Amend the Criminal Code.

Steed, L., & Bicknell, J. (2001). Trauma and the therapist: The experience of therapists working with perpetrators of sexual abuse. *Australasian Journal of Disaster and Trauma Studies, 1*, http://www.massey.ac.nz/~trauma/info/journal.htm.

Stein, H. (2002). Toward an applied anthropology of disaster: Learning from disasters—experience, method, and theory illness. *Crisis & Loss, 42*, 154–163

Stephens, C. (1997). Debriefing, social support, and PTSD in the New Zealand police: Testing a multidimensional model of organizational traumatic stress. *Australasian Journal of Disaster and Trauma Studies, 1*(1). Retrieved on October 12, 2000, from http://www.massey.ac.nz/trauma.

Stephens, C., & Long, N. (1999). Posttraumatic stress disorder in the New Zealand police: The moderating role of social support following traumatic stress. *Anxiety, Stress, and Coping, 12*, 247–264.

Stephens, C., Long, N., & Miller, I. (1997). The impact of trauma and social support on post-traumatic stress disorder in New Zealand police. *Journal of Criminal Justice, 25*, 303–313.

Sterling, P., & Eyer, J. (1988). Allostasis: A new paradigm to explain arousal pathology. In S. Fisher & J. Reason (Eds.), *Handbook of life stress, condition, and health* (pp. 629–649). New York: John Wiley & Sons.

Stokols, D. (1992). Establishing and maintaining healthy environments: Toward a social ecology of health promotion. *American Psychologist, 47*(1), 6–22.

Stout, K. D., & Thomas, S. (1991). Fear and dangerousness in shelter work with battered women. *Affilia*, 6(2), 74–86.

Strecher, V., Wang, C., Derry, H., Wildenhaus, K., & Johnson, C. (2002). Tailored interventions for multiple risk behavior. *Health Education Research*, 17(5), 619–626.

Stressed soldiers shunned. (2003, March 5). *Montreal Gazette*, A12.

Stroebe, M. S., Schut, H., & Finkenauer, C. (2001). The traumatization of grief? A conceptual framework for understanding the trauma-bereavement interface. *Israel Journal of Psychiatry and Related Sciences*, 38(3–4), 185–201.

Sullivan, T., & Frank, J. (2000). Restating disability or disabling the state: Four challenges. In T. Sullivan (Ed), *Injury and the new world of work* (pp. 3–24). Vancouver & Toronto: UBC Press.

Talbot, A. (1989). The importance of parallel process in debriefing crisis counselors. *Journal of Traumatic Stress*, 3(2), 265–277.

Talbot, A., Manton, M., & Dunn, P. (1992). Debriefing the debriefers: An intervention strategy to assist psychologists after a crisis. *Journal of Traumatic Stress*, 5(1), 45–62.

Tarasoff v. Regents of the University of California. (1976). 17 Cal. Rptr. 3rd (U.S.).

Tarrier, N., Pilgrim, H., Sommerfield, C., Faragher, B., Reynolds, M., Graham, E., & Barrowclough, C. (1999b). A randomized trial of cognitive therapy and imaginal exposure in the treatment of chronic posttraumatic stress disorder. *Journal of Consulting and Clinical Psychology*, 67, 13–18.

Taylor, S. E. (2002). *The tending instinct*. New York: Henry Holt.

Taylor, S. E., Kemeny, M. E., Reed, G. M., Bower, J. E., & Gruenewald, T. L. (2000). Psychological resources, positive illusions, and health. *American Psychologist*, 55(1), 99–109.

Tehrani, N., & Westlake, R. (1994). Debriefing individuals affected by violence. *Counselling Psychology Quarterly*, 7(3), 251–259.

Tehrani, N., Walpole, O., Berriman, J., & Reilly, J. (2001). A specific courage: Dealing with the Paddington rail crash. *Occupational Medicine*, 51(2), 93–99.

Terheggen, M., Stroebe, M., & Kleber, R. (2001). Western conceptualizations and Eastern experience: A cross-cultural study of traumatic stress reactions among Tibetan refugees in India. *Journal of Traumatic Stress*, 14(2), 391–403.

Thesenvitz, J., Hershfield, L. and Chirrey, S. (2000). *Changing Behaviors: A Practical Framework*. The Health Communication Unit, University of Toronto, available through www.thcu.ca

Thompson, J. (1993). Psychological impact of body recovery duties. *Journal of the Royal Society of Medicine*, 86, 628–629.

Thompson, A., & Bolger, N. (1999). Emotional transmission in couples under stress. *Journal of Marriage and the Family*, 61, 38–48.

Toseland, R., & Rivas, R. (2001). *An introduction to group work practice*. Toronto: Allyn & Bacon.

Tragedy at Gander. *Quartermaster Museum*. Retrieved July 11, 2003 from http://www.qmfound.com/gander/html.

Travis, K. (1993). Critical incident stress and the interruption of behaviour: A handbook for police personnel and those who support them. Burlington, Canada. Unpublished manuscript.

Truscott, D., & Cook, K. (1993). Tarasoff in the Canadian context: Wenden and the duty to protect. *Canadian Journal of Psychiatry*, 38, 84–89.

Turnbull, G. (1998). A review of post-traumatic stress disorder, part 1: Historical development and classification. *Injury*, 29(2), 87–91.

University of Toronto Joint Centre for Bioethics. (2003). *Ethics and SARS: Learning lessons from the Toronto experience*. Toronto, Ontario. Retrieved August 14, 2003, from http://www.utoronto.ca/jcb/SARS_workingpaper.asp.

Ursano, R., Fullerton, C., Vance, K., & Kao, T. (1999). Posttraumatic stress disorder and identification in disaster workers. *American Journal of Psychiatry*, 156(3), 353–359.

Ursano, R., Fullerton, C. S. and Norwood, A. E. (Eds.) (2003). *Terrorism and disasters: Individual and community mental health interventions*. Cambridge: Cambridge University Press.

Van der Kolk, B. (1997). The psychobiology of post-traumatic stress disorder. *Journal of Clinical Psychiatry*, 58, 16–24.

Van der Kolk, B., Hostetler, A., Herron, N., & Fisler, R. (1994). Trauma and the development of borderline personality disorder. *Psychiatric Clinics of North America*, 17(4), 715–730.

Van der Kolk, B., & van der Hart, O. (1989). Pierre Janet and the breakdown of adaptation in psychological trauma. *American Journal of Psychiatry*, 146(12), 1530–1540.

Van der Kolk, B., Weisaeth, L., & van der Hart, O. (1996). History of trauma in psychiatry. In B. van der Kolk, A. McFarlane & L. Weisaeth (Eds.), *Traumatic stress: The effects of overwhelming experience of mind, body and society* (pp. 47–76). New York: Guilford Press.

Van Emmerik, A., Kamphuis, J., Huisbosch, A., & Emmelkamp, P. (2002). Single session debriefing after psychological trauma: A meta-analysis. *Lancet*, 360, 766–742.

Verboski, S., & Ryan, D. (1988). Female partners of Vietnam veterans: Stress by proximity. *Issues in Mental Health Nursing*, 9, 95–104.

Violanti, J. (1995). The mystery within: Understanding police suicide. *FBI Law Enforcement Bulletin*, 64(2), 19–23.

Violanti, J. (1999). Death on duty: Police survivor trauma. In J. Violanti & D. Paton (Eds.), *Police trauma: The psychological aftermath of civilian combat* (pp. 824–826). Springfield, IL: Charles Thomas.

Violanti, J., & Aron, F. (1993). Sources of police stressors, job attitudes, and psychological distress. *Psychological Reports*, 72(3), 899–904.

Violanti, J., & Aron, F. (1994). Ranking police stressors. *Psychological Reports*, 75, 824–826.

Violanti, J. M., Paton, D., and Dunning, C. (2000). *Postraumatic stress intervention* Springfield, IL: Charles Thomas.

Watzlawick P., Weakland, J., & Fisch, R. (1974). *Change: Principles of problem formation and problem resolution*. New York: W. W. Norton.

Weine, S., Danieli, D., Silove, D., Van Ommeren, M., Fairbank, J. A., & Saul, J. (2002). *Psychiatry*, 65(2), 156–164.

Weiss, D., Marmar, C., Metzler, T., & Ronfeldt, H. (1995). Predicting symptomatic distress in emergency services personnel. *Journal of Consulting and Clinical Psychology*, 63, 361–368.

Wenden v. Trikha. (1991). 116 A.R. 81 (Altaedez. Q.B.).

Weisaeth, L., & Tonnessen. A (2003). Responses of individuals and groups to consequences of technological disasters and radiation exposure. In R. Ursano

(Ed.), *Terrorism and disaster: Individual and community interventions* (pp 209–235). New York: Cambridge University Press.

White, L. (2002). *The action manual: Techniques for enlivening group process and individual counseling.* Toronto.

Wilkinson, R., and Marmot, M. (Eds.). (2003). *Social determinants of health: The solid facts, 2nd edition.* World Health Organization. Retrieved August 11, 2004, from http://www.who.dk/document/e81384.pdf.

Williams, M. (1999). Impact of duty-related death on officers' children: Concepts of death, trauma reactions, and treatment. In J. Violanti & D. Paton (Eds.), *Police trauma: The psychological aftermath of civilian combat* (pp. 159–174). Springfield, IL: Charles Thomas.

Workplace Safety and Insurance Board (WSIB). (1998). Adjudicating mental stress. *Policy Report, 11*(3).

World Health Organization. (2001). *Rapid assessment of mental health needs of refugees, displaced and other populations affected by conflict and post-conflict situations.* Retrieved November 7, 2002, from http://www.acdicida.gc.ca/ .

World Health Organization (2002) *World report on violence and health.* Geneva.

World Health Organization. (2003). *Mental health in emergencies. Mental and social aspects of health of populations exposed to extreme stressors.* Retrieved May 2, 2003, from http://www.reliefweb.int/w/lib.nsf/0/b033de527788 ef35c1256ca90059b179/$FILE/who-mental-2003.pdf

Yassen, J. & Harvey. M. (1998). In P. Kleepsies (Ed.), *Emergencies in mental health practice: Evaluation and management.* New York: Guilford Press. 117–144.

Yeager, K., & Roberts. A. (2003) Differentiating among stress, acute stress disorder, crisis episodes, trauma, and PTSD: Paradigm and treatment goals. *Brief Treatments and Crisis Intervention, 3*(1), 3–25.

Yehuda, R. (1998). Psychoneuroendocrinology of post-traumatic stress disorder. *Psychiatric Clinics of North America, 21,* 359–379.

Yehuda, R. (1999). Biological factors associated with susceptibility to posttraumatic stress disorder. *Canadian Journal of Psychiatry, 44*(2), 34–39.

Yehuda, R. (2002). Clinical relevance of biologic findings in PTSD. *Psychiatric Quarterly, 73,* 123–133.

Yehuda, R., & McFarlane, A. (1995). Conflict between current knowledge of post-traumatic stress disorder and its original conceptual basis. *American Journal of Psychiatry, 152,* 1705–1713.

Yehuda, R., Schmeidler, J., Wainberg, M., Binder-Brynes, K., & Duvdevani, T. (1998). Vulnerability to posttraumatic stress disorder in adult offspring of holocaust survivors. *American Journal of Psychiatry, 115,* 1163–1171.

Zilberg, N., Weiss, D., & Horowitz, M. (1982). Impact of Event Scale: A cross-validation study and some empirical evidence supporting a conceptual model of stress response syndromes. *Journal of Consulting and Clinical Psychology, 50,* 407–414.

Zohar, D. (2000). A group-level model of safety climate: Testing the effect of group climate on microaccidents in manufacturing jobs. *Journal of Applied Psychology, 85*(4), 587–596.

Zohar, D. (2002a). Modifying supervisory practices to improve subunit safety: A leadership-based intervention model. *Journal of Applied Psychology, 87*(1), 156–163.

Zohar, D. (2002b). A group-level model of safety climate: Testing the effect of group climate on microaccidents in manufacturing jobs. *Journal of Applied Psychology,* 85(4), 587–596.

Zohar, D. (2003). Safety climate: Conceptual and measurement issues. In J. C. Quick & L. E. Tetrick (Eds.), *Handbook of occupational health psychology* (pp. 123–142). Washington, DC: American Psychological Association.

Index